AFRICAN

HOMICIDE AND SUICIDE

AFRICAN HOMICIDE AND SUICIDE

EDITED BY PAUL BOHANNAN

PRINCETON, NEW JERSEY

PRINCETON UNIVERSITY PRESS

1960

Dr. Paul James Bohannan is a former Rhodes
Scholar who has carried out extensive field research
in British Africa. He has been University Lecturer
in social anthropology at Oxford University and
an associate professor in the Department of Economics and Sociology at Princeton University. He
is presently an associate professor in the Department of Anthropology at Northwestern University
and Technical Director of the National Academy
of Sciences' program on Human Environments in
Central Africa.

Printed in the United States of America
by Princeton University Press at Princeton, New Jersey

PREFACE

I should like to express here my gratitude to the members of the several seminars, at Oxford, The London School of Economics, and Princeton whose members have made valuable suggestions, some of which have been incorporated into this book. I also owe a debt of thanks to my secretary, Adele Adlerstein, who painstakingly and with unbelievable good humor reduced the sprawl of data from its original form to one that could be reproduced as the Appendix to this book.

P.B.

Princeton
April 1959

CONTENTS

TABLES

Tables

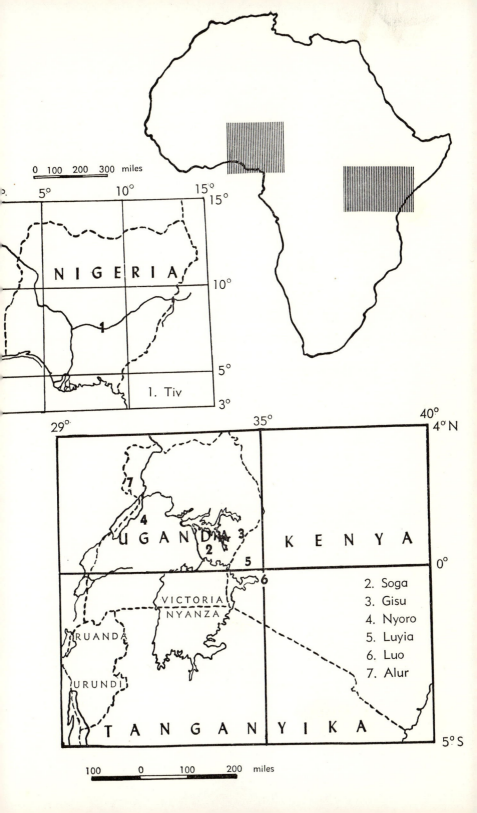

0 100 200 300 miles

5° 10° 15° 15°

NIGERIA

10°

1

5°

1. Tiv 3°

29° 35° 40° 4°N

7

4

UGANDA 3

2

5

KENYA 0°

6

2. Soga

3. Gisu

4. Nyoro

5. Luyia

6. Luo

7. Alur

VICTORIA

NYANZA

RUANDA

URUNDI

TANGANYIKA

5°S

100 0 100 200 miles

INTRODUCTION

PAUL BOHANNAN

ONE DAY in the spring of 1950 when I was going over files in the District Office of Tiv Division, Benue Province, Nigeria, where I was making a field study, I noticed a file labeled "Rex vs. Wannongo. Murder."[1] With all the sensations of the amateur sleuth—I recognized them immediately from descriptions in detective stories—I opened the file, dated 1932. One corner of the wad of papers inside it had been eaten away by termites, even though the files are kept in square kerosense cans. One set of papers among them was called the "P.I." or Preliminary Inquiry, a record of the proceedings in the Magistrate's court held to determine whether or not the case need be sent to the High Court of Nigeria.

As I read the file, I was struck by the fact that it contained invaluable ethnographic information. Here, set out in the form of a court case, was documentation of some of the most carefully guarded aspects of Tiv life.

Eagerly, I went to work: I found and noted, with more or less thoroughness, 122 such official investigations. They were all I could find.

When, after my last return from Tivland, I re-read these cases, I saw in them the beginning of a study in the comparative sociology of homicide. I also realized that both my system of note-taking and the administration's system of filing and registering were inadequate. The sample which I had was random—haphazardly so.

Such random samples, no matter how good the ethnography in them, could not be handled statistically, as are most criminological data. They required more orthodox anthropological methods—the "patterns of culture" concepts fit them neatly—but if they were analyzed anthropologically, they

[1] This case, one of the most dramatic I ever discovered in Africa, is retold briefly as Case No. 3 in Chapter 2.

would not be comparable with criminological studies in our own society. Since working in the traditional criminological mode, which is largely statistical, was impossible, the only way to bring the two sorts of study together was to re-appraise the body of criminological studies in anthropological terms.

Such a task was a formidable one. I did not embark upon it.

Several years later, in 1955, at a conference in Uganda of the research fellows of the East African Institute of Social Research, I read an informal paper about Tiv homicide. My main point was that official records of homicide are an invaluable source of ethnographic data. I mentioned the shortage of comparative data and the scarcity of theoretical considerations of the subject. The members of the conference were enthusiastic, and during the next two days we planned a book of essays on homicide in various tribes. The other contributors convinced me that suicide should also be included.

When I returned to the field a few days later—my wife and I were engaged in studying the Wanga tribe of the Baluyia in Western Kenya—I set about making a somewhat more thorough and orderly investigation of homicide than I had done among the Tiv. The other members of the conference made similar studies. We also sought contributors from other parts of Africa.

The problem in these studies was not primarily one of acquiring data. All district and provincial offices, police offices and court offices in British Africa bulge with it. However, the bulk of it is unusable anthropologically or sociologically by anyone not fully familiar with the ethnography of the area. Furthermore, we could not draw on the large body of anthropologists who had previously studied African societies because such material is not usually noted by anthropologists. For these two reasons we were limited to people then in the field. The only real disadvantage of such a scheme was that it did not allow us to get a good coverage of the African continent.[2] For example, although the late David Tait had agreed to write an article on the Dagomba, the Tiv are the only West African people actually reported in this book. A letter which I received from Dr. Tait throws into relief some of our losses of range:

> In fact, there is remarkably little suicide in the whole Tamale region [northern Ghana] and very little in Dagomba—three cases in five years. Up in Farafara country next to the Tallensi, we do get institutionalized suicide— the kind of suicide in which the offended person kills himself before the front door of his offender.

Unfortunately, we do not have data on this "institutionalized suicide." Neither do we have data on the institutionalized homicide known to occur in parts of East Africa. Indeed, we have no examples of ritual murder.[3] We have no material from Central Africa or from South Africa. The weighting is heavier than would be desirable on the Interlacustrine Bantu (the area of greatest concentration of fellows of the East African Institute). We have, in fact, barely scratched the surface.

Each contributor to this volume was "given his head." We asked each person to gather cases of homicide and suicide, arranging the data on charts with the following headings:

Homicide: File Identification
Date
Name, Sex, Age and Tribe, Clan etc., of Accused
Name, Sex, Age and Tribe, Clan etc., of Deceased
Relationship of Deceased to Accused
Weapon
Stated (by whom?) motive
Circumstances of Arrest

[2] See Map, p. xi.
[3] The best study of this subject is G. I. Jones, *Basutoland Medicine Murder*, London, H.M.S.O., 1951, Cmd. 8209.

Judgment and Sentence
Remarks

Suicide: File Identification
Date
Name of Suicide
Method
Stated (by whom?) motive
Remarks

These charts were to be used for purposes of comparison. We then asked each contributor to write an essay. The following paragraph was considered sufficient to set forth the frame of reference:

Each essay should cover the following points, but the order and relative importance of the points (and any others necessary) are left entirely to the writers, following their own material:

Homicide: (1) Words, categories and notions concerning homicide among the people studied.
(2) What emerges from the charts which accompany the article?
(3) Some half-dozen, more or less, cases which are typical, of special interest, etc., for the tribe or situation studied.

We requested the same range of information for the suicides.

We were fully aware, when we agreed on these "instructions," that the material would not all be completely comparable. One man could emphasize one point, another man another point. It was our opinion that some lack of comparability is more desirable than prejudicing our results by making our analytical categories in advance. Each person was to reach his conclusions from his own data and whatever reading he chose to do in order to clarify them. If it should be desirable to check an hypothesis reached by one field worker in one area against the data of another from a different area, it could be done in terms of the charts, which all had the same headings. Any prearranged outline for the essays would inevitably miss important points from one or all of the societies. Worse, it would lend an a priori arrangement to data which have, in one way or another, a folk arrangement which we sought to discover.

It is the purpose of the charts, reproduced in the Appendix, to provide comparable data for several societies. The purpose of the essays is to provide differing viewpoints, both of African peoples and of various anthropologists.

The sort of records available to the field worker differed from one country to the next despite the fact that all were dominated by English law and English methods of administration. When foul play is suspected in a death, police are called in. In Northern Nigeria this usually means "Native Authority" policemen. They merely arrest the man. They may make a few preliminary inquiries, but their notes seldom amount to more than a short letter to the District Officer. The District Officer, in his role as magistrate (and, later, magistrates who were especially appointed), makes Preliminary Inquiries. The formality of turning a case from the police to a magistrate is minimal. Nigerian District Offices (at least the one in Tivland) keep no registers, so that quantitative handling of the material is impossible.

In Kenya, on the other hand, both police records and magistrate's court records are full, the two departments are rigidly separated, and transference of a case is a more or less formal affair. The records of small, local police stations were greatly improved from the time of Mau Mau on. Therefore, though they have been of little use in this study, they will provide more material for subsequent studies.

The Preliminary Investigation could often be profitably supplemented by new evidence which emerged during the trial. In all the territories we have found that new evidence may be added during the trial which was not presented in the Preliminary Inquiry, but seldom does it contradict or nullify that set forth in the Preliminary Investigation. Moreover, information in trial records is invariably more distorted toward Western norms than is that in the Preliminary Inquiry. Obviously, data on sentences, and so forth, always come from the High Court or Supreme Court report, a copy of which is returned to the District Office.

In Uganda, records are better kept than in either Kenya or Nigeria. In many places, however, including those outside Buganda, they are kept in Luganda which sometimes badly distorts the facts. Nevertheless, they are kept. Uganda is the only country in our sample in which suicide cases are recorded with any degree of accuracy at all (Kenya after 1954 is probably adequate).

The difficulty arising from records that are not strictly comparable has, of course, always beset criminologists. It has beset us too.

The difficulties involved in the analysis of the material, once gathered, were far more serious. They hinged on the lack of theoretical background on which to base the comparative parts of the study. If one is to study homicide in Africa, one has to study homicide wherever else it occurs. Little of the meticulous care which sociologists and anthropologists have given social organization, kinship nomenclature, religious ideas like *totem* and *mana*, or *rites de passage*, has ever been expended on homicide.

The theoretical basis for studying suicide is, thanks to Durkheim and the psychoanalysts, somewhat better. Nevertheless, despite Durkheim's work, there is a great dearth of sociological theory for understanding suicide in comparative terms.

The first chapter of this book presents a brief summary of the theoretical points made in the literature on the subject of homicide and suicide. It will provide a framework for reading the essays which follow. The essays are in turn fol-

Introduction

lowed by a brief summary of the various points made in them; insofar as it is possible these points are then related to all of the societies considered here and to some considered in the literature. This summary raises problems of the nature of both criminal law and social pathology and their examination on a comparative basis. It investigates the possibility of a comparative criminology, and tries to state briefly the anthropological theory we have used for understanding crime.

AFRICAN

HOMICIDE AND SUICIDE

1

THEORIES OF
HOMICIDE AND SUICIDE

PAUL BOHANNAN

THE main question is this: do Africans kill themselves and one another for the same reasons and in the same situations as Europeans and Americans? If not, how and why do the conditions differ? Obviously, before such a question can be answered, it is necessary to know something about suicide and homicide in America and Europe.

It is an interesting fact that the literature on suicide is several times as extensive as that on homicide—if, of course, we omit fiction and legal documents. The laws of our society provide that cases of homicide be "handled" by "the law," and except for an occasional priest, no one else is directly concerned. "The law" has no such monopoly in matters of suicide. On the other hand, the mores of our society allow us to enjoy fictional homicide, but demand that, in fiction, we condemn suicide in all cases save those in which a sympathetic character would, otherwise, be executed or killed.

When in Western society people become "serious" about the study of homicide, they turn to lawyers, judges, and policemen. When they become "serious" about the study of suicide, they turn to sociologists, psychologists, and actuaries. As a consequence, in the field of homicide, a great literature exists on the nature of punishment and on the various conditions which allow of distinctions in the laws regarding killing. The psychological literature on homicide is small, and the sociological literature on it is smaller. On the other hand, the psychological literature on suicide is of a respectable size, and the

3

social literature on that subject might almost be described as ample.

One further factor should be noted. Social scientists have had relatively little trouble achieving a cool, dispassionate position when they study suicide; for the most part, they remain disengaged from actual instances of it. However, in studying homicide, one does not deal merely with killers, but with society as avenger. The literature on the two subjects indicates that it is less easy to be objective in homicide studies.

Although it has not, to my knowledge, been recently assembled on any large scale, there exists a truly prodigious amount of data on suicide among primitive peoples. The situation as regards homicide data is not so favorable. Although many cases of homicide are reported in ethnographic literature, they are not correlated with beliefs or with institutions in nearly such precise detail as are instances of suicide. As an example, I shall take only the best known suicide in the ethnographic literature: that committed in the Trobriand Islands, and reported by Malinowski, by a young incestuous lover when he jumped from the top of a palm tree after having been publicly denounced.[1] Malinowski has carefully correlated this event with beliefs and institutions: with the village structure, the tensions inherent in the matrilineal system of clan membership and inheritance, and the concepts of law which he is elucidating. No place in his writings does Malinowski give so careful an analysis to homicide.

It is of course possible to find societies for which homicide is better recorded and understood than is suicide—Hoebel's re-analysis of homicide as a legal mechanism of the Eskimo,[2] or Evans-Pritchard's analysis of feud among the Nuer,[3] are

[1] Bronislaw Malinowski, *Crime and Custom in Savage Society*, London, Kegan Paul, 1926, pp. 77-79.
[2] E. Adamson Hoebel, *The Law of Primitive Man*, Cambridge, Harvard University Press, Chapter 5, pp. 67ff.
[3] E. E. Evans-Pritchard, *The Nuer*, London, The Clarendon Press, 1940.

cases in point. Nevertheless, throughout ethnographic literature as a whole, suicide is better handled than is homicide.

Even more important is the situation as regards theoretical
bases for studying the two phenomena. Many hypotheses
about suicide are to be found in the works of sociologists like
Durkheim, Halbwachs, Cavan, and many others, and of
psychologists such as Menninger, Zilboorg, and Freud himself.
No Durkheim or no Menninger has ever studied homicide.[4]
In several standard textbooks of criminology neither "homicide" nor "murder" appears in the index. In none of them is
the subject treated systematically, as a unit.[5] There are legal
treatises on the law of homicide, but few books on the phenomenon itself. Although reports of murder trials abound—
some of them in discouraging detail—there has been little
attempt at generalization or theoretical analysis. What has
been done has been left to journalists or to amateurs. F. Tennyson Jesse, the English playwright and criminologist, has
made six pigeonholes for motive and the claim that all murder
fits into one or the other of them.[6] There are a few books—
like Brearley's[7] or Hoffman's[8]—that deal more or less ex-
haustively with what one can only call the demography of
the subject. There is some psychoanalytical theory on the
matter—most of it forensic, and highly debatable as well as
debated. But there is little sociological theory. Studies in homicide in individual societies such as Elwin's fine study of the

---

[4] Actually, Durkheim treated homicide in four pages of *Suicide* (see
note 12) and in thirteen pages in *Leçons de sociologie*, Presses Universi-
taires de France, 1950, pp. 131-143. These brief notes were never developed, so far as I know.

[5] In fact, most criminology books do not deal with crime at all, but
with criminals and penology. For an analysis see Clarence R. Jeffery,
"The Structure of American Criminological Thinking," *Journal of Criminal Law, Criminology and Police Science*, Vol. 46, No. 5, pp. 658-672.

[6] F. Tennyson Jesse, *Murder and its Motives*, London, Heinemann,
1924.

[7] H. C. Brearley, *Homicide in the United States*, Chapel Hill, University of North Carolina Press, 1932.

[8] Frederick L. Hoffman, *The Homicide Problem*, Newark, The Pru-
dential Press, 1925.

Bison-Horn Maria,[9] or Verkko's of the Finnish people[10] (unfortunately prejudiced by an a priori conclusion that "Finns cannot hold their liquor"), are all too rare.

A recent book by two sociologists, Henry and Short's *Suicide and Homicide*,[11] contains in its first appendix a review of the relevant literature on suicide under the headings of theory and fact. When these authors come to study homicide, they discuss the theory and fact *not* of homicide, but of "crime." They were in fact forced into this position, for there is little fact and less theory regarding a sociological literature of homicide. But it is a pity that they did not emphasize, instead of trying to ignore, the change of subject. Homicide is, of course, a crime. But probably the only point about it on which all criminologists agree is that it is a unique type of crime, that comparatively few killers in Western society are "criminals" in any other sense. Most criminological theory, of whatever sort, does not fit this particular crime as well as it does others.

Therefore, it becomes necessary to forge some theory for handling homicide data. We can do this best by first reviewing the various positions that have been taken on suicide, for it is in the theoretical literature on suicide that the first clues for a theory of homicide are to be found.

It has been sixty years since Durkheim published *Le Suicide*.[12] It is a tribute that can, probably, be paid to no other piece of social analysis to say that, far from having been superseded, it is after sixty years still the most vital book on the subject. Durkheim's statistical methods have become antiquated, but the conclusions which he reached by them have for

---

[9] Verrier Elwin, *Maria Murder and Suicide*, London, Oxford University Press, 1943.

[10] Veli Verkko, *Homicides and Suicides in Finland and their Dependence on National Character*, København, 1951.

[11] Andrew F. Henry and James F. Short, Jr., *Suicide and Homicide*, Glencoe, The Free Press, 1954.

[12] Emile Durkheim, *Le Suicide: étude de sociologie*, Paris, 1897.

the most part stood up in spite of them. His study has been annotated and enlarged by others, notably Halbwachs—Mauss remarked in his Introduction to Halbwachs' book that it forms with Durkheim's a single piece of analysis and study.[13] The remark could be made of most other books on the subject, even some which deny the association. Cavan, who does not fully acknowledge the extent of her debt to Durkheim, nevertheless still followed his principles. She worked in terms of "social disorganization," whereas Durkheim worked with an obverse statement of the same idea—the presence or absence of social integration.

In reviewing Durkheim's theoretical position in the light of the essays to be presented in this book, I have been acutely conscious of another stream of traditional theory: one stemming from Malinowski. Durkheim's notion of social solidarity or integration, and Malinowski's conception of the institution illuminate one another in such a way that I find it impossible to describe one without the other.

What might be called "Durkheim's law" of suicide reads: "Suicide varies inversely with the degree of integration of the original groups of which the individual forms a part."[14] The concept of "integration," which must still be explained today, is (for an anthropologist, at least) most easily illuminated by Malinowski's concept of the Institution—a word which Malinowski used with a meaning different from Durkheim's (or from those modern American sociologists, such as Talcott Parsons,[15] who follow him).

Malinowski's institution concept, like Durkheim's solidarity concept, is masterly in its simplicity. An institution, Malinow-

[13] Marcel Mauss, "Avant-propos" to Maurice Halbwachs, *Les Causes du Suicide*, Paris, 1930, p. vii.

[14] Emile Durkheim, *op.cit.*, p. 209 of the English translation, *Suicide: a Study in Sociology*, Routledge & Kegan Paul, 1952.

[15] Talcott Parsons, *The Structure of Social Action*, New York, 1937; pp. 399ff. of the 1949 edition by The Free Press.

7

ski tells us,[16] is a group of people united by a purpose. They have an organization necessary for achieving the purpose, and they either have or can make the material and technical equipment for carrying it out. They have, moreover, concepts and ideas which are communicable in words and in actions; some of these concepts and ideas deal with technology, others form what Malinowski called the "charter" of the institution—the ideas which make the purpose worthy of achievement.

Durkheim's "integration of social groups" is a pseudo-quantitative concept for the degree to which the members of the social group forming the core of an institution are held to the social roles and organization, to the ideas forming the charter, and to the event-cycle of activities characteristic of that institution. If the members are strongly committed to the institution, and hence to one another, the integration is high. If the institution is one to which they assign less value or less importance, then it is not a highly integrated institution.

There is an additional dimension: it may be that a society is marked by one or by several well integrated institutions, but is still characterized by a greater or lesser number of individuals who are not integrated into institutions of these sorts. That is to say, the family in Western society is a tightly integrated institution, but there is a large section of people in Western society who do not actually "belong to" an empirically existing family. Durkheim, thus, was talking about two things at once when he discussed the integration of society: he was talking first about the degree of institutionalization, and secondly about the proportion of people who were subject to the institutionalization.

If the individual is not satisfactorily associated with other persons in playing his roles in institutions, he can be said to be in a position of *anomie* (in English, "anomy," which the *Shorter Oxford English Dictionary* gives as "lawlessness" and

[16] Bronislaw Malinowski, *A Scientific Theory of Culture and other Essays*, Chapel Hill, University of North Carolina Press, 1944, pp. 39ff.

8

dates from 1775). Such a person is without the regulating pressures or laws of social institutions. When suicide occurred in such a situation, Durkheim described it as "anomic suicide." Suicide is, he postulated, one possible reaction to insufficient social pressures, and his data showed that he could, in all situations, show that absence or diminution of such social pressures is correlated statistically with increased suicide rates. Therefore, under certain conditions, the suicide rate is a diagnostic index of the degree of anomy in the social group. Putting this statement into Malinowski's terms, suicide is common in situations in which the institutions are inadequate to bind people to their purposes.

It also sometimes happens that large areas of the social life are left uninstitutionalized. This phenomenon is usually studied by social scientists under the heading of "individualism." In such a situation, institutionalization in some areas of life is not only absent, but its absence is considered normal and good. Such situations cannot and must not be called "anomic" for they conform to their own standards. Anomy results from inadequate functioning of recognized and valued institutions. "Individualism" is a situation in which large areas of life are purposely not institutionalized. If we call this an "open society," we can say that in an open society it sometimes happens that a person who is not closely bound or integrated to other people may commit "egoistic suicide." Put in Cavan's terms (which re-state Durkheim in quite another way) we have the "secret, personal suicide" of the West contrasted with the institutionalized suicide of some of the Eastern countries.[17] Thus, "egoistic suicide" is a concomitant of a type of social structure, not the result of social pathology.

Finally, Durkheim noted, there are some societies in which it was neither the failure of association with an institution nor the lack of close binding to institutions, but rather the very

[17] Ruth Shonle Cavan, *Suicide*, Chicago University Press, 1928, pp. 3ff.

strength of the association with the institution which resulted in suicide. When a person commits suicide because he is bound into an institution, part of the doctrine or activities of which extol suicide as one of the means of reaching the end valued by the institution, there is still another sort of suicide: Durkheim called it "altruistic suicide." Altruistic suicide is, like egoistic suicide, not found in a condition of anomy, but rather in one in which the institutionalization is considered adequate by the members of the society concerned.

The three Durkheimian social situations to which the individual can respond by suicide then are these: (1) an anomic situation, in which the institutionalization is faulty, and therefore the individual is not closely integrated into a social group; (2) the egoistic situation, in which the institutionalization is not faulty, but merely "open," and in which in certain areas the individual denies that he ought to be integrated into a group; (3) the altruistic situation, in which the institutionalization is sound and in which the individual espouses the purposes of the institution to a point that they outweigh considerations of self-protection when suicide is called for as a means to an end.

Obviously, suicide is an index of social disorganization (or lack of integration) only in cases of anomic suicide.

Durkheim had great difficulty in making an empirical separation between anomic and egoistic suicide, and had to postulate several stages of interval between them. Then, in order to make his scheme consistent, he postulated intermediate stages between altruistic suicide and the other two types: these last two stages were not as immediately necessary. His use of military figures to "prove" them is today the least convincing part of his book. The difficulty obviously arose from the fact that both anomic and egoistic suicide took place in the presence of weak integration. The difficulty disappears when we realize that one situation is pathological—the dissociation of a person from institutions which both he and the other members of his society respect and desire—while the other situation is individual, in which the culture does not recognize the right of the social groups to exercise any integrative influence on the person.

Most of the studies of suicide since Durkheim have utilized his categories. Some have rejected or ignored them only to smuggle them back in under another name. We have already mentioned Cavan, and we can add a thoughtful study of suicide in Ceylon by the Strausses,[18] who use a "loosely-structured : closely-structured" dichotomy suggested by John Embree to make the same distinction: that is, egoistic suicide occurs in a "loosely structured" and altruistic suicide occurs in a "closely structured" social situation.

There has been one truly original contribution which fits, if somewhat uncomfortably, into the Durkheim scheme. Some years ago, M. D. W. Jeffreys published a few short paragraphs pointing out that some suicides in Africa, also encountered in some other parts of the world, could not be fitted into Durkheim's tripartite classification of suicide. This new type of suicide he called "Samsonic suicide" because it was undertaken as an exercise in revenge.[19]

Vengeance suicide was mentioned in the literature as early as 1908 by Westermarck,[20] but it was nowhere stated with the same clarity as was given it by Jeffreys. Vengeance suicide is not to be confused with anomic suicide, in which the suicide neurotically attempts to get "revenge" by making a social group reject a second person thought to have "caused" the original suicide. Neither is it to be confused with the altruistic type in which the values of an institution can be brought

---

[18] Jacqueline H. and Murray A. Strauss, "Suicide, Homicide and Social Structure in Ceylon," *American Journal of Sociology*, LVII No. 5, 1953.

[19] M. D. W. Jeffreys, "Samsonic Suicide or Suicide of Revenge among Africans," *African Studies*, Vol. XI, No. 3, 1952, pp. 118-22.

[20] Edward Westermarck, "Suicide, a Chapter in Comparative Ethics," *Sociological Review*, I, January 1908, pp. 12-33.

to the notice of a wider audience by the act of suicide of one of the individuals involved in that institution.

Vengeance suicide results from the firm belief that as a ghost a man can take revenge on living persons. Suicide is a specific means to a specific end. Vengeance suicide resembles altruistic suicide in that the individual holds so fast to a belief that he commits suicide as a means of carrying out the purposes of an institution. However, the institution or its members do not demand the suicide, and therefore it resembles egoistic suicide, in which the individual gives his own ends priority over those of the group.

Jeffreys was, in my opinion, wrong however in saying that vengeance suicide is a fourth "type" to be classed with Durkheim's three types, because the criterion of vengeance suicide is not to be found in the degree and sort of integration of the social group, the primary criterion in the Durkheim classification. Vengeance suicide is, however, very difficult to evaluate in Durkheimian terms.

Durkheim's classification of suicide can be applied almost as it stands to homicide. Durkheim himself recognized this point. However, later scholars of homicide have not, so far as I am aware, picked it up.[21] There are homicides which occur in situations in which the institutionalization is inadequate for the purposes of its members. Such a situation can be called anomic homicide. But there are important differences between suicide and homicide in this respect. Homicide necessarily involves at least two persons, usually many more. Either killer or victim may be in an anomic situation. A neurotic individual who is at odds with his society may commit anomic homicide. On the other hand, a man who does not fit into any known category in a society, whose presence is an

---

[21] On pp. 356-359 of the translation of *Suicide*, Durkheim applies the words egoistic and altruistic to homicide. However, he himself said, "This is not the place to dwell on this important proposition in criminology" (p. 358). Neither he nor anyone following him seems to have found a place.

embarrassment, who is thoroughly anomic, may be killed; killing him may even be enjoined. Furthermore, anomic homicide can also be committed by members of "extra-societal" institutions which spring up when the recognized and approved institutions of a society are inadequate for the purposes of its members. Thus, members of the Chicago gangs in the 1920s, Mau Mau or other terrorist movements, may commit homicide to further the ends of their illicit institutions.

Homicide, like suicide, also occurs in situations in which the institutionalization of society is considered adequate by its members. When persons commit homicide in the "open areas" of the society, between the adequate institutions as it were, we can refer to it as egoistic homicide.

Finally, perhaps even commonly, there are instances in which institutionalization is adequate and is in fact so strong that it leads to homicide for the so-called purpose of protection of the institution. Examples can be cited from history—Mediterranean and Arab peoples have, in the past, required of men that they kill their unchaste sisters. There is an example quoted by Verrier Elwin of a Spanish nobleman who was hanged because he took personal revenge on his wife's lover by castrating him when he ought to have worked society's revenge by killing him according to the institutional norms.[22] We can certainly call these examples "altruistic homicide."

Obviously, if we follow such a method, we can but seek to classify homicide as well as suicide (and perhaps other "pathological" social acts as well) according to the degree and satisfactoriness of the institutionalization in which it occurs. The acts themselves can, thus, be characterized as "egoistic," "altruistic," or "anomic" with more or less precise meanings. However, to do so is ultimately the subject of social psychology—we are interested in how individuals fit into institutions, even though we may disguise that fact by saying that the institution itself is marked by a quality called "integration."

[22] Verrier Elwin, *op.cit.*, pp. 51-2.

13

Such, indeed, was Halbwachs' point about the Durkheimian classification.

Obviously, even when the anthropologist accepts Durkheim's classification, and any logical extensions of it, for what it is worth, his task is to study the relationship among the acts, institutions, and ideas of other people, not merely to classify the acts into an a priori scheme.

For the anthropologist, then, Durkheim's scheme provides a necessary background; it does not offer a workable methodology. There are two reasons: first, when "applied" outside the situations for which Durkheim evolved it, it is a-prioristic, and hence does not allow the anthropologist free rein in interpreting the ideas of the people he is studying; moreover, it demands a statistical approach for which the anthropologist rarely has adequate quantifiable data.

However, it is necessary for the anthropologist to have at his command the information which has been derived by statistical techniques, and specifically by the actuaries who have worked on the subject of suicide since Durkheim. The best actuarial book on the subject is that of Dublin and Bunzel.[23] They have either discovered or documented such facts as that the suicide rate is cyclical but tends to be increasing; that suicide is in the United States more common among whites than Negroes; that for males the suicide rate rises constantly with age while for females it rises only to age 19, and then levels off, rising only very slightly. They have given data which makes it possible to discover the methods of suicide most common in different countries, and to correlate suicide frequencies with socio-economic grouping.

In the long run, however, the actuaries have not created any theory—they have only made correlations. For their basic theory they have fallen back on psychologists. Dublin and Bunzel find that there are four "basic emotional patterns con-

[23] Louis I. Dublin and Bessie Bunzel, *To Be or Not To Be: A Study of Suicide*, New York, 1933.

14

ducive to a state of psychic disintegration that may readily lead to suicide": fear, inferiority, hatred and guilt.[24] Bunzel, in fact, in a later article, notes that "to understand suicide . . . one must uncover the basic causes of psychic conflict."[25] Therefore, although the actuaries have given us a great deal of information meticulously organized about suicide in Western civilization, their theory has been external and derivative.

The psychological theories of suicide provide an additional background of theory which the anthropologist can, with some reservations about cross-cultural application, accept.

With a few exceptions, the most important psychological writers on suicide have been psychoanalysts. Simpson has summed up their viewpoint admirably: "the most widely adopted view today in psychoanalysis is that suicide is most often a form of 'displacement'; that is, the desire to kill someone who has thwarted the individual is turned back on the individual himself. Or technically stated: the suicide murders the introjected object and expiates guilt for wanting to murder the object. The ego is satisfied and the superego mollified through self-murder."[26]

Simpson's summary, however, does not include the main contributions of Karl Menninger: that suicide is only an acute form of a more common tendency toward self-destruction which shows up in many non-acute forms in neurotic and psychotic patients. Menninger explains suicide entirely in terms of the Freudian theory of the death instinct, and notes that psychologically the act must contain three elements: a desire to kill, a desire to be killed, and a desire to die.[27]

[24] *Ibid.*, p. 282.
[25] Bessie Bunzel, "Suicide," *Encyclopaedia of the Social Sciences*, New York, 1934.
[26] George Simpson, "The Aetiology of Suicide," Editor's Introduction to the English translation of Émile Durkheim's *Suicide*, London, Routledge & Kegan Paul, 1952, p. 24. This view is expressed by Sigmund Freud, "Mourning and Melancholia," *Collected Papers*, Vol. 4, pp. 162-163 and by Karl Abraham, *Selected Papers*, p. 448 fn.
[27] Karl Menninger, *Man Against Himself*. On p. 71 (Harcourt, Brace,

On the basis of statements of the sort given above, it would appear to an anthropologist (but perhaps not to a psychologist) that homicide is psychically simpler than suicide. It is, thus, the more amazing—perhaps, though, it is the more understandable—that the psychologists themselves have not dealt at any depth with the psychology of murder. Bjerre, who was a prison doctor and psychologist in early twentieth century Sweden, has made the claim that all murderers show a fundamental "weakness" which manifests itself in an inability to "face reality"; rather the social situation is restructured to the murderer's own ends. He gives three extended case histories of "types." He specifically repudiates Freud, but it seems to this non-psychologist that he does so on the basis of a misunderstanding, and that nothing he says in any way nullifies or detracts from anything Freud ever said. The aetiology of the murderer's inability to "face reality" seems to me perfectly explicable in Freudian terms,[28] and it would also seem that murderers have no first claim on such an inability.

Wertham has, however, been at pains to show that homicide is a psychologically complex action, and that it is a culmination of a series of acts just as surely as Menninger has shown that suicide is inevitably a culmination of a series of acts. Menninger notes in a case history that: "This man began to commit suicide long before he took the pistol in his hand and long before he took the money from the bank. Suicide is the culmination of a process."[29] Wertham made the same point repeatedly for homicide in *A Show of Violence*.[30]

Anthropologists—at least those who are contributors to this book—are not psychologists. Psychological theory is, to

---

Harvest Books Edition) Menninger gives a 12-point statement of the psychoanalytical theory of suicide.

[28] Andreas Bjerre, *The Psychology of Murder*, New York, 1927. In objecting to Freud, Bjerre objected to "explanation in terms of sex," and emphatically rejected Freud's theories of the libido.

[29] Menninger, *op.cit.*, p. 21.

[30] Frederick Wertham, *A Show of Violence*, New York, 1949.

them, necessary background. We mention it here primarily so that it can be held fresh in mind while the essays are read. To test the hypotheses of psychologists cross-culturally would be extremely interesting but also very difficult and is not a problem we could set ourselves. However, keeping these hypotheses in mind adds a dimension to the case histories which follow.

There is one other factor which should be mentioned about the general theory of suicide and homicide before we proceed to an investigation of the material specifically relevant to primitive societies. That is the question of whether, and in what sense, the two phenomena are antithetical or "antagonistic." This point has been argued for over a century. Durkheim surveyed the evidence,[31] and Verkko has more recently given an interesting and lucid account of the vicissitudes of this idea.[32] Both point out that André-Michel Guerry, as early as 1833, considered suicides and crimes against the person as comparable phenomena and showed that they varied inversely with one another in the French Departments, suicide being high in the north and homicide in the south. French scholars for the next few decades extended their knowledge of this phenomena to other countries, and many of them constructed "explanations" for the facts they found. In the late nineteenth century this dispute became involved with the Italian criminological school. Verkko sums up Morselli by pointing out that the criminal type "blindly obeys his instincts and passions" and "because of the weakness of his mental structure" commits homicide. The non-criminal type, "in whom the sense of duty has been implanted," destroys himself instead.

In the nineteenth century, the negative correlation between homicide and suicide was more or less general, though Durkheim found exceptions. In the twentieth the negative correla-

[31] Émile Durkheim, *Suicide*, Part III, Ch. 2.
[32] Veli Verkko, *op.cit.* The next paragraphs are based on pp. 145-157 of his book.

tion disappeared in all parts of Europe save the south. Verkko points out that such nations as Finland, Estonia, and Latvia had both high suicide and high homicide rates. Others, like France, had medium rates, and still others, like Great Britain, Denmark, and Sweden, had low figures of homicide but only average suicide rates. Both Durkheim and Verkko refute the validity of the antagonism. Verkko claims that both homicide and suicide stem from a common cause (which in his case is foreseen—drink); Durkheim relates both to anomy.

Henry and Short have, more recently, also entered the arena of this particular dispute—and have brought a new weapon: the concept of "aggression" which they have taken over from the psychologists. Both suicide and homicide, they say, are "forms of aggression." Hence they can either increase or decrease in parallel, or show antagonism, and still be the same thing. Means of aggression, as well as quantity of aggression, may change.[33] Such a view seems to me to leave us right where we started. Von Hentig expressed a similar opinion, putting it into behaviorist terms instead of depth psychology terms: "Murder and suicide are complementary phenomena: the total amount of available destructiveness is discharged in two psychologically similar, socially distinct *Gestalten*."[34]

Although we shall be unable to make any statistically verifiable contributions to the question of the relation between homicide and suicide, again because of the nature of our data, the question forms a necessary part of the background against which any study of homicide and suicide must be set. It is an interesting point on which to compare the Luo or the Nyoro to the Tiv or the Alur.

Finally, we must note that homicide has a criminological dimension that suicide does not have, even when the latter is a crime. In English law, even today, "suicide" is defined as

[33] Henry and Short, *op.cit.*, "Introductory Statement," pp. 13-19.
[34] Hans von Hentig, *The Criminal and his Victim*, New Haven, Yale University Press, 1948, p. 390.

self-destruction by a person of unsound mind. Because such a person is by definition unable to commit a "crime," the act cannot be "punished." When persons of sound mind kill themselves, it is *felo de se*; it is a crime and may actually be "punished" by certain rights which the crown may exercise against the estate of the deceased. Suicide is a crime in many countries and attempted suicide is sometimes punished. Criminality in suicide is often reviewed by sociologists but has not given rise to any appreciable literature.

Homicide, on the other hand, is (with certain exceptions) always a crime in Western and European countries, unless it is committed by the State or its agents. Its being a crime is probably the most important thing about it in popular opinion; certainly its criminal aspect has given rise to the largest body of literature on the subject. This literature can be divided into three sorts: that large literature written from the standpoint of the criminal lawyer or comparative jurist, the smaller output of the criminologist, and the immense library of trial reports.

Of these literatures, the trial reports may be written by jurists or criminologists but are as often the work of journalists or other amateurs. Any given example of it may lean either to the exposition of the legal aspect or of the social pathology of the subject. Legal theory *per se* on the other hand is concerned, by definition, with law and not with social pathology. Criminologists, finally, must always be concerned with the interrelation of social pathology and the criminal law.

William Seagle's short, expert essay in the *Encyclopaedia of the Social Sciences* is a good example of the legal viewpoint. It begins with a legal definition of homicide: "Homicide is the killing of a human being. Such a neutral term must be considered an obvious necessity in view of the fact that homicide may be made punishable with reference to a great number of mental elements as well as external circumstances. The mere possibility of this should make it plain that there has never

19

been a universal concept of wrongful homicide." This quotation is fairly representative in that it immediately brings in the notion of punishment, and "mental elements" not of homicide but of homicide-as-a-crime. The article continues with interesting and significant details about the distinctions which have been made in various legal codes of the ancient and modern worlds for classifying various types of homicide by culpability. It ends with a short survey of the actuarial material on comparative homicide rates.

The legal literature is of very great interest to the anthropologist because it contains the categories which some of the greatest minds of historical and modern societies have patterned and on which they have acted in relation to homicide. However, in evaluating the present essays, one must remember that the "law" involved was British law. Cases of homicide and other important crimes, as well as civil cases which involve large sums or heavy fines, were at an early date taken out of the jurisdiction of "native courts" or any other African institution. The view expressed in the official records is always that of the British law so far as procedure is concerned. Substantively, in some cases, allowance is made for "native law and custom" and a judge always has expert advice, usually from tribesmen, when he hears a capital case. We have not made much effort to reconstruct the traditional treatment of homicides in the societies we have studied.

On the other hand, however the British may feel about what we have called the "social pathology" of homicide under various conditions, the ideas and mores of the Africans in these matters are still very much alive and can be studied. It is obvious, then, that if we take a legal view of homicide in the tribes we have studied, we would be taking up the British view. If, on the other hand, we take a purely criminological view, we are beset with the difficulty that any case records are marked by two variables: British law and African ideas of pathology.

In order to make this situation perfectly clear, we want to present another analysis of it. Jural or legal action in any society comprises a series of three sets of social acts: first, a breach of norm; second, a counteraction on the part of society or a representative body of it; and third, a correction which brings about either retributive justice or punishment.[35] These three series of acts always follow one another in a definite order, and can be diagrammed:

The idea of "breach of norm" necessarily involves two subordinate ideas: first, a social action, and second, a recognized norm of what is acceptable to the society and what is not. An action contrary to what is acceptable is a breach of norm. In the European or American situation, the laws and the jural acts are of a piece with the evaluation of acts which are considered pathological and which set the jural series of acts in motion. In the African situation, however, the legal machinery and the notions of social pathology may be at odds.

This situation adds a dimension to our problem: to study African homicides in such a situation, we must study not merely African ideas of what is wrong (i.e., social pathology) but African ideas of British law and African evaluation of that law in terms of their own ideas of wrongs, including homicide. We have gained some insight into this difficult problem, but it is a Herculean task, and its full realization goes far beyond the scope of these essays.

We have, however, been able to study homicide as an example of social pathology in various tribes. We are, thus, necessarily concerned with homicide not as an initial act that triggers off an event sequence which we can recognize as

[35] Paul Bohannan, *Judgment and Justice among the Tiv*, London, Oxford University Press, 1957.

21

jural, but rather as the final action in quite a different sequence of events. We are interested in murder as an end rather than as a beginning.

Because criminology studies not merely crimes but social reactions to crime, the preceding diagram can also refer to the three main branches of the study of criminology: there is that branch which treats of the criminal law, of acts labeled crimes, and of the criminals who perform the acts. There is, secondly, that branch of criminology which deals with the counteraction and its institutionalization: the police system and police methods, the court system and the operation of criminal courts. Finally, a third major branch of criminology deals with corrections, that is, it studies penology—prisons, parole systems, and punishment.

Homicide may occur in any of these three stages of jural activity. Homicide may be the crime—the act which is the breach of law. Homicide, legally excusable, may be committed by the police in the course of counteraction. Homicide, as a sanction and called "execution," may be a part of the social actions classed as "correction." On this very fact it might be possible to build a composite homicide rate which would be indicative of every society studied. We have, however, limited our discussion to homicide which is a breach of norm.

Having now made this brief introduction to the general sociological, psychological, and actuarial theory of homicide and suicide, we must next look to any statements of their occurrence specifically in primitive societies. In the writings of the authorities on suicide, one finds the most preposterously contradictory statements. Suicide is held to be common, indeed endemic, among primitive people and to occur without rational motivation. Briffault, to take only one example, tells us that "Suicide for all sorts of absurdly frivolous reasons is exceedingly common among all primitive peoples."[36] The exact

[36] Robert Briffault, *The Mothers*, London, 1927, Vol. II, pp. 143f. (cited in Elwin, *op.cit.*, p. 56).

opposite view is expressed as often. Cavan, after giving us the major European countries divided into three groups for "most," "middle," and "least" suicides per 100,000 population, follows with this statement: "Below these countries stand the primitive peoples, among whom suicide is almost non-existent."[37]

Indeed, one of the earliest articles on the subject with any claim to scientific analysis of data[38] states that its avowed purpose is to disperse the idea that suicide is rare or non-existent among primitive peoples. Steinmetz' conclusions are twofold—that anthropologists should gather more and better material on the subject (an admonition that they have not, for the most part, taken to heart), and that "there is a greater propensity to suicide among savages than among civilized peoples."

It was obvious, as early as 1908, that Steinmetz o'erleapt himself. In that year, Edward Westermarck pointed out that to hold either alternative as typical of primitive people as a whole or of "primitive society" as an entity was erroneous—that the range was as great as it was for more advanced societies.[39]

Many writers since that time have admitted this basic fact—that primitive societies vary as widely in matters of suicide as do record-keeping societies. However, they often go too far in searching for a single general "cause" of this variation. From Dublin and Bunzel, the actuaries, we get this statement: "To understand suicide among primitive people it is necessary to know the patterns of life that prevail in a given community." Admirable though that statement may be, the people who made it went on to vitiate it by adding: "In primitive communities . . . it will be found that where the emphasis is on individuality there will be more or less suicide. But in other groups where there is no striving for leadership or for attain-

---

[37] Ruth Shonle Cavan, *op.cit.*, p. 60.
[38] S. R. Steinmetz, "Suicide among Primitive Peoples," *American Anthropologist*, Vol. VII, 1894, pp. 53-60. The quotation is on page 60.
[39] Edward Westermarck, *op.cit.*, p. 12.

ing personal recognition and prestige [as in Zuñi] suicide will be almost unknown."[40] One of these authors stated, at a later date, "The determining factor, whether in primitive or sophisticated societies, is the emphasis that is placed upon individuality."[41] Obviously, what we have here is a non-scientific, folk restatement of the Durkheimian hypothesis: "individualism" and "striving for leadership" have replaced the more precise formulation in terms of integration which Durkheim himself made.

In the literature on suicide among primitive peoples, we get a few interesting statements like Bastide's that the Mina, Dahomeans, and Yoruba slaves in Brazil tended to kill their masters while Gabon tribes, Mozambique tribes, and 'les mysterieux Peules' [Fulani] tended to commit suicide.[42]

With the exception of a few studies, cited below, it seems fair to say that the only tenable position in the present state of the literature is that the suicide situation in various primitive societies is open to investigation, but has not been investigated. Therefore, we do not know what the suicide situation is in "primitive society."

There is one point, on which all of the authorities on suicide in the last few decades are agreed, with which we are in disagreement. That is in the matter of "motive." Durkheim and Menninger, from their different angles, both threw out motive. Durkheim's main problem was to turn scientific consideration of suicide away from the ethical speculation of the philosophers and demi-philosophers who had been concerned with it. One of the methods by means of which he sought to bring about this divorce between social fact and ethical speculation was to expose the falseness of "motive" as it had been discussed. Correctly enough, he was interested in suicide

[40] Dublin and Bunzel, *op.cit.*, p. 152.
[41] Bessie Bunzel, "Suicide," *Encyclopaedia of the Social Sciences*, p. 456.
[42] Roger Bastide, "Le Suicide du nègre brésilien," *Cahiers Internationaux de Sociologie*, 7 (12) 1952, pp. 79-90.

rates and the correlations which existed between them and other social "facts" and natural phenomena. In a long and often-cited passage, he eschews the method of examining "motivations" of a suicide. He claims, quite correctly of course, that an investigator can never know unequivocally just what the motive of a suicide may have been. He further justifies his rejection of this material by noting that the motivation assigned by French recorders of suicide did not change as the suicide rate changed. He did not believe, he said, that all of the "causes of suicide" increased or decreased in exact proportion every year. Therefore, the assigned "cause" was not really to be taken either as the cause or as the motive of the suicide.

Menninger was even more uncompromising. "In the popular mind," he wrote, "suicide is no enigma. Glib explanations are to be read with monotonous invariability in the daily newspapers, in life insurance reports, upon death certificates, and in statistical surveys. Suicide, according to these, is the simple and logical consequence of ill health, discouragement, financial reverses, humiliation, frustration and unrequited love."[43] Menninger, like Durkheim, overstated this objection in order to make his own, valid, point: that suicide is not an act which occurs on the spur of the moment, but rather one which has a long explanatory history. In an effort to elucidate types of the suicide process, his first step was, understandably enough, to reject "motive."

Very occasionally, one finds a weak note of protest. Dublin and Bunzel go along with the current, but add that "these commonplace accounts do furnish suggestive glimpses into human motivation."[44]

Yet neither Menninger nor Durkheim noticed that the word "motive" has two meanings: it means the psychic reason the suicide was committed; it also means the cause which is assigned to it by survivors. Now, we must agree with them

[43] Menninger, *op.cit.*, p. 16.
[44] Dublin and Bunzel, *op.cit.*, p. 6.

that the first sort of motive—that is, what was in the mind of the person who committed suicide—is of little scientific use because it is not knowable. However, the second sort of motive—the cause assigned by survivors—is of ethnographic interest. Durkheim, or at least some of his followers, should have recognized that these "motives" were important, not as *causes* of suicide, but as popular ideas (Durkheim would have called them *representations collectives*) about what is worth living for and what worth dying for. As such, these statements of "motive" made in suicide notes, by surviving kinsmen, by police officers and coroners, or by anyone else, are important. *Only* if they do not change from one society to the next can we say that they are of little anthropological interest. In short, the "motive" assigned to a suicide by a French coroner may, we all admit, tell us nothing about the "true motive" (that is, the psychic state or the social milieu) of the person who killed himself. But, for all that, it tells us quite a bit about French culture, and is therefore a suitable topic for study.

Just as "motive" in suicide studies is too easily associated with folk psychology, so motive in homicide studies is too easily associated with false jurisprudence. It should be noted that courts are not obliged to look for the "motive" of a homicide, but rather to determine whether or not there was intent. Psychologically the "motive" of a homicide is probably as diffuse, as deep-seated and as difficult of expression as that of a suicide. Popular ideas on the subject and the confessions of killers are, like suicide "motives," brought into line with prevailing modes of thought. The question is: are these idiomatic expressions of the common understandings that are popularly associated with homicide different from one society to another?

We must not confuse "motive" which means psychic aetiology with either intent or folk explanation. In order to avoid confusion, we shall talk of "folk explanations" of suicide or homicide instead of "motive." We can thus divorce them from pseudo-psychological and pseudo-legal contexts.

What we are doing here is to consider together Durkheim's notion of the correlates of suicide and Menninger's idea of the period of development of suicide to readmit "folk explanation" as the popular means of stating moral and evaluational ideas about suicide, homicide, and about "life" in general. We have, in fact, opened the way for a thorough "culture pattern" technique of studying either homicide or suicide.

A culture pattern is an action or series of actions which recurs recognizably in a social group as a mode of social relationships. It takes place in time, and in a given idiom of material traits and ideas. It may be institutionalized and recognized by the people of the social group in which it is found. On the other hand, it may be either uninstitutionalized or unrecognized or both.

Homicide is, no matter what else it may be, a social relationship. It might even be called the most definitive of social relationships. Like all other human social relationships, it must take place in terms of culture. It can, therefore, be studied with the ordinary tools of social anthropology, no matter what other tools may also profitably be brought to bear on it.

This fact about homicide has been only imperfectly recognized by criminologists, and at that only by a few of them. Von Hentig's *The Criminal and his Victim* and Wolfgang's *Patterns in Criminal Homicide*[45] are the best informed and best integrated statements of this recognition. Von Hentig makes a fundamental mistake, however. He states the obvious fact that homicide, along with a good many other crimes, is a dyadic social relationship between perpetrator and victim. He studies this relationship, and characterizes both perpetrators and victims. He is particularly good in showing the

[45] Marvin E. Wolfgang, *Patterns in Criminal Homicide*, Philadelphia, University of Pennsylvania Press, 1958.

social situation or characteristics which mark victims. However, he ignores the equally obvious fact that this dyadic relationship must be merged, to some extent—the very extent is instructive—with other social relationships into institutions or free areas of social action on the one hand, and into personality totalities on the other. Wolfgang did not correct this view sufficiently.

Thus, we agree with von Hentig that the criminal-victim relationship is an extremely important one. We go further, however—the criminal-victim relationship is interlocked with other social relationships. These other social relationships may be as indicative of a criminal situation as is the criminal-victim relationship. Sociological or anthropological analysis must start with that assumption.

Suicide has been shown by Menninger and the other psychoanalysts to be just as uncompromisingly an activity in a framework of social relationships as is homicide. It necessarily takes place in terms of culture, and just as necessarily is evaluated culturally.

Since social relationships, social acts, and cuture do not take place *in vacuo*, we are endeavoring to find the concatenations of social relationships and the accompanying idiom of culture which are associated with homicide and with suicide in different human groups. It is "culture patterns" in this sense that we are investigating. We are interested in whether or not killings, either of the self or of another, form many or few patterns, how the patterns compare, and whether they vary significantly from one society to another.

This idea is, of course, not new. It is its very traditionality which we wish to stress. Granted its wide acceptance in many fields, it is a strange fact that it has so seldom been applied to the phenomena of social pathology or of crime. It has, indeed, been used there a few times: Erminie Voegelin has used it in a small-scale study of suicide in northeastern California.[46] Her findings will help to illuminate ours in the final chapter of this book. Wyman and Thorn also used it in studying Navajo suicide.[47] Yet, this obvious technique of studying homicide has been taken up but seldom.

We are now ready to proceed to the essays: our aim, restated, is to provide description and analysis of the culture patterns which involve homicide and suicide in several African societies. In the summarizing chapter, we shall look for patterns in the social relationships and in culture represented by the data we have gathered on the several African societies. We shall also include whatever comparable data we have found from other parts of the world if it elucidates our own. We are interested in comparing patterns of culture. We might, had Dr. Ruth Benedict been alive so that we might ask her blessing, have called this book *Patterns of Murder*.

[46] Erminie W. Voegelin, "Suicide in Northeastern California," American Anthropologist, Vol. 39, 1937.

[47] Leland C. Wyman and Betty Thorn, "Notes on Navajo Suicide," American Anthropologist, Vol. 47, 1945, pp. 278-287.

HOMICIDE AMONG THE
TIV OF CENTRAL NIGERIA

PAUL BOHANNAN

THE Tiv are a semi-Bantu people of central Nigeria who number about 800,000 when they were studied in 1949-1953. They are subsistence farmers who live in compounds containing from 5 to 120 or so persons. They are organized in agnatic lineages based on the principle of segmental opposition. The smallest lineages associated with a discrete territory contain from 150 to 1500 persons, on an area which tends to be about two square miles or a little less. According to samples which I took from several parts of Tivland, 83 per cent of the males resident within such an area are members of the lineage associated with the area. Thus groups of neighbors are composed for the most part of agnatic kinsmen and their wives.[1]

The traditional political system of the Tiv was based on their lineage system; there was no hierarchy of "responsible offices," and the "law" was kept through *ad hoc* meetings of groups of elders associated with lineages, and by self help. Outside the compounds, there was no one in the indigenous system who was granted legitimate authority, although of course there were men who had more prestige (*shagba*) or power than others, and there were leaders who could command something of a following within varying sizes of lineages. These

---

[1] Details of Tiv settlement patterns, law, and political system are to be found in Paul Bohannan, *Tiv Farm and Settlement*, London, H. M. S. O., 1954, and *Judgment and Justice among the Tiv*, Oxford University Press for International African Institute, 1957, and Laura Bohannan, "The Political System of the Tiv" in *Tribes without Rulers*, edited by John Middleton and David Tait, London, Routledge and Kegan Paul, 1958.

leaders, however, acquired and retained their followings on personal grounds; they did not occupy any formal position, office, or status. They wielded influence in terms of the political system, but not by means of it. There were no chiefs or any other sort of official among the Tiv.

Today, a foreign government has introduced the ideas of legitimate authority, responsibility, government, hierarchy, and courts. It has at the same time removed the treatment of major crimes from any Tiv institution, and has established institutions based on British models (but purporting to recognize "native law and custom") to deal with crimes and criminals, including killers.

As a result of this re-institutionalization along British lines, there is some uncertainty among Tiv about the legal processes which ensue after a homicide, and what one can only call amazed wonder that Europeans execute a man whose only fault was killing another. However, the Tiv substantive norms of homicide have been comparatively unaffected.

Records of 122 homicide cases were available in February 1950. All had occurred between 1931 and 1949. The sample is by no means complete; some of the early case records were lost, but it was not possible to estimate the proportion. This sample is random if the vagaries of African filing clerks and termites can make it so. The substantive norms of homicide were sometimes exposed and occasionally clouded in the records of these cases.

The Tiv phrase for homicide is *or wuan* or "man killing." Distinctions within the concept are made by a set of adjectives by which Tiv distinguish degrees of culpability in most serious breaches of norm. A man can perform a breach of norm, including homicide, "by accident" (*sha aikor*), or "through ignorance" (*sha lanegh*), but he can also perform it by purposely going against the known norms of Tiv society (*sha apela*). When these terms are compared with the English words, we find that the first two are more or less coextensive with man-

31

slaughter as it is legally defined, and the last more or less coextensive with murder. The two sets of distinctions are not
precisely parallel, however.

In examining the Tiv cases in search for repetitive social
and cultural patterns, those which are unequivocally manslaughter to the English judges and "killing a man by accident" to the Tiv can be considered first.

The most important pattern of "accidental killings" in Tivland is that which occurs in communal hunting. Before it was
made illegal, Tiv carried out large communal hunts during
the latter part of the dry season—usually from January through
April, although smaller hunts might be organized at other times
of the year. Usually the grass was fired; Tiv formed a ring
around the burning area and shot the game with poisoned
arrows as it rushed out.[2] It is small wonder that many accidents occurred; since the arrows were poisoned, even minor
accidents often proved fatal.

There are 21 of these hunting accidents in the sample. In
my hurried notes on them I did not record sentences in 9
cases. Of the remaining 12, one was acquitted, one discharged
for want of evidence, one released after having been given
12 strokes administered on order of the court by his father,
and the rest received sentences of between 4 months and 18
months at hard labor.

A second, but much less common, pattern of accidental
killing occurs in the handling of firearms. Four of five killings
in which the weapon was a gun, were accidents. Tiv make
their own muzzle-loading "Dane guns," importing only the
barrels. The mechanism is not always safe in itself, or safely
used.

There were eleven other "accidental" killings, but no well-
marked patterns emerge from them: four occurred in the
course of beer-drinks and gambling brawls; two resulted from
blows that would not normally cause death; one man was ac-

[2] R. C. Abraham, *The Tiv People*, London, Crown Agents, 1940,
pp. 134ff.

cused of beating his child, but the judge decided that there was no evidence to indicate that the child did not die of convulsions, and that there was certainly no intent to kill. One man was accidentally killed by bumping into a poisoned arrow held by one of his kinsmen in the dark; another was killed by a horse in a market place during a show of prestige items—the owner of the horse was reprimanded for bringing it into the market place. In the final case, a man set fire to a hut in anger; a woman dashed in to recover her belongings and the roof collapsed on her.

These 35 "accidental" killings will be omitted for most of the subsequent analysis. We are left with a sample of 87 homicides which cannot be classified unequivocally as "accidents."

The weapons with which Tiv commit homicide are overwhelmingly arrows and knives, even when the accidents have been removed from the sample (see Table 1). Figures such as

TABLE 1. WEAPONS USED IN TIV HOMICIDES

Weapon	Total sample		Accidents omitted	
	No. cases	Per cent	No. cases	Per cent
Arrows	47	39.2	26	30.0
Knives and Matchets	33	27.0	29	33.3
Beating	19	15.5	15	17.2
Gun	5	4.0	1	1.1
Spear	3	2.3	3	3.5
Axe	3	2.3	3	3.5
Adze	1	.7	1	1.1
Miscellaneous	11	9.0	9	10.3
TOTAL	122	100.0	87	100.0

these tend to be more meaningful in comparison than as characteristic of a single society. Compared with my own samples from North Nyanza of Kenya, the number of Tiv killings by beating is very small, and those done by cutting and piercing instruments is correspondingly large.

Arrangement of the homicides by month of the year (Table 2) reveals that killings are most numerous in February, March, and April, the months of the late dry season. When the hunting accidents are deducted—most of them occur at this season—there is still a slight increase in killings in those months. No single pattern accounts for the increase, which is a general

TABLE 2. TIV HOMICIDE BY MONTH OF OCCURRENCE

Month	Number of killings	
January	4	
February	9	
March	9	[2]*
April	12	[4]
May	6	
June	3	
July	6	
August	5	
September	6	
October	4	
November	6	[1]
December	6	
Date not recorded	46	[14]
TOTAL	122	[21]

* Hunting accidents

one. This period is the one in which Tiv have the largest amounts of food, perform the most ceremonies, and give the most parties. The period from May to December, which shows a slightly lower incidence of homicide, is the time of heaviest agricultural labor, tasks in which mainly small family groups take part. In any case, the differences by time of year are small, and seem to be of less importance than they are in Europe or America.

The relationship between a killer and his victim is a subject which all who have studied it insist is not adequately documented in European and American statistics and case histories.[3] This factor is one of the first to strike an anthropologist, because the relationship among the actors is one of the first things which he studies about any social situation. Especially in those societies which hold kinship more important than we do, and which use it as a fundamental organizing principle to a greater extent than we, this factor is of an importance that cannot be exaggerated.

In studying the killer-victim relationship, I shall provide several sets of analyses in order to bring the data as nearly as possible into line with other studies in the field. We shall first examine the total sample from the standpoint of the sex of the killer and that of the victim. We shall then examine the specific relationships, whether kinship or some other sort, between those in the smaller sample, from which "accidents" have been omitted.

Three noteworthy facts emerge from Table 3, which sets forth the killers and victims by sex: women are involved in homicide even less than they are in European countries, the

TABLE 3. SEX OF KILLERS AND VICTIMS

Killer Victim	Man kills—	Several men kill—	Woman kills—	Unknown person kills—	TOTAL
Male	87	4	2	1	94
Female	16	2	1	–	19
Several males	1	–	–	–	1
Several females	2	–	1	–	3
Both males and females	3	–	–	–	3
Child of unknown sex	1	–	1	–	2
TOTAL	110	6	5	1	122

[3] Hans von Hentig, *The Criminal and his Victim*, New Haven, Yale University Press, 1948; Marvin Wolfgang, *Patterns in Criminal Homicide*, University of Pennsylvania Press, 1958; and Kaare Svalastoga, "Homicide and Social Contact in Denmark," *American Journal of Sociology*, LXII, No. 1, pp. 37-41.

number of killings done by more than one person is very small, and the number of "unsolved murders" is very small indeed.

Of a total of 122 killings, only five, or 4 per cent, were done by women. When accidents are omitted, women were responsible for a little under 6 per cent. Although the percentage of killers who are women is small in every society, this figure is unusually small. It is unusual in another way as well: four of the five women killed with a knife or arrow. The fifth, who was released by the High Court for want of evidence of intent, hit her husband on the head with a log; he fell into a stream and drowned. Of the first four, two women killed their children, and two killed their agnatic kinsmen, one a man and one a woman. Of the several conclusions that may be drawn from these cases, the most apparent is that only certain types of cases ever came before a magistrate. In many countries, women are believed to use poison as the predominant weapon. Whether this situation also exists in Tivland it is impossible to say. There are few post mortem medical examinations on victims; moreover, doctors say that among those few there is little likelihood of finding a non-metallic poison (the most common sort in West Africa). Even more important, one cannot ask the Tiv, for they do not distinguish as we do between "poisoning by substance" (what they would call "medicine" and we "poison") and "killing by witchcraft." They consider that both are necessary, at least to some extent, in many deaths which we would consider natural. They further believe that women often "poison" their husbands in this mystic sense, but that the women are mere tools of the witches. In a country in which all death is believed to be homicide in one form or another, it is difficult to examine any except the most obviously overt forms of killing.

Of the four cases in which women were convicted of homicide, all were adjudged guilty but insane. One of the four was a known case of sleeping sickness.

The number of female victims of homicide is also very small

36

by the standards of Western society. Of the sixteen female victims of male murderers, eight were wives or recognized mistresses, two were mothers. Analysis of these cases will be made below, in association with the other kinship relationships.

Omitting the accidents, we have 87 cases. There were two double killings, and one case in which there were two relationships of importance between one set of persons.[4] We thus have a total sample of 90 relationships between killer and victim in non-accidental situations. In these cases we find the distributions as they are set forth in Table 4. Important patterns are to be found in the first and second categories.

TABLE 4. RELATIONSHIPS BETWEEN KILLERS
AND VICTIMS

Victims were thieves (or were mistaken for thieves) stealing from accused	8
Victims were kinsmen (including affines) of accused	48
Victims (other than thieves) were stated not to be kinsmen of the accused	13
Residual category: "relationship unknown" (includes one case in which the killer is not known)	21
TOTAL	90

Killing of thieves is a comparatively rare but regular occurrence in Tivland. Tiv say that in the past such killings may have led to war, but it is not a moral wrong, especially if the thief stole agricultural produce or other food. As one man told the magistrate, when accused of killing the thief of his wife's yams, "I was following an old custom that if a man

[4] There is one multiple killing (Case No. 10 below) in which a man killed his mistress' three daughters. I have counted this as a single relationship to avoid overweighting the evidence on the basis of a unique case.

caught a thief he should kill him. If I was wrong, then kill me, but first pay for my wife's yams."[5]

In seven instances, thieves were caught red-handed and were beaten until they died. It seems doubtful that intent to kill could be proved in any of them, and as a matter of fact, in two of these seven cases the accused were released or given short sentences for unlawful wounding because there was insufficient evidence that the wounds caused death. In one instance, however, four men were convicted and hanged for killing a thief; this particular theft included a very powerful fetish referred to in the English account as a "head" (it was probably the fetish called "father's head," *ityough ki ter*). The official who carried out the Preliminary Inquiry in this case did not understand what the issues were, and his record is unsatisfactory from the anthropologist's standpoint; I was unable to find a copy of the trial records.

Of the total of six crimes by more than one accused person, four were beating of thieves, their victims being both male and female.[6] The entire neighborhood may be brought out to punish thieves, as the following case indicates:

Case No. 1. Rex *vs*. Girgir and four others, for killing a thief.

Imenger, the head of a compound, was sleeping alone in his reception hut one night when he was wakened by the sound of clinking metal. He put his hand up to the point on the half-wall of the reception hut where he had placed some hoes the evening before and found that they were gone. He raised the five accused (his sons and brothers' sons) by his calling; they pursued the thieves. They caught one of four men and,

[5] The subject of thieves is discussed at length in *Judgment and Justice among the Tiv*; other murder cases are also described in that book.

[6] In the fifth instance of multiple killers, two men combined to kill and rob a Hausa trader; in the other, two men killed an Udam woman and took her head.

in the process, the thief used a knife on one of them, thus angering them all. They beat him severely. He died before he could be returned to Imenger's compound. The man whose hand had been cut proceeded immediately to the District Headquarters and informed the District Officer. The five accused were committed to the High Court on a charge of murder. They were found not guilty of murder but guilty of manslaughter and each was sentenced to four months' hard labor.

In those cases in which there is a kinship relationship between killer and victim, two important patterns appear. Table 5 lists the total of 48 instances in which a kinship relationship was found. The figures for affinal kinsmen have been swollen because I have included with them 2 victims who were publicly recognized mistresses rather than "legal" wives of their killers, and seven men who were lovers of their killers' wives. These persons, especially the latter, are not affines, strictly speaking, but including them has the advantage of throwing together all cases of sexual jealousy and adultery, and all cases which occur within the family institution.

In discussing killing of affines, we must distinguish two groups: (1) those cases in which the victim is a spouse's kinsman or a kinsman's spouse, and (2) those in which the victim is the killer's own spouse (or mistress), or wife's lover. The first group shows no regular patterns. The man who killed his father's wife (see Table 5) was declared insane, suffering from sleeping sickness which had reached a violent stage. The one who killed his mistress' daughters was not legally insane, but certainly was what would be called psychotic in our society (see Case No. 10). The man who killed his wife's elderly guardian with a knife claimed to have been aiming at someone (otherwise unidentified in the Preliminary Inquiry or trial record) who had been "spoiling his marriage." The man who killed his brother's wife did so while insane. The one who killed his wife's brother did so when the latter jeered at him for living uxorilocally—uxorilocal residence is very rare in Tivland, and is very much despised.

TABLE 5. KINSHIP RELATIONSHIP OF VICTIMS
TO KILLERS

	Agnates		Non-agnatic cognates		Affines		TOTAL
Ascending generation	FaBr "compound head" Other	4 1 1	Mo MoBr MoAgnate	2 1 1	WiGuardian FaWi	1 1	12
Ego's generation	Br FaBrSo Other	7 1 1	–		Wife BrWi WiBr Hu Mistress WiLover	6 1 1 1 2 7	27
Descending generation	BrSo Da Child FaBrSoSo	4 1 1 1	FaBrDaSo	1	Mistress' Da	1	9
TOTAL		22		5		21	48

There is, thus, some unusual circumstance in each of these cases.

In the second group—those persons who kill spouse or wife's lovers—some regularity appears. There are 6 cases in which men killed their wives. In one of them the husband was declared insane (see below, Case No. 9). Of the five remaining, two cases concerned adultery, two definitely did not, and in one instance the issue was doubtful. Thus, in at least half of the cases in which men killed their wives (including that in which the husband was insane) sexual motives were not directly involved. The questionable case is the most instructive:

Case No. 2. Sughgba killed his wife, WanItyo (1938).

Sughgba married WanItyo, who was a ward of Igbedde. She bore one child, a daughter, and then had no more children. Sughgba consulted a diviner on the matter of his wife's infertility, and was told that she had been bewitched, and that the matter must be taken care of by her lineage. He therefore took her home with the necessary animals and money to have the rites performed [though the wife's kinsman must perform the rites, the husband must pay for them].

The guardian said that he had no opportunity to cure her at the moment, and suggested that Sughgba leave her and the animals. He did so. In about a month's time he went back and returned his wife to his own compound. Two days later she ran back to her guardian. When Sughgba went for her the second time she refused to go home with him but said she wanted to marry someone else. The guardian told her to go with her husband—obviously he was unwilling to refund the bride-wealth.

Husband and guardian forced the wife to return to the husband's compound. Two days later she asked for permission to return to her guardian's compound to get her property which she had left there. The husband refused it. She said that she was going anyway. A fight ensued. Neighbors and bystanders separated them. She hit him with a stick while he was being held, and shouted at him (according to the husband's evidence) "You beat me like this—kill me today!" His statement continues: "She took a stick and beat me. I caught hold of the stick but MbaAkurga came up and took it from me and told me to stop. She hit me on the neck and head. I fought to get rid of them and throw them off. I asked why they had caught hold of me when my wife was beating me. I then drew a knife and threatened to strike anyone who beat me.

My wife came and beat me on the wrist with a stick. Kpelaun caught my knife hand. I snatched the knife hand back and inflicted a scratch on her. I then stabbed my wife. Her intestines came out. I said, 'I have killed myself.' My heart bled. I bandaged her wound. I told MbaAkurga to go and tell the others quickly, this is a bad thing." The wife died a few days later at the dispensary to which she had been taken.

In a community in which 83 per cent of the adult males are agnatic kinsmen of one another, the chances that a woman's lover will be a kinsman of her husband are obviously extremely high. Of the two uxoricides in which adultery was involved, one adultery was with a man unrelated to the husband, the other was with the husband's "brother" (the exact relationship cannot be traced, but it was either a half-brother or a father's brother's son). In the eight cases in which men killed their wives' lovers, only this case and one other show any kinship relationship between the husband and the lover. Any field worker in Tivland realizes that adulteries between women and their husbands' kinsmen occur frequently. Tiv do not suggest that such adultery does not occur. They insist, however—and the cases prove them right—that a wife's adulteries must not be allowed to disturb relationships among kinsmen. If a woman continues to commit adultery with her husband's kinsman, she is made to leave.

The sentences for killing a wife's lover range all the way from 18 months at hard labor for the man who killed the lover whom he found *in flagrante delicto,* to death for the killer who told the court, "X had committed adultery with my wife. For four months now I have determined to kill him. I have."

Another pattern of murder, and this one is more characteristically Tiv, appears among agnates. In 9 of the 22 instances in which victims were agnates of their killers, witchcraft was involved. Also in 9 of them, insanity was present. In 5, insanity and witchcraft ostensibly overlap. If we count insanity as a form of illness, as Tiv do, in 8 of the 9 instances of witch-craft, the syndrome "illness–agnates–witchcraft–murder" appears. The pattern is also found among non-agnates of the ascending generation. It is impossible to define the limits of this pattern because many cases besides those so considered in official investigations can be analyzed in light of it.

In examining the killing of agnates, it is necessary to look into the generation differences, as we have done in Table 6.

TABLE 6. GENERATION DISTINCTIONS AMONG
AGNATICALLY RELATED VICTIMS OF HOMICIDES

Persons who killed agnates of— generation	Witchcraft	No witchcraft	TOTAL
Ascending generation	4	2[a]	6
Ego's generation	1	8[b]	9
Descending generation	4	3[c]	7
			22

[a] 1 bride-wealth dispute, 1 mistaken identity.
[b] 2 insanity, 2 "unreasonable impulse," 2 fights, 1 adultery, 1 mistaken identity.
[c] 1 adultery, 2 insanity.

In the single case in situations involving witchcraft, in which a man killed an agnate of his own generation, it was an elder half-brother who stood to him *in loco parentis*. We have here a documentation of a very overt Tiv belief: it is one's agnates who bewitch one, but not the agnates of one's own generation who are, rather, one's protectors against the elders of one's agnatic lineage.

Investigation of cases which display this pattern requires some background information about Tiv religious and cosmographical belief. Tiv explain much of their cosmography and most of their notions of illness and misfortune by reference to *tsav*, which is sometimes translated into English as "witchcraft substance." *Tsav* is said to be a growth on the heart of some persons, indicating special talent and ability, including ability to perform acts which Westerners would have to consider "supernatural." Tiv say that some of the elders of the community, who have *tsav* and form the *mbatsav*, meet at night in order to carry out rituals which are to the advantage of the lineage and all people who live within its area. However, in order to carry on their work they must make human sacrifices from time to time, and it is as *mbatsav* that the elders decide who is to be sacrificed. Tiv also say that some elders use their *tsav* for personal, individual, and *ipso facto* evil purposes, bewitching persons without the consent of the *mbatsav* of the community. All illness and death is ultimately attributable to *tsav*; usually it is the *mbatsav* among one's agnates who have reason and power to kill one. The tensions of neighbors and those of agnates are combined and are expressed in terms of *tsav* and the men who "grow" it on their hearts. The best way further to elucidate the matter is to look thoroughly into the cases.

Case No. 3. Wannongo killed his kinsman, Jabi, with an axe.

As a child, Wannongo had suffered from epilepsy. His father believed that the *mbatsav* were using the *ikungu* fetish against Wannongo, and countered the evil which he assumed to be at work among his agnates by taking the boy to live with his mother's lineage. Wannongo "drank medicine" and suffered no more attacks. He was circumcised there and lived there until he became adult.

When Wannongo was grown he left his father's mother's lineage; without going back to his own lineage, he went in search of a wife. He married a woman of MbaTiav and went further west, to Shangev Tiev, where he settled down for

44

some years. He was fit and healthy with no sign of the epilepsy that had troubled him during childhood.

Several years later, Wannongo's elder full brother, Itibo, was killed by snake-bite. He had lived in his agnatic lineage area all his life. Tiv say that snakes are like arrows—they have poison on them but do not hurt anyone unless they are shot at him. Snakes are the arrows of the *mbatsav*; snakes never bite without having been set by the *mbatsav* to do so. Since only agnates can readily bewitch one, the obvious assumption was that Itibo had been killed because his agnates had set a snake to bite him.

Wannongo now went back to take up his brother's inheritance: his wives and his farms. He refused to live in the area of his agnatic lineage, but rather moved into the compound of an elder in an adjoining area. A few months later he was struck by an epileptic attack—while working on the farm in the area of his own lineage. The attacks recurred. His hosts became afraid for his life and refused to let him stay any longer for fear they would be involved in the witchcraft discussions and accusations that would follow his probable death. Wannongo could do nothing but move to his agnates [though I do not know why he considered it impossible to return to his western friends].

The attacks grew worse; soon it was impossible for Wannongo to work. In such a situation it is Tiv custom for the compound head to send someone to a diviner to determine the source of the epilepsy. After consultation, ceremonies should be carried out and perhaps a moot held to discuss witchcraft, if the consultation indicated its presence. However, Jabi, the compound head, was desultory in sending to the diviner. Wannongo, in his statement to the magistrate, says that he asked Jabi again and again to send someone to a diviner. When finally Jabi did send to a diviner, it was determined that the *ikungu* fetish in the lineage of Wannongo's mother had to be repaired. This meant it was necessary to get someone from that lineage who was capable of carrying out the ceremony. Little was done.

Several months later, an old man was found living in a nearby lineage who was an agnate of the lineage of Wannongo's mother. He could not perform the ceremony, but he could touch Naaga, a fairly close agnate of Wannongo's, while Naaga performed it. On the day of the murder, the old man who was Wannongo's kinsman came to carry out his part of the ceremony but Naaga refused to come because he was going to a beer-drink.

During that day Wannongo was particularly ill. He dug a hole in the ground behind his hut, lay down in it and howled for his "brothers" to bury him. He howled that he was being bewitched and that his kinsmen were obviously bewitching him because they would take no hand in curing him.

Toward evening, he seemed to be better; watch over him was relaxed. Soon after dark, he picked up an axe, went to Jabi, the compound head, and asked, "Why did you send away my mother's kinsman?" Jabi replied that the old man would return the next day for the ceremony. Without further words, Wannongo struck Jabi on the forehead with the axe, cleaving his skull and killing him instantly. He set up a shout that "they" were killing him with epilepsy. However, he had turned the tables on "them." He had killed Jabi, and if there was anyone else who wanted to kill him, they should come to try it now in open combat.

Wannongo, in his statement, is quoted in English as having said in Tiv, "I was convinced that my brothers were killing me by witchcraft. I saw strangers coming for me in great numbers like evil spirits. I felt that they had entered my belly and went through my body, some coming out of my head, some coming out of my feet. . . . In the early evening, I was better, but later I again began to see evil spirits. So I went to Jabi to remonstrate with him for sending Angiche [the mother's kinsman] away. I did not intend to kill him. . . .

I felt certain when I spoke to Jabi that he meant to kill me by witchcraft, and lost control of my reason and killed him."

At his trial, Wannongo was declared guilty but insane.

This case shows clearly that a man, already insecure from his childhood illness and subsequent removal, took up physical weapons in defence of his life against what he conceived to be stronger weapons.

This killer was declared legally insane under the McNaughton rules. But the values in terms of which he acted were sound Tiv values: agnatic kinsmen are loved and respected because they are your kinsmen and neighbors, but they are also feared because they share a common patrimony with you and because, as a group, they must renew themselves spiritually and ceremonially through spilling the blood of one of themselves as a sacrifice.

A constant but usually latent fear of one's agnates results. When illness strikes, fear immediately springs up. One distrusts those persons whom one considers to be one's closest kin. They may be basing their chances of survival on one's own life.

Most Tiv, in this situation, run to their mother's lineages, where they consider themselves safe from their agnates. A man's age-set sometimes comes to his aid at this time: the age-mates consult a diviner about the causes of illness, and they "ask" the elders of his lineage, in a moot, why they have allowed him to be bewitched in this way. Before the British Administration, age-sets sometimes mauled and even killed elders whom the divination apparatus showed to be guilty of bewitching their members if the elders would not in the course of a moot agree to a settlement and withdraw their power.

Tiv are always drawn toward their agnates because their rights as citizens to land, to law, and to social position can be claimed only in the area of their agnatic lineage. At the same time, the jealousies, frictions, and hatreds that exist among kinsmen, especially those who are close neighbors, are expressed in mystical terms centering on the notion of *tsav*. The leaders of Tiv society are the elders of the lineage. Their wisdom is necessary; their protection of the community is necessary; their ceremonial "repairing" of the community is necessary. Yet, their wisdom incorporates the knowledge of how to kill, and their protection must be withdrawn from at least one member of the community from time to time in order that a sacrifice may be had for "repairing" the community as a whole.

How much homicide occurs in order to carry out these rites is, of course, unknown because it would not be reported. However, we can assume that it is extremely rare, for the *mbatsav* kill not by material but by psychic weapons. Murder occurs when a man who suspects he is a victim takes matters into his own hands and fights back with material weapons.

In a much smaller number of cases, kinsmen other than one's agnates enter into this pattern. Duels and deals between the *mbatsav* of several communities ("fought" out in the course of moots in the daytime) make it possible occasionally for even one's mother's people to turn on one.

Case No. 4. Abo killed his mother's brother's compound head (1949).

Abo's statement to the magistrate: "About four years ago I took my younger brother Aerga to the house of Amema, my mother's brother, as Aerga was unwell. About three months ago I went to see Aerga and found him no better. I thought that he was neglected and began to reproach Amema, but he said that it was not his fault and told me not to bother him. I said that it was his business, as he had taken care of Aerga, and he was doing nothing to help him. Then Amema slapped me. I lost my temper. I rushed to Ugenyi's house to tell him, as he is head of my mother's family. Ugenyi told me that I had done wrong to quarrel with my relatives and he did not want to hear me. He began to hit me. I saw an arrow and picked it up. Ugenyi tried to catch hold of me so I stabbed him the arrow. . . ."

Tiv suspect their mothers of bewitching them, probably more often than any other non-agnatic kinsman. There are two bases for such beliefs: every woman, Tiv say, owes one child to the *mbatsav* for sacrifice; once she has given it, her other children should be allowed to live in peace. But Tiv are uncertain about whether the mother designates the particular child. I have heard Tiv women complain to the elders of their husbands' communities when "too many" of their children die; it is a standard reason for leaving the husband. In addition, it is believed that women are easier than men to trick into flesh debts. If a person, by a trick, is made to eat human flesh, he must provide victims to "repay" his "debt" (*ikpindi*). A man in such a position can choose from among his agnates. But a woman, in such a position, has only her children to give.

Case No. 5. Ngur killed his mother because he was bewitched.

Ngur was accused of killing his mother, Wanikyar. His full brother recalled helping Ngur to make a knife and haft it at a blacksmith's forge, and that as they were going home afterwards, Ngur said to him, "Do you know[7] what is wrong with me? Do you know what caused my illness?" The younger brother, Ihembe, said that he did not know, and Ngur asked, "Does our mother, Wanikyar, know the cause?" Ihembe replied that the divination apparatus had been consulted and had not in any way involved their mother. "If you were older," Ngur told his brother, "I would tell you something."

When they reached home Ihembe went into the reception

[7] In these contexts, Tiv use their word for "know" (*fa*) to mean "to have guilty knowledge" and by implication some degree of guilt.

hut, while Ngur went into his mother's hut and lay down on the bed. His mother was sweeping. Ihembe was sitting in the reception hut wanting very much to know what Ngur might have to say to him when screams came from the house. Ihembe's evidence runs: "I jumped up at once to see what was happening. I opened the door and went in and saw that Ngur had stabbed our mother Wanikyar on her right side just below the ribs [demonstrates position]. He had pulled the blade out and was trying to stab her again, but Wanikyar was struggling with him. I caught hold of him and tried to get the knife away from him. It was the same knife that he had made. In doing so, my fingers were cut. I told Wanikyar to go outside and she did so. When the women who were sitting in the compound saw her, they ran away. Ngur was too strong for me and went outside with his knife in his hand. I followed him and again tried to get hold of the knife. He told me to leave him alone. He said that he would not stab Wanikyar again, but would go after Iwer and Wantsegha who had caused his illness. He was too strong for me so I left him." Ihembe turned to aid their mother; she was carried to a dispensary where she died a few hours later.

Meanwhile, Ngur looked for but failed to find the two persons, Iwer and Wantsegha, whom he believed had caused his illness. He attempted suicide.

In cross-examination by the magistrate, Ihembe said, "Ngur had been ill for two years and sometimes when the illness was bad he would talk foolishly. He would not answer questions, and he used to talk to himself." He said that his body often trembled and that "some people said he was mad, but we said that the *mbatsav* had bewitched him."

Later evidence showed that when Ngur became ill, his kinsmen consulted a diviner who said that the trouble was due to the *akombo twer* and the *akombo chigh*. These fetishes were propitiated in a ceremony that involved sacrifice of goats and chickens. Since there was no effect, he consulted the elders and Agwabi, the compound head, consulted the divination apparatus again. This time Wantsegha and Iwer were shown to be responsible for Ngur's illness. The elders thereupon summoned these two and they, together with Ngur's mother, were made to swear on *swem* that no harm should come to Ngur. The illness failed to get any better. A short time afterwards the murder took place.

Ngur was declared to be "a person of unsound mind," and was not tried. He died after five years in an asylum. He was acting in accordance with Tiv values, even when he took his defense into his own hands.

This point becomes clear by comparison with a case in which witchcraft was involved, but in which legal insanity did not enter.

Case No. 6. Ngaghen killed the daughter of a man he thought was bewitching him (1949).

Ngaghen's own evidence, as taken down by the magistrate, contains all the necessary information about this case, and much of the equally necessary ambiguity: "About two months ago, Wakwagh came up to me and told me that Yemeer would kill me. I went off with the intention of telling our kindred head [a man occupying the government office of *ortaregh*], but on the road I met Alia who told me the same. I then went to the kindred head and he said, 'Yes, I have heard the same thing. But I am the kindred head, working for the District Officer. You must go to Mtegh the elder, who will collect all the other elders and investigate the matter [in a moot].' I went to Mtegh's house and told him what I feared. Mtegh said that it was true that all MbaTerem [agnatic lineage] had met and decided to kill me. I asked Mtegh, 'Am I seeking death myself or has my mother said I must be killed?'[8] Mtegh said, 'Get away from here. I have not accepted money to kill you. Yemeer was paid!' Then I left and took a matchet and went to Yemeer's house with the intention of telling him, 'You have taken money to kill me, so try to do so!' I did not find Yemeer at home. I set out for home but on the way I met one of Yemeer's daughters on Yemeer's farm, and I killed her."

Except for the absence of mental disease or legal insanity, this case differs little from the foregoing cases. In all, a person who believed himself the victim of witches took matters into his own hands. The symptoms of the presence of witchcraft may be delusions, mental disease or epilepsy, or the person may be warned that he is the next victim of the *mbatsav* of his community. However he comes to believe that he is being killed by his kinsmen and neighbors, his reaction is much the same: to "get them before they get me."

It sometimes happens that a person kills because he has been accused of being a witch rather than because he fears witches. Again, insanity may or may not enter.

Case No. 7. Akperaku is accused first of witch-craft and then of killing her two children (1938).

Akperaku left her husband, took her two children and re-turned to her agnatic lineage. About a month later she appeared again at the compound of her husband in a weakened and demented condition. She told him that two of her kinsmen had killed their two children. The husband and one of his kinsmen went to the place she indicated and found the bodies

---

[8] It would seem that Ngaghen's mother had never lost a child, but the exchange marriage of his mother may have affected the situation, so that "my mother" refers to her lineage.

of the two children, one girl about 5 and another of about 10.

Akperaku charged two men of her agnatic lineage before the court, with killing her children. They both established alibis. Her lineage said that she killed the children and she said she did not. She had been accused of stealing and had tried to kill herself. With great skill and patience the magistrate determined that she had been called a witch, not a thief.

She had been locked in a hut with her children but escaped with them. One of her lineage kinsmen found her next morning, near a stream, trying to kill herself again—she had cut her own throat, but had not severed the arteries. As this kinsman was looking for the children, Akperaku ran away and walked all that day and the next night to her husband's compound.

Akperaku was found guilty but insane, and was assigned to the insane asylum. The judge's summing up contains the statement: "The horrible consequences of such an accusation, which are well known did, I am convinced, drive the accused into such a state of frenzy that she did not know what she was doing, though there may have been in her subconscious mind a desire to relieve her children of the taint that would be communicated by her being proved a witch."

Akperaku was released three years later and returned to her family. Her husband refused to have her back, but her agnatic kinsmen agreed to look after her.

Although Tiv do not believe that the "taint" of witchcraft is heritable, as some African peoples do, the judge may be right that she murdered and attempted suicide in a frenzy resulting from the accusation of being a witch.[9] Such cases, to be thoroughly understood, must be accompanied by medical and psychological evidence. The culture patterns are, however, clear enough.

Only one case in which a person killed a non-agnatic kinsman does not conform to the pattern centered on witchcraft.

[9] A similar case is recounted in *Akiga's Story*, pp. 277-278.

It is instructive to look at all of the cases in which insanity plays a part. Of a total of 87 killings, there were 19 in which the accused person was declared unfit to plead, guilty but insane, not guilty and insane, or in which the accused died, presumed insane, in the course of the hearing. Furthermore, one case (never solved—a kinsman was charged but released) concerned the murder of a mad man. Three more cases concerned mental illness either of the accused person or as a contributing factor in the evidence. Thus, in 23 out of 87 killings in Tivland, mental illness was involved.

Of these 23 killings involving mental illness, 11 present the pattern: illness–witchcraft–murder. In three additional cases, the accused were known to suffer from sleeping sickness, which may reach a violent stage at one point of its course. Two were pronounced epileptics. Both sleeping sickness and epileptic cases were associated with the witchcraft pattern.

Epilepsy is fairly common in Tivland, at least in comparison with Buluyia. There is no record of epilepsy in 125 cases of Buluyia homicide. There are half a dozen among the Tiv cases. More convincing to me, I saw no epilepsy among the Buluyia but saw several attacks in Tivland and knew several other people who were said to be subject to such attacks.

It is a well known fact that epilepsy and homicide show a positive association, although it is not known just why the association is present. Hill and Pond note that murder is seldom associated with an epileptic seizure, but that nevertheless there are 32 times as many epileptics in a sample of 110 British murderers as appear in the general population. Epilepsy appears 35 times as frequently in a sample of juvenile criminals as in the general population in a Chicago test quoted by Gillin.[10]

Tiv describe epilepsy by the symptoms: "to fall to the

[10] Denis Hill and D. A. Pond, "Reflections on One Hundred Capital Cases Submitted to Electroencephalography," *Journal of Mental Science*, No. 98, 1952, pp. 23-43. John L. Gillin, *Criminology and Penology*, London, 1927, p. 127.

ground" or more commonly "to fall into the fire." *Kungu* is the name of the fetish which is said to cause, more accurately, to *be*, epilepsy or any other fainting fits. Tiv are afraid of epileptics; women and young men almost always run away when a seizure occurs. One of the six cases involving epilepsy has been recorded above.

Tiv also suffer considerably—or did until about 1949—from sleeping sickness. There is no evidence that they recognized sleeping sickness as a "disease" before it was pointed out to them by Europeans; certainly they did not know its carriers. Today it is called by a term which is a direct translation of "sleeping sickness."

Sleeping sickness causes, I understand, the deterioration of the gray cells of the spinal column and the brain, and hence one of its symptoms in advanced stages is madness, often accompanied by violence. Until the discovery of pentamadine and other modern drugs, its cure or arrest required as many as 15 injections given over a period of time. Authorities have told me that it was very difficult to insure that Tiv finished such a course of injections, because the first third or so of them removed most of the gross symptoms. Hence, lapsed cases were common.

Case No. 8. Jonki, who suffered from sleeping sickness, killed his father's wife.

Jonki lived alone, with his father and his father's wife, in a small compound containing two huts and a reception hut. His own mother had died of sleeping sickness when he was a small boy. According to his father's evidence, they lived happily until Jonki got sleeping sickness, whereupon he became grouchy, nagged at Ikuan, the wife, who nagged back. Jonki's father told the magistrate: "On the night this happened, I was sleeping in the reception hut with my wife. I was suddenly wakened by my wife crying out, 'I have been shot.' I

55

saw an arrow in her left side; it had not penetrated deeply. I pulled out the arrow and went outside and got some medicinal leaves and gave them to my wife to drink as a potion, but she died before very long. When I pulled out the arrow I saw the remains of some old poison on it, but not very much. I then ran after Jonki but could not find him until sunset next day. He had nothing in his hands but would not answer why he had done it. He seemed sick and not his true self." The father added that it was Jonki's illness which made him say "annoying things" and he had often told his wife to pay no attention.

Jonki himself is quoted: "Since I became ill I used to sleep from morning to night. Later I became so ill that I could not sleep. I was very ill. My mouth and throat were sore and I could hardly hear. I did not know what was happening at all until after I had been taken to Makurdi and treated by the doctor."

Jonki got medical treatment; it would seem that he was released afterwards, but the records in the file do not say definitely. Several cases describe men and one woman going berserk in the course of sleeping sickness and killing those near at hand. Tiv put violent cases of sleeping sickness, like all violent lunatics, into stocks where they are cared for and guarded.

This case, like the last, makes no mention of witchcraft as a motive for murder, and I have therefore not counted it in the number showing that pattern. I personally think, however, that its presence must be assumed because Tiv associate almost all madness with witchcraft. The presence of sleeping sickness —like the presence of epilepsy or of any other serious disease— indicates *tsav*. The number of cases which have been assigned to this pattern is a minimum. Had I been able to investigate them on the ground, I think the number would be very much higher.

There are, in addition to cases of epileptics and persons

suffering from sleeping sickness, several cases in which "berserk" behavior occurred.

Case No. 9. Shirkwagh kills his wife.

The first witness in this case tells the story briefly and well: "Six days ago I got up at dawn and went to the stream to supervise a fish trap. I stayed near the stream till night fell. I left the bed of the stream and came to the banks. I saw Shirkwagh and his wife and Age—they were approaching the stream. Shirkwagh's wife was in front, followed by Shirkwagh. Age brought up the rear. Shirkwagh and his wife crossed the stream. When they had got over, I saw Shirkwagh draw a knife and stab his wife in the stomach. She cried out to Age, 'Death has overtaken me.' Age helped the woman to move along the path. I went and caught hold of Shirkwagh and took his knife from him. I went to Agondo's house which was close to the stream. Age was in front with the woman, helping her walk. She did not get as far as Agondo's house. She stopped and sat down. At cockcrow next morning she died. . . . When Shirkwagh stabbed his wife they were not arguing or quarreling. He struck only one blow."

Other witnesses described Shirkwagh as a wanderer and said that he had been ill. "Accused has lived in my household for three months. I sent him to Jov market to sell some meat. On his return he started weeping and said something had happened to him on the road. He would not say what. I saw his mouth was cut. He then started to talk nonsense about nothing whatever that I could understand. When I saw he had the appearance of being demented, I sent him to Iger with the request that he should administer medicine against witchcraft, evil spirits, and madness. Iger told me he had given him medicine for evil spirits and madness, but I should send him a fowl for the witchcraft ceremony. I sent Iger 2d to buy a [baby] fowl. Iger did the rites. Shirkwagh did not quarrel with his wife until the last few months. He had been perfectly healthy."

The statement of Shirkwagh himself runs: "I was returning from Iger's house with my wife and Age. When we crossed the stream, I found my wife was not pleasing to me. She seemed to have a fish stuck to her side by the lower ribs. I thought someone must have been trying to kill me with witchcraft. I thought the fish was trying to bite me. Then something took my wife away back across the stream and she disappeared. Then when I got to Agondo's house they arrested me.

Shirkwagh died in the insane asylum about a year later.

Seven cases involving insanity were not in any way involved with witchcraft. One of these was the unsolved killing of a mad man. This is one of only two cases in which the police and magistrates did not receive the cooperation of the community in which the killing occurred. The other six seem to me to bespeak social maladjustment and probably psychoses, which I am not competent to analyze psychologically. The most interesting of these cases is given here:

Case No. 10. Ashietsa kills his mistress' three daughters (1936).

Ashietsa, a man apparently about 45, was a misfit in his own society: "He has no house of his own, and no wife of his own. He wanders about and lives with other people." A man without a house, without a farm and without a wife is by Tiv definition mad.

Ashietsa came to the compound of Kuragba, and stayed for about ten days during which time Kuragba "fed him and treated him well." There was a woman in Kuragba's compound, one of his "sisters," who suffered from elephantiasis of the leg. Her name was Ingor. She had three daughters, one of whom was recently married, another about ten years old, and another of five or six. Ashietsa slept with Ingor during these ten days. Ingor's testimony at the preliminary inquiry runs: "Ashietsa came to our house and slept with me. He asked Kuragba for me [as a wife] but Kuragba told him to ask my guardian. Ashietsa gave my father ten shillings so that I could go to [the Dutch Reformed Church Mission hospital at] Mkar to get treatment. I went with Ashietsa to my father who gave him back his ten shillings and told him to take me to Mkar himself. Next morning my daughter brought him food and he ate it and then went off saying he was going to drink beer at the house of Huma. After a short while I heard crying in the stream. My daughter Asemtsa came running with an arrow sticking in her. We ran into our huts and another daughter of mine, Nguto, a young girl thus (indicates about ten years of age), came running up and got into the hut. As we were looking out, I saw Ashietsa shoot an arrow into the hut; it hit Nguto in the neck. It went in deeply. I tried to get it out, but it broke off, and after a little while she died in my arms. The other daughter came up and fell down outside. She had an arrow in her side. She was a girl just past the age of puberty. We took her up. The arrow was deeply in and we could not get it out. After a short while she died. She did not say anything, only wailed. My other daughter too, a married woman, was shot. She came up and we took her in. The arrow had gone in at the back and was sticking out in front. She died in the hut."

One of the witnesses said that some time before effective administration [any time before the end of the First World War], Ashietsa had killed the brother of a man whom he suspected of having committed adultery with his wife. "Ashietsa ran away to Tongov. The Gatiev called the elders of Tswarev and they sent for Ashietsa. Having discussed the matter they decided that a woman must be paid as compensation."

Unfortunately, nothing further is said about Ashietsa in the files beyond his own statement: "Kuragba and his family were my friends; I cannot say what made me do this thing. I have been a wanderer for years because people are afraid of me. I could not get a wife. I had no reason for shooting these people. I had had a bad dream in which I was beaten on the head four times."

Ashietsa was found guilty of murder; sentence was commuted to life imprisonment.

In Table 4 we discovered that there were 13 victims other than thieves who were stated definitely not to be kinsmen of the Accused, and a residual category of 21 in which the relationship was unknown. The absence of a kinship relationship does not, obviously, mean that no relationship existed at all. In order to discover the nature of some of these non-kinship relationships, we shall first examine how many victims in these two categories were strangers to their killers, and how many were acquaintances (Table 7).[11]

TABLE 7. RELATIONSHIP OF VICTIMS TO KILLERS

Victims are—to the killer	
Acquaintances	18
Strangers	4
Unknown	10
Unclassifiable	1
Unsolved	1
	—
	34

The unclassifiable case deals with a man who exposed an infant whose mother had died in childbirth. The relationship of the man to the mother is nowhere stated, though it is prob-

[11] Insofar as it is possible, I have followed the lead of Svalastoga—an acquaintance is someone whom the killer had met before the day of the murder.

ably that of compound head to wife of a compound member.

That only four of the 87 cases, or a little more than 4.5 per cent, unequivocally had victims who were formerly not known to their killers is noteworthy. The percentage in Denmark is about 10 per cent, which corresponds with that in England.

Although the number of ritual killings in this sample is small, the problem deserves mention. "Ritual killings" are of several sorts among Tiv. As we have noted, Tiv believe that human sacrifice is necessary for preserving prosperity. It is my opinion that such "legitimate" human sacrifices are never actually made in the ordinary course of events. However, Case No. 6 concerns a man who feared being sacrificed and said that he committed murder as a result of his fear. Another sort of "ritual murder" is that which is performed in order to acquire pieces of the human anatomy for the purpose of establishing the "great fetishes" (*akombo a tamen*). Several of these great fetishes require human parts (it is this fact, indeed, that makes them "great"): the *ityough ki ter* (part of the *po'or*) needs a skull, as does the *wuna ingbianjor*. The *imborivungu* demands a human tibia. Another fetish requires a knee cap; still another a fresh human brain; the great arrow fetish demands female genitalia, preferably from a woman of an enemy tribe. I have two cases in this complex. One of them involved the murder of a seven-year-old boy (an agnate of the murderers) to obtain a skull for the *Ingbianjor*. His murderers were detected and hanged. The other man was murdered, apparently for a tibia to make an *imborivungu*. An investigation was made into his death, but no charge was ever made.

Finally, there is one case in my sample which deals with taking a head. Head-taking seems to have occurred only in southern Tivland, and seems to have been an importation from the south. Information about this case is scrappy; the preliminary investigation of the case established the overt facts and the three accused were tried, found guilty of murder, and hanged.

These are the most important patterns that emerge from the Tiv material. Several which are common in our own society are lacking: there is only one case in which economic gain was primarily, or even secondarily, the motive. In that case, two Tiv murdered a Hausa trader and stole his goods.

Lack of "economic motivations" for murder is associated with the sort of community life which Tiv live. One would find it impossible to keep or enjoy anything which he might have gained by murder. Even the goods of the Hausa trader mentioned above were found to have been distributed among kinsmen of the murderers when official attempts to collect them were made.

We have found, thus, that the four most important patterns of Tiv homicide are (1) the communal hunt killings, (2) killings which involve adultery or sexual jealousy, (3) killings which result from illness, as it is explained by Tiv ideas about cosmography and witchcraft, and (4) killing thieves. The first and third are typically Tiv and reflect Tiv culture; the second and fourth are as typical but show no peculiarly Tiv characteristics.

Killing thieves is in Tiv eyes a jural mechanism, not a crime. They know, however, that the new administration considers it a crime. They sometimes voice their disapproval of an ethic that allows a man to be executed for killing a worthless wife but will not allow killing a thief caught in the act of stealing. Of the killings which Tiv regard as crimes (*ifer*), those which involve adultery and sexual jealousy occur for the most part within the institution of the household. The witchcraft killings occur within kinship groups. Although the communal hunt killings often occur among kinsmen, they are a function of neighborhood and not of kinship. When kinship is a basis for local grouping, and one of the most important values in a culture, homicide, like everything else, is cast into a kinship idiom.

Homicide among the Tiv of Central Nigeria

My material on Tiv suicide is very thin. I found no records of government investigations of suicide (though I did not search for them). There was only one instance of suicide which came to my attention during my stay in Tivland. In this instance, an Udam girl, who had been married to a Tiv less than a week when war broke out between her tribe and his, tried unsuccessfully to cut her own throat. She said later that she was afraid of Tiv because she had been told as a girl that Tiv would kill her to "make medicine." My Tiv informants—comparatively few of whom knew the "secret" of the great *akombo* —were incredulous. "After all," one elder, who did know them, remarked ironically, "we might not have done it, so she had nothing to lose by waiting to see whether we would or not." Tiv women were particularly upset by her action, and found it difficult to explain.

This case led me to make inquiries about suicide. I was assured by all that Tiv never commit suicide. Although such a claim is obviously untrue, none could or would give me cases. When asked to do so, they always referred to the Uge, a people to their south who, Tiv said, would commit suicide on the slightest provocation, or even without reason "if their hearts are sad."

The only case material I have on the subject is that four of the homicides (two cases of which are described above) tried unsuccessfully to commit suicide: two women and two men. Both women and one of the men were found guilty of murder but insane; the other man had killed his wife, was found guilty of murder and executed. All stabbed themselves either with arrows or with knives. In his book on his own people, Akiga notes in passing two instances in which suicide might occur: when women were required by the rules of exchange marriage to marry old men, and when men were falsely accused of *mbatsav* activity. In both contexts, he mentions, as the natural method, stabbing with arrows.

This "sample" is unusual in only one respect: every suicide in it was performed or attempted with a piercing or cutting instrument. If this is indicative of a more general pattern, the Tiv are a very unusual people in what suicide they do commit. Unfortunately, all I can safely say at the moment is that Tiv consider suicide rare, inexplicable, and un-Tiv.

3

HOMICIDE AND SUICIDE IN BUSOGA

L. A. AND M. C. FALLERS

LIKE several of the other peoples discussed in this book, the Basoga of southeastern Uganda are members of the great Bantu-speaking group which covers most of Africa from the southern margins of the Sudan to the Cape of Good Hope. More particularly, they belong to a cluster of Bantu peoples who inhabit the region around Lakes Victoria, Albert, Edward, and Tanganyika in east-central Africa and who, consequently, are known to ethnologists as the "Interlacustrine Bantu." The unity which the term denotes is more than linguistic; it is also cultural and social. As over against neighbouring Bantu groups, the Interlacustrine peoples share common patterns of value and belief with regard to the natural and supernatural worlds and common institutional forms. All regard a hierarchical form of society, with its division of men into such categories as "ruler," "chief," "prince," and "peasant," and its emphasis upon correct and courtly behaviour, as part of the natural and proper order of things. All share a similar pantheon of gods and spirits, who both control human affairs and may be manipulated by men for personal or group ends. In some of the Interlacustrine states, these patterns are worked out on a tiny scale; in south Busoga and in Buhaya are found "kingdoms" of no more than a few thousand souls. Elsewhere, as in modern Buganda or nineteenth century Bunyoro, several hundred thousand people may be united under a single ruler.

Before looking more closely at the Basoga themselves and at their characteristic forms of murder and self-destruction, it will perhaps be well, in order to facilitate understanding, to add a word concerning the structure of the Bantu words which we will have occasion to use. The word in Bantu languages usually consists of a root and one or more prefixes to indicate number, person, tense and the like. (It may have suffixes as well, but these are more apt to be familiar to speakers of European languages.) Thus the people who concern us here are called *"Basoga,"* while an individual among them is called a *"Musoga."* The country is *"Busoga"* and the language *"Lusoga."* These variations are essential and, once the principle is grasped, easy to remember. There are, however, many others which would simply create confusion if we tried to follow them in English. When, therefore, an adjectival form is required to denote attributes or possessions of the Basoga, the root "Soga" will have to suffice. To Bantu ears this is, of course, a barbarism comparable to speaking of "Eng china" or "Americ cars," but some compromise is necessary. Most of the Bantu words which we shall have occasion to use belong to one or the other of the two major dialects of Lusoga. Some, however, come from Luganda, the language of the neighbouring Baganda, who have often dominated the Basoga both culturally and politically. Since the languages are basically similar and have long been in contact, many words are common to all three.

Soga society is most simply described as a series of petty kingdom-states peopled by peasant cultivators who are distributed among a number of patrilineal clans and lineages.[1]

[1] Soga political institutions are more fully described in *Bantu Bureaucracy: A Study of Integration and Conflict in the Political Institutions of an East African People*, W. Heffer and Sons, Cambridge, for the East African Institute of Social Research, 1956. The peasant economy is discussed in "The Politics of Land-Holding in Busoga," *Economic Development and Cultural Change*, Vol. III, No. 3, 1954. The tensions and conflicts which beset Soga marriage are the subject of "Some Determinants of Marriage Stability in Busoga: A Reformulation of Gluckman's Hypothesis," *Africa*, Vol. XXVII, No. 1, April 1957. As will be seen presently, this last is particularly relevant to the present discussion because

Homicide and Suicide in Busoga

Before the coming of British administrators at the end of the nineteenth century, there were within the territory occupied by the half million present-day Basoga some twelve to fifteen states—their precise number is now difficult to determine because of the de-population of certain areas by sleeping sickness. Each was headed by a ruler, whose position was hereditary within a lineage of a royal clan and who ruled through a hierarchy of household officials, territorial chiefs, and village headmen. The local community, under a headman, consisted of homesteads scattered over the low, flat hill which usually made up the village territory, each homestead set in among its own plantain gardens and plots of millet and sweet potatoes. Most homesteads consisted of a man, his wife or wives, and their children, with the addition, perhaps, of an odd younger brother or sister, widowed mother or aunt. Often the homestead of a chief or headman—certainly that of a ruler—would be substantially more complex, including servants and many more dependent relatives.

Inheritance, succession, and marriage were the province of the neighborhood group of lineage mates. Although much wider groups of putative patrilineal kinsmen were recognized —including the clan as a whole, which often was scattered over the whole of Busoga—it was this local group of close patrilineal relatives which most often figured in the round of peasant life. Sitting as a corporate body at a member's funeral, they might alter his testament and assign guardianship over his widow and children. A young man intending marriage might go to his lineage mates for aid in gathering the marriage

---

conflicts arising out of marriage are among the commonest causes of homicide and suicide.

All these accounts of different aspects of Soga life are based upon fieldwork carried out during 1950-52. We are most grateful to the U.S. Educational Commission in the United Kingdom (the "Fulbright Program") and to the East African Institute of Social Research for providing us with the necessary funds and facilities. Most of the field data were gathered by L. A. Fallers, while most of the documentary research on suicide and murder was carried out by M. C. Fallers.

payment demanded by his bride's people, and he would certainly draw upon the genealogical knowledge of senior members in order to make certain that the marriage did not involve a breach of the customary incest rules. Lineage and local community were not, however, coextensive. The headman, who controlled the distribution of land and acted as the local arm of the state hierarchy, exercised his authority over kinsman and nonkinsman alike. Neighborhood lineage groups cut across village boundaries.

British administration has brought political stability, a new technology, cash crops; missionaries have brought education, Roman Catholic and Protestant Christianity, and Islam. Rulers, princes, and chiefs have become civil-servant chiefs, administering justice and collecting taxes in the name of the Busoga African Local Government and presiding over elected councils. In the villages, peasants grow cotton for sale as well as the traditional subsistence crops. These changes have, as we shall see, brought new forms of violent death, but in the main modern Basoga, like their forefathers, kill themselves and each other for reasons which are rooted in the traditional social structure.

ATTITUDES AND FREQUENCIES

The commonest word for murder in Lusoga is simply *okutta*, "to kill"; suicide is the reflexive form of the same word, *okwetta*, "to kill one's self." Both are unequivocally bad.

Life, *bulamu*, is a prime value in Soga culture, but the feeling-tone associated with the term is not quite that of *joie de vivre*. Rather the idea of the good life is closer to "success" or "well-being," with a tinge of "sobriety," "politeness," or "respectability." The wealthy man, the man who is kind, well-behaved and consequently popular, the man who rises in the social hierarchy through cleverness: these have made good use of life and are admired. Earthly life is prized as an opportunity to pursue these goals. There is, in traditional belief,

68

an after-life, but it is of greater significance for others, who may be affected for good or ill by one's ghost (*muzimu*), than for one's self. The notion of "a better world beyond" as reward for earthly virtue or a resting place from earthly suffering is limited to particularly devout Christians. Thus, to take a man's life is to rob him of his dearest possession. Killing is justifiable only in self-defence or as an act of war; uncontrollable passion, such as that which possesses a man when he finds his wife in adultery, may partly, but can never fully, excuse it. Likewise, suicide is an act of utter irresponsibility, a foolish discarding—again perhaps as a result of momentary passion— of that which reasonable men consider most worth preserving. Basoga are, in fact, rather more intolerant of suicide than most Western peoples. The youth who kills himself for unrequited love and the sick and aged parent who dies to relieve his children of a burden are recognised as familiar types, but such motives are not considered to excuse self-destruction.

In the past, it is said, a certain amount of "self-help justice," including killing in revenge, was accepted and even approved. Some types of dispute were formally tried in the courts of chiefs, where there was a set procedure for argument and re-buttal and a system for tallying with small sticks the debating points made by the respective litigants. In other cases, apparently, individuals or kinship groups were free to seek private revenge for wrongs suffered. But in just what spheres the "chief's peace" or the "ruler's peace," to adapt a medieval European concept, applied and in what spheres it did not is today impossible to discover. Today it is accepted that private revenge is wrong. Disputes must be taken to the courts of the chiefs or (in cases where death is alleged to have occurred) to those of the British magistrates and judges.

Both suicide and murder may have supernatural aspects, though the sharp line which modern Westerners of a secular-scientific persuasion draw between the "natural" and the "supernatural" would not readily occur to a Musoga. Sorcery

69

(*bulogo*), poison (*butwa*), and arson (*kwokya*) are similar means of deliberate killing because all are carried out in secret, usually at night. Poison may be either a substance introduced into a victim's food (which Western science would recognise as physiological poison), or it may be a substance placed on the path or over the doorframe which has effect without "physical" contact. These forces, as well as nature spirits (*misambwa*) and ghosts (*mizimu*) may drive men mad and cause them to commit either murder or suicide. To deal with them, there are practitioners of several types—doctors (*basawo*), seers (*balaguzi*), anti-sorcerers (*bayigha*), and spirit mediums (*baswezi*). The belief in the efficacy of such supernatural forces does not, however, detract from the immoral character of murder and suicide, which are *wrong* and not merely *unfortunate*. Whatever the supernatural pressures, murder and suicide are offences which must be punished. Traditionally, the body of a suicide was punished by being burnt, along with the tree or hut where the hanging—the almost universal method of suicide in Busoga—took place or by being buried at a cross-roads or in waste land. No funeral feast was held and no heir chosen. Today public health rules govern the disposal of the body, but the attitude remains. Nor is homicide justifiable—at any rate today—in reprisal against supernatural attack. Unlike those of some African countries, Uganda's courts, while not accepting the actual efficacy of witchcraft and sorcery, recognise their anti-social nature. The Criminal Law (Witchcraft) Ordinance of 1912 provides penalties of up to seven years imprisonment for attempt to injure through the use of "witchcraft, sorcery, enchantments, or the use of charms."

In sum, supernatural forces are not a field apart from "physical" means of killing and injuring; rather, as we shall see when we examine actual cases of homicide and suicide in Busoga, they form part of the total situation of interpersonal conflict in which killing occurs.

70

Homicide and Suicide in Busoga

The attitude of the Basoga toward murder and suicide is, therefore, quite simple and familiar: homicide is wrong except in self-defence or war. Suicide is always wrong. Both, however, occur each year in Busoga in substantial numbers. Tables 8 and 9 show the frequencies of homicide and suicide respectively for the years 1952-1954.

TABLE 8

HOMICIDES COMMITTED BY BASOGA IN BUSOGA
1952-1954

	1952	1953	1954	Mean	Mean per 100,000*
Convictions for murder and man-slaughter, excluding motor vehicles cases, plus homicides with suicide	19	13	17	16.3	4.0

* Basoga in Busoga District numbered, at the 1948 census, 405,110. See *African Population of Uganda Protectorate*, East African Statistical Department, 1950.

TABLE 9

INQUEST FINDINGS OF SUICIDE BY BASOGA IN BUSOGA
1952-1954

	1952	1953	1954	Mean	Mean per 100,000
Among inquest reports examined	23	23	39	28.3	7.0
Projection from proportion of suicides among inquest reports examined	33	25	46	34.7	8.5
Assuming all un-located reports to be findings of suicide	93	40	80	71.0	17.5

The data presented in these tables were made available through the kindness of the Registrar of the High Court in Kampala, who gave us access to the records in his keeping. They require a word of explanation. In the case of homicides, only actual convictions for murder or manslaughter have been included. Convictions for manslaughter arising out of motor vehicle "accidents" have been excluded, since it is the practice not to include these "homicides" in international cause-of-death statistics and we shall presently want to compare the Busoga figures with some of these. In later tables such cases will be included. Finally, cases where, according to inquest reports, persons committed suicide after having killed someone else have been included, even though such persons could not, for obvious reasons, be convicted of murder or manslaughter.

In the case of the suicide figures given in Table 9, the question of definition is simple; included are simply all cases in which the inquest resulted in a finding of suicide. There is, however, a problem of incompleteness in the data, because it proved impossible to locate all the inquest reports for the relevant years. We have therefore given three sets of figures: those for findings of suicide actually located and examined, those which would result if the proportion of suicide findings were the same for all inquests as it is for the inquests which were located and examined, and those which would result if all the unlocated inquest reports were to be findings of suicide. It is likely that the first set of figures is the more accurate. The commonest reason for our inability to locate inquest records, apparently, was that homicide had been found, or had been suspected to be, the cause of death and the records were still in the hands of the police or the courts. Since Basoga almost always commit suicide by hanging, the cause of death in suicide cases is usually obvious and the inquest reports quickly come to rest in the High Court archives where we worked.

The numbers of suicides and homicides which are reported

to the police probably reflect quite accurately their actual frequency in the District. As African countries (and not *only* African ones) go, Busoga is well administered by its hierarchy of chiefs. There is, of course, evasion of unpopular laws and rules and there is occasional corruption, but death is considered too serious a matter for either of these to seriously influence reporting. Again, as we shall see, death usually occurs in catastrophic fashion; emotions flare, a life is taken, and the neighbors set up a hue and cry and rush off to report the event to the village chief, who in turn reports to his superiors in the hierarchy and to the Protectorate Police. Even if it were desired to keep a death secret, this would not be easy, for neighbors tend to be well-known to each other and are almost always within shouting distance. It therefore seems unlikely to us that many cases of homicide or suicide go unreported.

On the whole, the inquest reports and case files from which our data come are remarkably rich and clear from the point of view of the student of social relations—a fact which reflects considerable credit upon the African police constables who usually investigate reported deaths and take down the statements of witnesses. With our background knowledge of Busoga acquired through fieldwork, we found that in most cases the story which unfolded itself had a familiar and plausible ring. People behaved as we had learned to expect Basoga to behave in similar circumstances. In a few cases, however, the material simply made no sense. It was clear, perhaps, that Leubeni Wambuzi had stabbed Maliya, his wife, but no clear pattern of motive emerged from the statements of kinsmen and neighbors. In some cases, no doubt, the latter were actually ignorant of the trouble which ended in killing. Unlike peoples who live in compact villages, Basoga do not lead the whole of their lives in public. Though homesteads are seldom more than a few dozen yards apart, each is tucked away in its own plantain grove and each has its own "private affairs of the house" (*eby'omu ndhu*), which outsiders are not meant to know about.

Before passing on to consider some of the reasons why and ways in which Basoga kill themselves and each other, we may note that there is nothing unusual about the *frequency* with which they do either. Tables 10 and 11 show, for purposes of comparison, the frequencies of suicide and homicide in Busoga and in a scattering of countries outside Africa. No serious statistical conclusion can of course be drawn from such a short list, but it is enough to show that the Basoga are not out of the ordinary.

TABLE 10. FREQUENCY OF HOMICIDE*

Country	Homicides per 100,000
Chile (1953)	8.2
Ceylon (1954)	5.2
United States (1953)	4.8
Busoga (1952-54 mean)	4.0
Japan (1953)	2.0
Italy (1953)	1.8
England and Wales (1953)	0.6

* *Demographic Yearbook*, Statistical Department of the United Nations, 1955, pp. 710-24.

TABLE 11. FREQUENCY OF SUICIDE*

Country	Suicides per 100,000
Japan (1953)	20.5
England and Wales (1953)	10.8
United States (1953)	10.1
Ceylon (1954)	8.0
Busoga (1952-54 mean)	7.0
Italy (1953)	6.6
Chile (1953)	4.4

* *Ibid.*

74

Homicide and Suicide in Busoga

In our search for patterns of murder and suicide in Busoga, we examined one hundred instances of each, beginning, in both cases, with the last instance recorded for the year 1954 and working backward in time. In the case of suicide, we had to go back only as far as 1951 to reach one hundred; to find one hundred homicides, on the other hand, we had to go back to 1947. (This, incidentally, is the reason why frequencies for only the three years from 1952 to 1954 are given in Tables 8 and 9. Only three full years' suicides were recorded, and it was, of course, preferable to give homicide frequencies for the same period.) Let us examine these two hundred case records for the light they may throw on the manner and motive of Soga killing.

TABLE 12

ONE HUNDRED SUICIDES: PLACE AND METHOD

Method	Place				
	House	Tree	Other	Unknown	Total
Hanging					
Men	29	29	1	7	66
Women	10	15	–	5	30
Other					
Men	2	–	1	–	3
Women	1	–	–	–	1
TOTAL	42	44	2	12	100

Nearly all Basoga suicides hang themselves—only four in our sample of one hundred used any other method—either from a hut rafter or from a tree nearby. As Table 12 shows, men are as likely as not to hang themselves inside the hut, while women tend to prefer a tree. Hanging, as carried out by many Basoga, requires a good deal of tenacity. Often the branch or rafter to which the rope is tied is too low for the

75

body to drop freely. The suicide must draw up his feet until the pressure of the rope has taken effect. In most cases the act is carried out impulsively, but occasionally it is clear that there has been a modicum of preparation. In a number of the cases in our sample, notes were left giving reasons for wishing to die, sharing out property, and bidding farewell to friends and kinsmen.

TABLE 13. WEAPONS USED IN ONE HUNDRED HOMICIDES

Weapon	Men	Women
Stick	21	–
Knife	17	–
Motor vehicle	7	–
Hoe	6	–
Panga (machete)	5	–
Axe	4	–
Rope or cord	3	–
Spear	3	–
Pestle	1	1
Hand or foot	2	–
Canoe paddle	2	–
Whip	1	–
Bill hook	1	–
Adze	1	–
Medicine	1	–
Stone	–	1
Unknown	23	–
TOTAL	98	2

Methods of homicide are much more variable. The general impression left by the list given in Table 13 is that killing is carried out with the aid of whatever hard, sharp, or heavy instrument is nearest at hand. This impression is reinforced by the accounts of witnesses, which make it clear that in most of the cases in our sample the deed could not have been planned in advance, but rather was committed on a sudden impulse. Most murder weapons are consequently common household or agricultural implements. The presence in the list of seven cases of homicide by motor vehicle perhaps requires the comment that these were ordinary road accidents of the sort which are common the world over, and not deliberate killings. The one case of killing by medicine was not, apparently, deliberate; the killer was genuinely attempting to effect a cure and consequently was charged only with manslaughter for practising medicine without a license. In view of the frequency with which Basoga talk about poisoning, both physiological and supernatural, as a means of aggression, it is perhaps surprising that no cases of deliberate poisoning appear in Table 13. In fact, however, poisoning and sorcery as practised in Busoga are thought not to cause sudden death, but rather to bring on wasting diseases and madness, which may result in suicide.

Motive is, of course, extremely difficult to assess, particularly from the pages of a case report. Even if one had perfect knowledge of the events, one would still have the problem of classification. There are nearly as many classifications of crime as there are students of crime. Our answer to this difficulty will simply be to evade it and to accept the explanations of motive offered by kinsmen and neighbors to police investigators. The resulting scheme of classification will lack analytical logic, but it may be expected to have a certain relevance to Soga circumstances. Sometimes, of course, different witnesses offer conflicting accounts. In such cases, we have tried to follow the dominant view or the view of the witness who appeared to be best informed. The results are shown in Tables 14 and 15, where our two hundred killers are classified by age, sex, and motive.

Of most relevance for the theme of this book are those killings which arise out of, or at any rate whose circumstances are greatly influenced by, the peculiarities of Soga institutions. This seemed to be particularly so in the case of those homicides and suicides which we have classified in Tables 14 and 15 under the headings "quarrel with spouse or lover," "quarrel

TABLE 14. ONE HUNDRED HOMICIDES: AGE, SEX,
MOTIVE OF KILLER

| Motive | Age | | | | | | |
	Under 21	21-35	36-50	51-65	Over 65	"Adult"[a]	Total
			M E N				
Quarrel with spouse or lover	1	21	15	1	–	8	46
Quarrel with in-law	–	1	2	–	–	–	3
Quarrel with patrilineal kinsman	1	1	–	–	1	1	4
Accident	–	3	1	–	–	4	8
Revenge upon criminal, usually thief	–	13	1	–	–	1	15
Killing in connection with other crime	–	2	–	–	–	1	3
"Just drunk"	1	5	2	–	–	4	12
Other or unknown	1	2	3	–	–	1	7
TOTAL MEN	4	48	24	1	1	20	98
			W O M E N				
Quarrel with spouse or lover	–	–	1	–	–	1	2
TOTAL WOMEN	–	–	1	–	–	1	2
TOTAL	4	48	25	1	1	21	100

[a] Classification given in official records; exact age unknown.

with in-law," and "quarrel with patrilineal kinsman." In these
cases, witnesses tended to give the *relationship* as the *reason*;
they clearly felt that this was a more satisfactory explanation
than the immediate precipitating cause of violence, which
might, they implied, be almost anything. In much the same
way, an American will say: "George is having mother-in-law

TABLE 15. ONE HUNDRED SUICIDES: AGE, SEX, MOTIVE

	Under 21	21-35	Age 36-50	51-65	Over 65	"Adult"	Total
			MEN				
Quarrel with spouse or lover	–	4	7	1	–	–	12
Quarrel with in-law	–	–	1	–	–	–	1
Quarrel with patrilineal kinsman	–	1	–	–	–	–	1
Disease	–	5	6	2	3	4	20
Impotence	1	3	3	–	–	1	8
Shame	–	–	1	2	–	2	5
Insanity	–	5	1	–	–	–	6
Old and unwanted	–	–	–	1	1	–	2
Grief	–	1	2	–	–	–	3
Other or unknown	2	4	4	–	–	1	11
TOTAL MEN	3	23	25	6	4	8	69
			WOMEN				
Quarrel with spouse or lover	3	4	1	–	–	1	9
Disease	–	3	2	4	2	–	11
Insanity	–	2	–	–	–	–	2
Old and unwanted	–	–	–	2	–	–	2
Grief	–	–	2	–	–	1	3
Other or unknown	–	3	1	–	–	–	4
TOTAL WOMEN	3	12	6	6	2	2	31
TOTAL	6	35	31	12	6	10	100

trouble," and this will be felt to be sufficient explanation of whatever particular misfortune George has suffered in consequence. In offering such explanations, Basoga and Americans recognise, perhaps implicitly, that in their respective societies there are certain relationships—certain "trouble spots" in the social system—which place persons involved in them under such strain that conflict may result. No doubt every society has such weak spots, though their "location" in the social system probably varies widely. No doubt, also, the interpersonal conflict which results is everywhere one of the precipitants of homicide and suicide.

TABLE 16

SUICIDE FOLLOWING ASSAULT UPON OTHER PERSONS
(NUMBER OUT OF 100 SUICIDES)

After killing spouse	10
After attacking spouse	3
After attacking in-law	2
TOTAL	15

In Busoga, it is apparent from Tables 14, 15, and 16, a major focus of conflict is the relationships arising out of marriage. Quarrels between spouses or lovers account for 48 per cent of the homicides in our sample and 21 per cent of the suicides. In fifteen per cent of the suicide cases, the fatal act was carried out after an attack upon the individual's spouse or in-law. Another three per cent of the homicides and one per cent of the suicides arose directly out of quarrels with in-laws. In the case of suicides, a further 8 per cent were due to impotence, which condition may, in the present context, be thought of as an inability to fulfill the expectations of the male role in marriage. Marriage in Busoga is clearly a dangerous undertaking.

The difficulties which beset marriage in Busoga have been analysed in some detail in another article on the causes of divorce.[2] The stability of Soga marriage, we think, is constantly threatened by the divided loyalties of the two spouses, arising out of the system of patrilineal lineages. A person remains, for life, a member of the lineage into which he or she was born, and members of the same lineage may not, of course, marry one another. Marriage partners are thus inevitably members of different lineages and, as we noted earlier, lineage membership is one of Soga society's strongest bonds. Apparently, in some societies which have kinship groups of this kind, there exist means of socially absorbing the wife into the husband's group. Philip Mayer describes how among the

[2] See Footnote 1, page 66.

Gusii of Kenya, for example, the last phase of the marriage ceremonies consists of a ritual separation of the bride from her own people, who now become "enemies," and her attachment to her husband's group.[3] In Busoga, however, the wife's attachment to her own group remains strong, and she tends constantly to be drawn back to her natal home. To express the point slightly differently, the father-daughter and brother-sister relationships are strengthened at the expense of the husband-wife relationship. At the same time, Basoga men have, in theory, extremely great authority over their wives. Wives may not absent themselves from the home without explicit permission. They may not hold real property, and husbands have the right to punish them by beating.

A common result is that a wife feels oppressed and tries to escape by running away to father. Father may accept her back into his home, and thus involve himself in conflict, and possibly litigation, with her husband; or, because accepting her would involve his repaying the bride-wealth, he may force her to return to a strife-filled existence with her husband. Husbands, for their part, are sensitive to the fact that their theoretically great authority over their wives is in reality insecure and is often flouted. In reaction, many become household tyrants. For both husbands and wives, the sexual act itself tends to become involved in the conflict of authority which centres upon their relationship. For the rebellious wife, extra-marital affairs become the symbol of freedom—an assertion of personal autonomy against a domineering husband. For the husband, whose position seems threatened, intercourse with his wife becomes an act of authority. When he feels his dominance slipping away, he may imagine himself to be losing his virility (and consequently may, in fact, lose it) as a result of sorcery directed against him by his wife. In a number of

[3] Philip Mayer, "The Lineage Principle in Gusii Society," *Memorandum XXIV*, International Institute of African Languages and Cultures, 1949, p. 7.

the cases in our sample, sexual intercourse appeared to have immediately preceded homicide or suicide.

Social age also influences patterns of killing. In our sample, for instance, it is the young or middle-aged man who kills himself because of impotence, whereas we may assume that the condition is actually more frequent among older men. It is, of course, the younger man who is thus rendered unable to play adequately a role expected of him; for the older man, impotence is accepted as an inevitable concomitant of advancing age. The point is emphasized when we look at the age distribution in Table 15 of suicide due to physical disability of other kinds ("disease"). Here we find the aged well represented. Unlike impotence, the wasting diseases such as syphilis and leprosy, which are so common in Uganda, are *not* accepted as inevitable for the old. We may also note the skewed age distribution of "insanity." It is here that "supernatural" forces are most prominent, for the commonest cause of madness, in the view of Basoga, is sorcery, and one of the main fields for sorcery is marriage. Husband-wife conflict and jealousy between co-wives or rivals are often accompanied— or are believed to be accompanied—by supernatural aggression. It is in younger middle age that these conflicts are most likely to occur.

One further instance of the influence of age upon patterns of killing may be noted. In Table 14, "revenge for criminal act" means, in most cases, the beating to death of persons caught in the act of theft. Although, as we noted earlier, self-help justice is not accepted as legitimate, it does occur often enough to form 15 per cent of the homicides in our sample. It is, however, only the younger men who engage in this sort of spontaneous physical violence against criminals. After the age of 35, Basoga males are unlikely to kill outside the context of marital conflict.

Much the same pattern of age and sex factors is apparent in Table 17, where homicides are classified according to the

TABLE 17. RELATIONSHIP BETWEEN KILLER AND VICTIM

Victim's relationship to killer	Age of Killer						
	Under 21	21-35	36-50	51-65	Over 65	Adult	Total
			M E N				
Spouse	–	14	15	1	–	7	37
Lover	–	1	–	–	–	–	1
Rival	–	2	1	–	–	1	4
Patrilineal kinsman of same sex	1	2	–	–	1	1	5
In-law	1	5	1	–	–	1	8
Step-parent	–	1	–	–	–	–	1
Step-child	–	–	2	–	–	–	2
Unspecified kinsman	–	3	–	–	–	–	3
Neighbor	–	4	1	–	–	–	5
Pupil	–	–	1	–	–	–	1
Public official	–	–	–	–	–	1	1
No previous acquaintance	–	7	1	–	–	2	10
Unknown	2	9	2	–	–	7	20
TOTAL MEN	4	48	24	1	1	20	98
			W O M E N				
Lover	–	–	1	–	–	–	1
Rival	–	–	–	–	–	1	1
TOTAL WOMEN	–	–	1	–	–	1	2
TOTAL	4	48	25	1	1	21	100

relationship between killer and victim. Indeed, because of the prominence of marital conflict as a cause of killing, the classification in Table 17 comes to much the same thing as that in Table 14. The correspondence is not exact, because the person one kills is not always the same as the person with whom the conflict began. One sometimes kills one's father-in-law as a result of quarrelling with one's wife, and *vice versa*.

It is apparent from Tables 14, 15, and 17 that Basoga quarrel with patrilineal kin, as well as with wives and in-laws, and that these conflicts also, though less commonly, result in killing. One suicide and four homicides were the result of such quarrels, and five patrilineal kinsmen were killed. As in some other societies where descent is reckoned patrilineally and where groups of patrilineal kinsmen have corporate rights and responsibilities, the very closeness of the bond thus created may be productive of conflict. In Busoga, jealousy between brothers over inheritance matters is common, and so also is father-son conflict arising out of the desire of sons for independence and the contrary desire of fathers to maintain their dominance. Death, however, results much less frequently from quarrels between lineage mates than it does from marital conflict. Killing a patrilineal kinsman, or even using the sanction of suicide against him, is a terrible thing which few Basoga would even contemplate. The unity and solidarity of the lineage, in spite of the conflicts which often rend it, have a sacred quality—a quality which traditionally was strengthened by a well-developed ancestor cult. For most Basoga, it is the unity and solidarity which are dominant, not the conflict.

In analyzing the social patterning of murder and suicide, we have been concerned to emphasize the strains and burdens which societies place upon their members, but it must not be forgotten that these killings are carried out only by the tiny minority who "couldn't take it"—the wastage of imperfect human institutions. For most people, most of the time, the rewards of following society's rules far outweigh the impulse to break them.

It is interesting to note, however, that, in present-day Busoga, the breaking down of traditional institutions appears to *reduce* the frequency of homicide and suicide rather than to increase it. In many parts of southern Busoga, population shifts resulting from sleeping sickness epidemics have scattered local lineage groups, and in such areas lineages have come to play a relatively minor role in the everyday lives of peasant villagers. Table 18 shows the homicide and suicide rates for the eight counties of Busoga, grouped into northern,

84

central and southern areas. The southern area (see map) consisting of Butembe-Bunya, Bukoli and Bugweri, has been demographically very unstable during the past half-century, so that today only a minority of its people live in the villages where they were born. The central area, consisting of Luuka and Kigulu, was subject to substantial population shifts only along its southern margins, while the population of the northern three counties of Bugabula, Bulamogi, and Busiki has remained quite stable. In Table 18 both homicide and suicide are shown to occur more frequently in a gradient from south to north. The differences are, of course, not large, but there is a suggestion here that with the loosening of the traditional structure there is also a decline in the severity of some of the conflicts which, we have argued, are inherent in it. We do not, needless to say, suggest that social change always has such consequences, either in Africa or elsewhere, but merely note that *thus far*, in *Busoga*, such appears to have been the case.

TABLE 18. FREQUENCY OF HOMICIDE AND SUICIDE IN
THREE AREAS OF BUSOGA, 1952-1954[a]

Area	Mean Annual Homicides per 100,000	Mean Annual Suicides per 100,000
Northern (Bugabula, Bulamogi, Busiki)	4.2	6.5
Central (Kigulu, Luuka)	1.9	4.3
Southern (Bugweri, Bukoli, Butembe-Bunya)	1.7	3.1

[a] Four cases of homicide and seven of suicide could not be allocated by county. These figures are not, therefore, comparable with those for the whole district give in Tables 8 and 9.

Not all killings are readily explicable in terms of the peculiarities of Soga social structure. In Table 15, five persons committed suicide out of shame—surely a common motive for self-destruction the world around, though of course the things which are considered shameful vary widely. Of our five cases, one involved a man whose son had been caught stealing chickens. When the son was arrested, the father tried, unsuccessfully, to bribe the chief. Seeing no other way to escape public disapproval, he hanged himself. In another case, a man hanged himself because he could not find the money to redeem his daughter from an unhappy marriage by repaying the bride-wealth. Again, Basoga, like other people, occasionally kill themselves because of grief. In our sample, three men and three women did so, in each case, apparently, because of the death of a close relative—sibling, parent, child, or spouse. Senility, too, is everywhere a burdensome state, both to the senile person and to his family. The Basoga, like most African peoples, make much better provision for the aged than do many Western societies, for the elderly man or woman can nearly always find a welcome with children or other kinsmen. Nevertheless, a few old people (four in our sample) come to feel hopeless and unwanted, and so end their lives.

Among homicides, too, there are some which are sociologically rather uninteresting. The "accidents" in Table 14, for example, are for the most part motor vehicle accidents in which drivers were found guilty of manslaughter. The rather large number of these is a measure, not of any peculiarity of Soga institutions, but simply of technical progress and of its hazards in a country where those who man the machines are nearly all inexperienced. Then there are the "real criminal" killers. On the whole, Basoga killers, like the majority in other countries, are amateurs; they kill in a sudden fit of anger or outrage, out of a gradually mounting sense of grievance or depression, or simply by accident. There are also, however, the few who kill deliberately and toward a definite criminal end. Of these there are only three in our sample: two who killed in the course of armed robbery, and one who did so while trying to escape from prison. Finally, as elsewhere in the world, there are the drunkards with quick tempers. It is quite possible that in some of the killings in Table 14 that witnesses attributed simply to an excess of beer or *waragi* (bootleg spirits), there was a dormant dispute which flared up under alcoholic stimulation. Doubtless if our information were more complete some of these cases could be assigned to other categories. In seven of the twelve cases, however, killer and victim were said never to have seen one another before the beer party at which death occurred. It should be added that in Uganda the high incidence of enlarged spleens due to malaria adds greatly to the number of deaths which result from beer party altercations. An unlucky blow which ruptures an enlarged spleen may cause death where otherwise no serious injury would have resulted.

SOME BRIEF CASE HISTORIES

We may end this account of homicide and suicide in Basoga with brief summaries of a few of the stories which emerge from the case records, beginning with some of the many involving marital conflict. Names are, of course, fictitious.

Case No. 1. Combined homicide and suicide.

On the morning of December 31, 1953, Mako Mukama and his wife Yezefina were found dead in their hut, Mako having hanged himself after killing Yezefina. Jeneti, Mako's other wife, denied that there had been trouble between the two wives: "Each of us had her own hut and Mako stayed with each of us in turn. We had plenty of property." She added, however, that Mako had consulted a doctor about impotence. This was confirmed by a neighbor, who said that Mako and his mother had sacrificed a sheep "to the spirits" in an effort to cure the condition. Yezefina's father added that Mako's impotence was "well known in the village": Mako was "very worried about it."

Whether Mako suspected Yezefina of being the cause of his impotence we do not know, but according to our experience of village life this would not have been unusual. Jealousy between co-wives does not seem to have been the difficulty here; most likely the trouble started with Mako suspecting Yezefina of infidelity—almost an obsession with Basoga husbands. Sometimes, however, straightforward co-wife jealousy *does* result in death:

Case No. 2. Suicide of a co-wife.

On April 29, 1951, Nambi was found hanging in her hut. The police constable's questioning of a neighbour elicited the following story: Nambi and her sister Getulida were both married to Yozefu. The sisters quarrelled and Nambi began to feel that Getulida was receiving greater favour from Yozefu. On one occasion, she was heard to say that Yozefu always slept in Getulida's hut. On the night before the hanging, Yozefu told the investigator, his two wives quarrelled about "domestic matters." The village chief commented: "It always happens in this country that women with little brain will kill themselves when they are angry."

On the other hand, a lack of affection for her husband and inability to escape from him may also lead a wife to suicide:

Case No. 3. A wife commits suicide.

Esitera had been married to Semu, but for a time had been allowed by him to return home to keep house for her brother and widowed father. Finally, Semu asked that Esitera return to him, but she refused, saying that she no longer loved him. Against her will, and in spite of her brother's pleas on her behalf, her father forced her to return to Semu, scolding her "for not being a good wife." On July 5, 1953, she was found to have hanged herself on a tree in the plantain grove. Again wisdom from the village chief: "This kind of incident is always occurring with the women of this country. They commit suicide for the simplest reasons."

We have noted the tension which tends to characterize relations between in-laws due to the division of women's loyalties between their husbands' and their fathers' groups. Perhaps as a means of controlling this tension, in-laws are expected to behave toward one another with greater-than-usual politeness and respect. There are elaborate rules with regard to visiting and gift-giving. The following case shows how near to the surface, in relations between in-laws, hostility and even homicide may lie:

Case No. 4. A man kills his father-in-law.

Fesito was married to Ana, daughter of Abusolomu. Yowana, Abusolomu's son, told how on April 9, 1952, Fesito had invited them to come and drink beer with him: "When we arrived, Abusolomu waited outside the door for Fesito to come and formally greet him. Fesito, who was drunk, did not do this, but called out to Abusolomu to come on in, saying that he would present him with a chicken, the customary gift to an in-law, when he departed. When the time came for us to leave, Abusolomu asked for his chicken, but Fesito refused. Abusolomu thereupon said that he would take Ana home with him since, by refusing to give the customary gift to her father, Fesito was denying the marriage." Fesito took up a spear and killed Abusolomu. He gave himself up to the chief, and while in jail awaiting sentence, he committed suicide.

Sometimes a father takes his daughter's part against her husband, with fatal consequences:

89

Case No. 5. A man kills his wife.

Sala and Nasanaeri had been married for many years and Sala had borne five children, but one day they quarrelled and she returned to her father. Several times, as is customary in marital disputes, Nasanaeri went to Sala's father and asked that he "judge the case" between them and send Sala back to him, but the father refused. On March 20, 1952, Nasanaeri came again and found Sala sitting on a mat with a stranger. Infuriated by the thought that she had, with the connivance of her father, taken up with the stranger, Nasanaeri stabbed her to death.

In most cases, perhaps because of linguistic difficulties (statements are always translated into English), the tangle of human motivation which goes to make up a murder or suicide appears in the court records in highly simplified form. Death appears to occur, as our village chief said, "for the simplest reasons." Occasionally, however, the record is full enough to reveal something of the confusion of love and hate which characterizes marital conflict:

Case No. 6. A man kills his youngest wife.

Sitefano had three wives. Each had a hut in the compound, and Sitefano visited each in turn for three days. According to the other wives, the youngest, Babirye, began to quarrel with Sitefano. A contributory factor, perhaps, was that they had been married for four years and Babirye was still childless. One day Babirye appeared with a new dress. Sitefano took it from her, accusing her of visiting other men. Finally, Babirye ran away to her older brother. On June 5, 1953, Sitefano came for her and they left her brother's house on a bicycle, apparently reconciled. Next morning, everyone thought that Sitefano behaved strangely. He told his other wives and children not to cry, that Babirye had not died but was only ill.

He told her brother, who lived nearby, that she had a "bad cold." In the evening, he was discovered in Babirye's hut, sobbing, and holding her body on his lap. He had strangled her.

This story serves to emphasize the superficiality of much of our analysis. No doubt the ambivalence which is apparent here is present much more often than would appear from the records.

A final marital conflict case illustrates the close connection which we noted earlier between violence and the sexual act:

Case No. 7. A wife in mourning commits suicide.

Samwili had two wives, Mbwali and Aliba. On November 11, 1952, Mbwali was found to have hanged herself. Aliba, the elder, related how Mbwali had gone to mourn at the funeral ceremonies for her aunt. "When she returned, she had not shaved her head to show that the mourning was finished. According to our custom, Samwili could not have slept with her because the mourning period had not been finished by the naming of a successor to her aunt. I suspect that he was trying to force her. He loved her more than me. He used to spend two weeks in her house, only one in mine. I asked him to have intercourse with me just before Mbwali came back, but he refused." Her husband's brother, who found the body, commented: "Her armlets were covered and she had no *butiti* beads (worn around the waist for sexual attractiveness). During the period of mourning, women cover their armlets and do not wear *butiti*. She was still mourning when she died."

We have said that homicide and suicide result much less often from conflict between lineage mates than from marital troubles. The following story, however, illustrates the tension which may arise between brothers:

Case No. 8. Suicide following conflict between brothers.

Waiswa, a village chief, and his brother Misaki had been quarrelling. On February 24, 1953, they attended a beer party together and after drinking for a time they began to fight. According to the statement given to the police by Waiswa's wife, Waiswa at one point demanded of Misaki: "Why do you always treat me so scornfully?" Misaki, in a rage, shouted back: "I will chop my bicycle to bits so you won't be able to inherit it!" Misaki then broke away and ran off. He tried to hang himself with a strip of plantain fibre, but was prevented by Waiswa and another brother. During the night he was more successful. In the morning his body was found hanging in his hut.

We have here only the bare skeleton of the story, but it is clear that there was jealousy between brothers. A father's testament, subject to confirmation by the local lineage group, may name any of his sons as heir. One son usually receives all or most of the land and the choice is often not known until the father's death. Smouldering jealousies often result.

We may appropriately end with a case which illustrates the uncertainty which is often the consequence of change in society's methods of securing order. "Self-help" or "vigilante" justice is, as we pointed out earlier, not accepted in present-day Busoga. That is to say, any Musoga, upon being questioned, will insist that criminals should be turned over to the authorities for trial. Faced with the actual thief breaking into his house, however, he and his neighbours very often respond in terms of an older set of standards, according to which the village community had to provide for itself security of life and property. (It is only fair to add that the Protectorate Police, often members of other tribes and for the most part trained for other tasks, are not very effective in preventing theft in the closed world of the peasant village.) Thus, on April

20, 1948, members of a village in southern Busoga took matters into their own hands:

Case No. 9. A thief is beaten to death.

Asani, finding a thief in his compound, raised a hue and cry and together with several of his neighbours gave chase. The thief was caught and bound to a tree. Asani and Petero, a neighbour, beat him with sticks until he died. Petero was released on bond of Shs. 100. The judge, sentencing Asani to nine months in prison for manslaughter, commented: "You have taken part in a practice which more responsible [men] than you regard as desirable, but I tell you that this practice of cruelly beating helpless men, even if they are thieves, is a savage and wicked practice."

Thus what in traditional Busoga was a legitimate form of punishment is slowly coming to be regarded as a kind of crime.

HOMICIDE AND
SUICIDE AMONG THE GISU

JEAN LA FONTAINE

THE Gisu are a Bantu people living on the western slopes of Mount Elgon, on the eastern border of Uganda. There are about a quarter of a million of them and they are mainly agriculturalists, though they also practice some animal husbandry, particularly on the drier and less densely populated plains. Their social organization is based on a series of localized lineages.

Before the introduction of British forms of law, disputes in Gisuland were settled by the heads of the lineages acting with an *ad hoc* council of elders.[1] Nowadays there is a hierarchy of native courts—sub-county, county, and district—set up by the British Government. There is also a series of Magistrates' courts on the British model, of which the lowest is the District Commissioner's court and the highest the High Court of Uganda. Appeal is from the highest native court to the District Commissioner's court. Cases are tried in the various courts depending on the magnitude of the offence; certain offences, of which the most important is homicide, are dealt with only in the Magistrates courts. In effect, therefore, there are two types of court: the purely British one, and the native courts which are intended to replace the traditional forms of legal organization.

Officials of the Police and Administration say that drunkenness is at the root of most crimes of violence. To a certain

[1] LaFontaine, J. S., *The Gisu of Uganda*, London, International African Institute, 1959.

extent they are justified, for a beer-drink is often the scene of an act of this sort. It is noticeable that in Gisu society killing is only rarely the result of a premeditated act; it is not murder in English law. Of the 99 cases studied here there are only four which can be said to be premeditated; this is less than five per cent of the total.

An analysis of the weapons used also supports the thesis that Gisu tend to kill in a fit of anger.

TABLE 19

WEAPONS USED IN GISU HOMICIDE

Stick	22
Panga	9
Knife	14
Axe	1
Spear	12
Bow and Arrow	2
Blows	9
Hoe	4
Piece of Wood	5
Household Tools	6
Not Stated	15

Ordinary domestic implements are the most commonly used. The two cases involving a bow and arrow, a weapon that is rarely used now that hunting is no longer a major occupation, were cases of premeditated murder.

There are only ten cases (roughly 10 per cent of the total number of murders in seven years) which can be attributed to drunkenness alone. There may be even fewer, as in several cases a motive for the crime was not uncovered in the trial and only became apparent as the result of the District Commissioner's investigations for the Death Report. Without allowing for the fact that there might have been an undiscovered or unrecorded motive, there are far fewer cases of murder attributable to drunkenness alone than would be expected if it were true that Gisu killed blindly in their cups. There is, in all cases, an ancient grudge or long-standing ill-feeling, suppressed because of social conventions, that determines who attacks whom in a brawl.

The cases on which this essay is based represent the total number of recorded homicides involving Gisu in Mbale District[2] during the years 1948 to 1954 inclusive. For purposes requiring a larger number of cases, those for 1945, 1946, and 1947 will be added. There are 99 cases in the detailed sample. The wider sample consists of 141 cases.

GISU NOTIONS OF DEATH

Formerly, and to a large extent today, all deaths were considered murder in that responsibility for them was laid at someone's door. At the ceremony ending the mourning period there is a formal consultation of the dead man's kin at which his goods and obligations are distributed among his heirs, and the reason for his death determined. Accusations and counter-accusations of witchcraft and sorcery are hurled. This is not to say that in traditional Gisu society a scapegoat was found for each and every death in the community. It was and is an essential feature of beliefs of this sort that there be a vagueness in the accusations. There does not have to be agreement on the subject; each man believes what it suits his social situation to believe. If a man were believed to be a sorcerer, and many deaths were attributed to him, he might have been beaten and even killed. Nowadays, if the accusations are all levelled against one person the death may be investigated by the police. The charge is usually one of poisoning: the Gisu term for the ingredients of sorcery being generally translated by the English word "poison." There were several cases of this type of accusation in the years under investigation but they are not included in the sample because in each case the medical officer's finding was death from natural causes.

There were, formerly, several ways to bring to book a killer who used material weapons: a retaliatory killing might be

[2] Now divided into Bugisu and Bukedi Districts.

made, blood-wealth might be paid, or war between the two parties might ensue. The choice of alternatives depended on the structural distance between the groups of killer and victim. The onus of exacting compensation for a death lay on the dead person's minimal lineage relatives whether the victim was a man or a woman. A man was not entitled to seek revenge for his wife, whatever factors of personal sentiment were involved. This duty belonged to her lineage, though he might assist them. Roscoe[3] speaks of the ceremonies necessary to cleanse a man who has shed blood and implies that before these rites were performed the killer was in a state of ritual impurity which cut him off from the normal everyday life of the community. Such an idea does not seem to be important today. The main emphasis in dealing with homicide is the necessity to restore the balance in group relations, and I suspect that this was always so. Therefore, should one lineage lose a member at the hands of a member of another lineage, the balance between them could be restored if one of the murderer's lineage were killed. The victim's lineage would kill a man of the murderer's lineage as nearly equal as possible in age and social standing to their dead agnate. A woman was killed in revenge in only one situation: if the dead man had been a lineage elder, his lineage might choose to kill a woman of the killer's lineage at the height of her reproductive powers.

Once a vengeance killing had been made, the matter was considered settled. There should be no further retaliation. There is no institutionalized feud in Gisu such as is found elsewhere in Africa in which no balance is achieved, but each generation seeks to add to the score.

The payment of blood-wealth was generally made where the bonds uniting the two groups were so strong that hostile relations could not continue until they culminated in a vengeance killing. Information as to the amounts paid varies according to the locality of the informant, but it is consist-

[3] John Roscoe, *The Bagesu*, 1924, p. 42; *Northern Bantu*, 1915, p. 170.

ently given as higher for a man than a woman. All informants agree as to the purpose it fulfills. Blood-wealth is paid in stock collected from all members of the murderer's minimal lineage. The animals are used to enable the brother of the dead man to marry and beget sons who will bear the dead man's name.[4] Moreover, the maternal kin of the deceased must be compensated for the loss of their kinsman. Blood-wealth tends to be one or two beasts higher than bride-wealth in the area concerned. After the blood-wealth had been paid or vengeance executed, peace was made between the two lineages concerned. The rites included the sacrifice of a cow and participation in a communal meal.

The killing of a man from a genealogically distant, or unrelated lineage, would result in an outbreak of hostilities between the two lineages. Blood money would not be offered, and the murderer's group would prepare to defend themselves against a vengeance killing. The war that ensued would be concluded only by the defeat of one side.

We have said that the course of events following a murder was determined largely by the structural distance between the two groups involved; the action followed a pattern very like that described for peoples possessing an institutionalized feud. The murder of a member of one's own family, excluding the spouse, was said to have "spoiled kinship"; informants say that the offender would always have been put to death and some sort of ritual performed to cleanse the lineage of the impurity. In fact this course of action does not appear to have been taken often. In one case of this sort, in which a man killed his own full brother, local opinion as consulted by the District Commissioner deplored the killing but said that it would be a pity for one family to lose two of its male members and they therefore considered that the culprit should not be executed. Killing a member of one's own minimal lineage seems to have met with sterner treatment. Blood-wealth could

---

[4] This is not a true ghost-marriage; the genitor is the children's *pater*.

not have been paid, for the receiving unit would have been identical with the paying unit, but the culprit would have been driven from the community to seek refuge with his maternal kin, or he would have been killed. Blood money was paid between lineages resident in the same village and, in certain circumstances, between lineages of different villages within the same village cluster. Vengeance killing took place generally between lineages in different village-clusters of the same district. The killing of a man of another maximal lineage could only mean war.

The motive for the act was not entirely irrelevant in deciding the course of events after a murder took place. It determined whether the murderer would have the support of his lineage-mates. The proposal to pay blood-wealth might forestall a vengeance killing but, if the murderer was habitually of a violent, troublesome nature, his lineage would not consider his life worth redeeming. They might kill him to prevent the victim's lineage taking vengeance on one of themselves. At the other extreme, the complete mobilization of a lineage in support of one of its members might mean that war rather than an isolated vengeance killing ensued. Finally, there are three sets of circumstances under which, in Gisu belief, homicide was justifiable, and no action would be taken by either party. If a man found a thief stealing his property or a man in adultery with his wife and killed him, he was subject to no retaliation. Furthermore, if a man earned the reputation of a sorcerer, his death at the hands of some member of the community was considered generally beneficial. Perryman writes in his article on witchcraft in Bugisu that the first "witch-doctor" he saw was hanging on a tree and "he was very dead."[5]

There were traditional means by which sorcerers were killed. Of these, the two most often cited by Gisu are: impaling on a sharpened stake, and pinning the tongue to the chin with thorns. Both were usually accompanied by a severe beating.

[5] *Uganda Journal*, 1937.

The latter method was supposed to prevent the victim's using his last breath to utter curses against his murderers. A modern example of this is seen in the following case.

Case No. 1.

Two sons of Muzaka, Musufa and Nabitere, were tried for the murder of an elderly man whom they had beaten and then killed by driving a nail into his head. They denied the killing but said they had beaten him "because he was a witch." From their evidence, it was clear that the witnesses considered the use of the nail a modern development of traditional methods of killing such malefactors. Moreover, they all expressed the belief that the old man had been both a sorcerer and a witch. He had been found late at night in the compound of one of the accused, sufficient evidence for a Gisu that he was there with evil intent. Local opinion had it that the two men had done a good job in ridding the community of an evil character.

The difference between killing men who wield evil supernatural powers and killing thieves is indicated by the fact that Gisu, when asked to give an instance when homicide would be justified, will instance the killing of a thief or adulterer but not of a sorcerer. Most Gisu agree that sorcerers should be killed; they are reluctant to take the responsibility themselves. Action against a thief or adulterer is defense of individual property; the responsibility lies on one man. Action against a sorcerer is the result of a series of acts which have lost him the support of the community; in a sense, his killers are agents of the community at large. It is said that elders of a lineage might even, after consultation, depute some young men to kill a recognized witch or sorcerer who was considered a public menace.

Homicide in these three instances is largely a matter of social control in that it is the ultimate sanction for conformity with social norms. An attack on another's personal property,

100

including his wife, or anti-social behavior which lays a man open to the charge of being a witch or sorcerer, both threaten the norms of Gisu society. The killing which may follow is then just.

CASES OF JUSTIFIABLE HOMICIDE

It is interesting to note the frequency of the killing of thieves, adulterers, and sorcerers in the sample of cases we are examining. Of 79 cases where the relationship between murderer and victim is stated, only two involved sorcery. One has already been cited. In the other, a man while drunk killed another for bewitching his wife.

In three of the 79 cases, men killed their wives' lovers. There is a set compensation recoverable in the native courts but violent action is considered understandable, if perhaps foolish. The following case is taken from outside the main detailed sample because it shows more clearly the principles involved.

Case No. 2.

Bulugwa Wamini, a youngish man from a remote hilly part of Bugisu, went, as many Gisu do, to Buganda to find work on the cotton farms there. He left his wife behind to look after his property. Three months later he returned and when he reached his hut he heard voices inside—his wife's and that of a close relative, Yowani Mudama. Mudama could be there for no innocent purpose. No Gisu man goes into another's hut when the wife is alone; such an action is considered adulterous and treated as such. Bulugwa, furiously angry, hammered on the door and his wife opened it. He pushed past her and seized hold of Yowani, who had tried to escape. There was a struggle, during which Bulugwa hit the other man on the head several times with his stick. When he saw that he had killed him he went and reported himself to

the nearest Police Station. In his statement he admitted everything and obviously considered that he had had ample justi-
fication.

I discussed the case with an elderly man who had a reputation for knowledge of traditional law. He said: "What! The
man was actually in his brother's hut? With the door closed?
Then serve him right!" The offense was the more heinous, he
explained, in that the adulterer was a close agnate of Bulugwa's. A man trusts his close relatives to look after his property, including his wife, and if that trust is abused, then there
is every cause for anger. However, from this and other evidence it seems likely that for homicide in this sort of situation
to be completely justified, the couple must be caught *in flagrante delicto*.

The largest number of cases in the category of what we
might call, according to Gisu ideas, justifiable homicide, is
that of killing thieves. Twelve out of 79 cases are of this sort,
of which the following is a good example.

Case No. 3.

The accused was Waniaye Masaba, an elderly pagan of
some fifty-odd years who came from a cattle-keeping part
of Bugisu. He had suffered many times from the depredations
of thieves and to prevent any further losses he took to sleeping at night in the byre. On this occasion, he woke and saw
a figure, with a bundle on its head, creeping stealthily from
the compound. He called out; the figure began to run, whereupon Waniaye seized his spear and speared it twice. The
victim fell to the ground and his attacker raised the alarm,
which was answered by Petero, his son, whom he sent to the
chief. The intruder was dead by the time the chief arrived
so Waniaye was arrested. At the trial, Waniaye admitted the
spearing but said in defense that he wished to stop the man
running away. The Judge did not allow this and sentenced

him in these words: "The accused has probably reached manhood in a society which regarded the killing of thieves as a praiseworthy act. I much doubt if he understands what all this fuss is about. However, he is not entitled to acquittal as the extent of the wounding far exceeded that necessary to apprehend a thief."

Altogether, there are seventeen cases of "justifiable" homicide, less than a quarter of the total cases, where the records allow of a reasonably clear understanding of motive.

TABLE 20

MOTIVES IN GISU HOMICIDES

1.	Victim a thief	12
2.	Victim an adulterer	3
3.	Victim a sorcerer	2
4.	Quarrel over land rights	3
5.	Quarrel over property rights including distribution of beer	12
6.	Quarrel over sharing of bride price	2
7.	Quarrel over control of women	5
8.	Revenge	4
9.	Marital disputes	10
10.	Resentment of authority	5
11.	Intervention in quarrel	2
12.	Drunken brawl	10
13.	Response to provocation	10
14.	No apparent motive	1
15.	Others	5
	TOTAL	86 + 13 unknown = 99

Although fighting over land used to be rife and there is now over-population in many areas, fatal disputes over land are rare—3 in seven years. There is one dispute over fishing rights in a river (classified in Category 15) which is really an inter-lineage fight. Quarrels over property rights, which include quarrels between debtor and creditor, and disputes over the right to distribute beer at a beer-drink are more numerous. These, together with two cases of quarrelling over the distribution of a sister's bride-wealth, form roughly 15 per cent of the total. As we have said above, there are 10 cases where a death has occurred after a fight and no motive has been adduced for the brawl except drunkenness. There are also 10 cases where the murderer responded to provocation in the form of attack, drunken abuse or serious insult. One case to illustrate this last category is needed.

Case No. 4.

Efulansi, who was her husband's first wife, was barren. His brothers were urging him to take another wife who would give him children. Gisu say that a woman always objects to her husband marrying a second time, and from the evidence it appears that Efulansi was strengthening her case with the argument that she was a Christian. However, her husband took a mistress, who one day passed by Efulansi's hut and taunted her with barrenness, saying that she should allow her husband to marry a second wife for it was obvious that she would never bear children. Efulansi's husband's brother came on the scene. He threatened to beat her or even kill her if she did not consent to the second marriage, and he advanced menacingly towards her. Efulansi seized a hammer which was lying nearby and hit him on the head with it. The judge considered that she had had ample provocation, but that she had been too handy with a very dangerous weapon, and sentenced her to four years at hard labor.

Gisu say that there are certain insults that will surely produce violence on the part of the person against whom they are directed, so that the user is, to some extent, responsible for what follows. To taunt a man or a woman with childlessness is one of these supreme insults; the man whom Efulansi killed was said to have brought it on himself. In another case a man killed someone who accused him of being a coward at circumcision.

104

Category 7 contains the cases where the quarrels which preceded the murder were between a man and his father-in-law for control over the wife; between a man and his son, whom he suspected of having an affair with his youngest wife; between a man and his mother, whom he accused of encouraging his sister to leave her husband, thus placing the burden of returning the bride-wealth on him.

Marital disputes account for ten of the killings—four of them are cases in which the wife killed her husband in self-defense. In two cases, it was the wife who provoked the quarrel by defying her husband's authority. These latter two cases might almost be classed with Category 10, as the driving motive seems to have been the murderer's resentment of authority exercised over him by a senior. Finally, there is one case where there was no motive for the crime that was discovered. The culprit was not drunk; it was said that he had been bewitched by his father's age-mate for rudeness to him. Gisu believe that witchcraft or sorcery can make a man mad so that he does things that no normal person will do.

From an analysis of motive, whether it was expressed by the accused himself at the trial or whether it was implicit in the evidence of witnesses, no clear picture emerges. A study of individual motive gives only the pattern of precipitating causes, but it is my view that a pattern can be found which will show the sociological factors operative.

CRUCIAL RELATIONSHIPS

If we analyze the relationship between murderer and victim—where it is shown—we find that the majority of women murderers kill their husbands, but men their patrilineal kin. The relationship between killer and killed in the cases examined are summarized in Table 21.

It would almost seem that the marital relationship is more prone than any other to drive women to murder. Women kill less than men—there are only 9 cases of women killing as

105

TABLE 21

RELATION OF KILLER AND VICTIM IN GISU HOMICIDES

Relation of victim to murderer	Killer is male	Killer is female
Thief	12	1
Wife's lover	3	–
Kinsmen:		
Ascending generation:		
Father	7	–
Class. father	4	–
Mother	4	–
Class. mother	1	–
Mother's brother	1	–
Ego's generation:		
Brother	5	–
Sister	–	–
Descending generation:		
Son	–	–
Daughter	–	–
Other:		
Same village	5	1
Same lineage	11	–
Affines:		
Ascending generation:		
Father-in-law	2	–
Mother-in-law	1	–
Own generation:		
Spouse	7	4
Brother-in-law	1	1
Sister-in-law	–	–
Not known	26	2
TOTAL	90	9

against 90 men in the sample. Of these nine women, four killed their husbands (nearly 50 per cent) whereas seven men killed their wives (just under 8 per cent). The husband-wife relationship is an unequal one. In marriage a man gains full rights over his wife's sexual and reproductive powers, her labor, and any economic gains she makes. A woman has only the right to enough food for herself and her children. She must share digging rights and her husband's sexual attention with any other wife he acquires. A woman may have considerable *de facto* control over the domestic economy, but she

106

has no jural right to it. A woman must also treat her husband with great respect and should obey his orders without questioning them. There is, moreover, a potent source of conflict in the fact that husband and wife both utilize the same resources, but with different ends in view. She is primarily concerned with getting the best she can for her children; his aim is to use his economic resources to improve his own status in the society. His advancement necessitates the use of property which she considers reserved for her and her children. Where this property is used by the husband to acquire another wife, the situation is fraught with inter-personal tensions. The formal structure of rights and obligations between them merely emphasizes the asymmetry of the conjugal relationship.

One-third of the men killed by men were agnates. This number (32) includes those men "from the same village" who, in a system of territorially organized lineages, are usually lineage relatives of some sort. The data are not complete enough on this point for meaningful conclusions to be drawn, but it is significant that, where the exact relationship is known, there are eleven fathers and father's brothers killed to only five brothers. In two cases in which the father's brother was killed, the father was dead and the victim of the murder stood *in loco parentis* to the murderer. Three of the brothers are elder brothers and hence in a position of some authority vis-à-vis the murderers. As in most patrilineal societies, a man is subject to the authority of his senior male agnates who also control property, land, and cattle, which is the means by which status is acquired in this society. Identity of interest, mutual loyalty and cooperation between agnates are continually stressed, and the fact that these very mutual interests may feed personal rivalries and jealousies for which there exists no outlet, means that the actual relationship is very different from the ideal. Conflict results in a greater strain on the junior party because legal and jural rights secure the position of the senior, whereas ideals of what is just are the only safeguards of the junior man's claims. Thus, a "good" father in Gisu society provides his son with land and the cattle with which to obtain a wife, but the son cannot sue his father if he fails in this duty. He can extort what he considers his due only by resorting to means which are socially disapproved.

Further evidence on this point is provided by a study of the ages at which men commit murder. Determining age among Africans, particularly those who are today over 30 or so, is notoriously difficult. Undoubtedly, ages are more accurate for the younger age-grades, and it may be that age is mentioned more often for young men than for older men. Be this as it may, I think that the general picture which emerges is a true one: that homicide is primarily committed by young men.

TABLE 22
AGE OF GISU KILLERS

Up to 20	3
21-25	5
26-30	12
31-35	6
36-40	1
41-45	1
46-50	2
51-55	–
56-60	1
60+	–

The peak period appears to be between 25 and 30.[6] The ethnographic facts show that this is a difficult period for Gisu men. By this time they have achieved adulthood, by undergoing the rites of circumcision. There being no further gradation of men into formal age sets, a young circumcised man has the same formal status, in the society as a whole, as his seniors. After circumcision, a man is entitled to the privileges of an adult male and the chief of these is the headship of his own

[6] The wider sample 1945-1954 was used for this table as data on ages is sparse.

family. In order to set up his own family, a man must have his own land and cattle, and it is his father's duty to provide him with them. However, the possession of large herds and much land mean power and high status in the community. An old man who is still vigorous is reluctant to relinquish to his son what he has acquired. To this rivalry is added another element which makes for conflict: although a man does achieve a change in ascribed status by passing through the *rite de passage* of circumcision, the structure of authority within the social group does not change. He is still subordinate to the authority of his seniors. But the inequality in terms of formal status that formerly supported this inequality of power no longer exists. Not only has the formal position changed but the newly-circumcised man begins to demand actual equality. Conflict between a man and his father is increased.

To conclude, there appear to be two aspects from which murder as a social phenomenon in Gisu society can be considered. One is the very real sense in which killing the transgressor can be considered as the ultimate sanction for conformity with social norms. However, as we have seen, the social control explanation does not cover all cases of murder that occur. A rise in the annual number of homicides does not appear to indicate a disruption of the system of social control and a failure of less stringent means to check individual rapacity. In 1949, there was a rise of nearly 50 per cent in the incidence of homicide (from the yearly average of 14 up to 20), but the proportion of thieves and adulterers killed remained the same as in other years.

Murder is also related to conflicts of interest which occur at certain points of the social structure. For Gisu men, it is largely a matter of competition between generations for control of the means of acquiring prestige; for Gisu women, it is the conflict between the interests of their husbands and their children which is crucial. Due to the influence of external factors, these conflicts have become intensified to a point where they result in violence. When we come to examine suicide in the second part of this essay, we shall see that these two relationships—between males of adjacent generations, and between husband and wife—are again crucial.

SUICIDE

"A person commits suicide if he finds too much trouble" Gisu say. Suicide, in their eyes, is a choice between the alternatives of life and death. Mental illness or insanity is not therefore considered to be a cause of suicide. A mentally unsound person is thought to be incapable of weighing the pros and cons of living and could have no inducement to commit suicide.

However, suicide is not entirely a reasoned decision. It is also a manifestation of *litima*, which is best translated "temper." This is a personal characteristic which, Gisu say, results in the possessor's being liable to fits of anger or violence, or unreasonable jealousy and spite. Gisu believe that traits of character are inherited and therefore a whole lineage or a group of kinsmen may be referred to as bad-tempered, in the sense of possessing *litima*, although they are reluctant to push the argument to its logical conclusion and say that a tendency to commit suicide may be inherited. They are equally reluctant to admit that a member of their own lineage or a close kinsman has committed suicide. Suicide is considered to be evil, for it results from strife, from bad relations between men, or between men and the ancestors.

Suicide is also thought to be contagious in the sense that physical contact with the body or surroundings of a suicide may cause the person who suffered contagion to commit suicide. For this reason the dead body must be removed from the place of death by someone entirely unrelated to the dead man and his kin; the service is repaid by the gift of a bull. A sheep must also be killed to pacify the spirit of the suicide, which is evil. A suicide's hut may be pulled down; it will certainly be smeared with the contents of a sheep's stomach, which is the material used for purification in all cases of ritual defilement. The chyme will be smeared on the agent of death (usually a rope or cord) and thrown round about the spot where the suicide took place. If the suicide hanged himself on a tree, it will be cut down and burnt. Nothing must be left which might cause another suicide by its contagious evil. Relatives of the dead man and his close patrilineal kinsmen are particularly susceptible to the evil influence for two reasons. The *litima* which was the precipitating cause of the suicide is also dormant in their natures and therefore the contagion of a suicide may make this quality active. Also, the suicide may have been a form of ancestral vengeance directed against the lineage group as a whole. The wrath of the ancestors, if not appeased, may cause another member of the lineage to commit suicide.

It is only the ancestors that can make a man kill himself. Witchcraft and sorcery can impel a man to kill another but not himself. This belief is connected with the idea that the measurer of a man's allotted span of existence, who metes out life and death, is the creator-god, Nabende or Were, who may work through the ancestors. The ancestors are thus intermediaries between him and the patrilineal descent groups whose founders they are. The ancestors can cause a man to commit suicide in one of two ways: either they may cause him to feel such shame at some anti-social act that he will kill himself, or they may involve him with hostilities with his close kinsfolk so that he commits suicide out of *litima*. Gisu do not formulate their ideas in quite this way. They say, "What makes one man in a certain situation commit suicide, while another, in an identical situation, does not? It must be the anger of the ancestors."[7] Thus, most men will say that an

[7] Of course, all Gisu theory on this subject is designed to explain individual cases of suicide, rather than suicide per se.

immediate sacrifice to the ancestors is one of the essential precautions to take when cleansing the community after a suicide.

Suicide, then, causes a state of ritual uncleanliness which must be purged or more evil will follow. This fact is also emphasized in the lack of ritual surrounding the disposal of the body. Gisu say that no one except very close kin will go to the funeral of a suicide; this is unusual, for there are strong obligations on neighbors, maternal kin, and affines to attend mortuary ceremonies. By their presence they show that they are not guilty of causing the man's death by witchcraft or sorcery.[8] No drums are beaten for the burial and no mourning observances are carried out. No one must name a child after a suicide victim, and his name is not mentioned in sacrifices to the ancestors. Formerly, before the introduction of burial practices, the corpse was thrown into thick bush where no one would be likely to come across the bones, for they, too, were ritually dangerous. The skull was not placed in the lineage depository with the skulls of honored men and women of the lineage. The net result was to blot out as quickly as possible all memory of the person who brought the evil of suicide into the community.

In part, the refusal of the wider community to attend the funeral of a suicide is a reflection of the idea that the people in daily contact with the dead man were responsible for the death. The most frequently cited cause of suicide is quarrelling with those people whose hostility makes an individual feel that life is no longer worth living. That is, those people with whom, in the Gisu social system, a man must be on good terms. One's father and brothers, one's spouse, should be loyal and appreciative and, at the very least, fulfill their obligations towards one. Thus, when a suicide takes place there is a feeling, not usually formulated precisely, that these people are to blame.

---

[8] One cannot, as has been said, cause a suicide by the use of supernatural powers.

A threat of suicide may occasionally be used to impose demands on relatives. One such threat came to my notice, which I will give in detail: Wosukira,[9] the son, by a young wife, of an influential minor chief, was at secondary school. He had already been expelled from two schools for making girls pregnant and this was his last chance. After two defections, his father refused to pay further school-fees, but would permit him to continue at school if his mother paid the fees out of what she could earn in agricultural work. Then he made a third girl pregnant and wanted to marry her, in part to pacify the school authorities. His father refused to pay the bride-wealth and expressed his disapproval of the whole affair. At this, Wosukira threatened suicide and left his father's homestead. His mother was worried and sent his sister to find him; she also did her best to persuade the father to relent. Wosukira did not carry out his threat, but had he done so, his mother, and probably others, would have blamed his father.

Gisu say that suicide must be prevented if possible, but this does not mean that the threat of suicide is either condoned or often used as a weapon to enforce one's demands. In the sample of cases which we will examine here,[10] there are only four in which previous threats of suicide were mentioned. Gisu do not hold the idea that by committing suicide a man may revenge himself on others by releasing an evil spirit to attack them. The spirit of a suicide is thought to be evil, but rather in the way that the spirits of anyone who dies an untimely death is evil.

Gisu will readily construct a hypothetical situation to illustrate common motives for suicides. The reasons given for men and women differ slightly, but there are three broad categories: failure to have children, quarrels with close relatives or

[9] This is not his real name.

[10] These cases are taken from the Police Death Enquiry Files for 1945 to 1955 inclusive. Any death in suspicious circumstances is investigated by the Police, and a report made. The cases examined are the total number recorded.

spouse, or the death of several children or siblings. Each of these situations is found among the cases in this sample.

Gisu say that if a man has no children and particularly no sons, or if he has a series of unsuccessful marriages and can get no woman to stay with him long enough for him to achieve a stable family unit, his state is indeed bad. At beer parties he will be chaffed or ridiculed, at councils no one will listen to him; generally, he will count for nothing. This will cause him to feel bitter against fate and jealous of others who are more fortunate; he will feel *litima*, and may well commit suicide. Case 1 is an example of this, in a more dramatic form than usual.

Case No. 1.

Wangobi, son of Mafwabi, aged about 35, had not been able to marry until this, by Gisu standards, late age; he had remained a virgin until his marriage. When he did marry, he proved to be impotent. His wife said that he had been in despair and had tried several remedies, but to no avail. Talking over this case with informants, I got a large measure of agreement that he had taken the only way out of an impossible situation.

A woman who is barren or whose children all die in infancy may suffer ill-treatment from her husband, even if he does not divorce her. Her co-wives and neighbors will treat her with contempt. This treatment may make her feel the *litima* that will cause her to kill herself.

Case No. 2.

Lozita Nagudi was barren. Her husband had taken a second wife who had a child and Lozita was very jealous of her. The husband seems to have been fond of Lozita and was scrupulously fair in his treatment of both. On this occasion

114

he brought back two pounds of meat from the market and divided it between them. Lozita refused to take her share saying: "Give it to your favorite wife, the mother of your child." He remonstrated with her, saying that they each had equal rights, but she persisted in her refusal. He got angry and boxed her ears, whereupon she tore herself away and ran towards a high cliff in the neighborhood. Her husband followed her but, despite his efforts, she threw herself over the edge and was killed.

However, Gisu say that fewer women than men commit suicide because they are childless. This is related to the fact that a women can escape from the situation by returning to her natal home, where her family will support her, and may even accuse her husband's lineage of bewitching her, for they will not believe that she is barren. Moreover, she has always the hope that taking a new partner may result in a more productive union. "A woman can always find a husband but a man who cannot keep a wife is indeed unfortunate" is a common saying.

But if a woman's natal family do not support her in quarrels with her husband and his lineage, whatever the cause, a woman is likely to kill herself. This is the type-situation for female suicide. One man gave me an example from his experience which I quote in full; it is not in the sample but is closely paralleled by one which is.

Case No. 3.

A girl of my informant's acquaintance, from a hills area, was married to a man who lived at some distance from her home in the plains. There are more cattle in the plains than the hills and her father had been able to get a large number for her bride-wealth. The woman did not get on well with her husband who beat her and did not fulfill the obligations of a husband. She went home to her father. He was not pleased to see her for he had used the cows of her bride-wealth to marry a wife for her brother. He refused to let her stay with him, which would have signified his willingness to repay the bride-wealth and obtain a divorce for her. Her brother, naturally enough, was equally unsympathetic, and the two men told her to return to her husband and not leave him till she had proof that he had sent her away, an action which would mean that he forfeited the bride-wealth. She left her father's homestead and hanged herself.

It is clear that Gisu ideas on suicide do relate to the facts. One can pick actual cases which correspond exactly to the "ideal type." Moreover, there is an institutionalized way of committing suicide, by hanging. Of the 68 cases in this sample, an overwhelming majority used this method, as Table 23 indicates.

TABLE 23

METHODS OF GISU SUICIDES

Hanging	64
Stabbing	1
Drowning	1
Setting fire to the house	1
Jumping over cliff	1

One can say, then, that suicide is a recognized, if not socially approved, course of action; it is a possible way out of certain difficult situations. The crucial point, however, is that Gisu do not win esteem by committing suicide. The "way out" is not thought to be the "noble way out." Gisu suicide cannot be classified in Durkheim's category of altruistic suicide.

An examination of the alleged motives for the 68 cases of suicide in our sample is set out in Table 24.

Two points emerge from a consideration of this table. The first is that a strikingly large number of suicides, both male and female are attributed to the person's having a long-standing, painful, or incurable disease. Gisu ideas on suicide make no mention of this condition as a possible motive. This factor is intelligible in the light of the importance of physical fitness for participation in the social life of a society such as that of the Gisu. A man or woman who is ill is, to a large extent, outside

TABLE 24

ALLEGED MOTIVES IN GISU SUICIDES

Motive	Men		Women	
	Number	per cent of total	Number	per cent of total
Physical distress	16	40	8	28.5
Mental disorder	2	5	5	17.9
Quarrels with kin	–	–	3	10.4
Fear of results of own misdeed	10	25	3	10.4
Other	4	10	2	7.1
Not known	8	20	7	25.7
TOTAL	40	100	28	100

the society, unable to take part in communal activity. When illness first attacks an individual, the support of the community is felt by him or her in the efforts that are made to cure the disease. If all remedies fail, the attitude changes; some people may even attribute the affliction to a supernatural punishment for evil doing. The isolation engendered by this situation may well lead to suicide.

However, the data provided by the analysis of alleged motives does not show clearly the sociological factor involved. Further, the attribution of seven suicides to mental disorder is quite contrary to Gisu theory and throws doubt on the reliability of the data.[11] In fact, the categories of motive show a marked similarity to those into which Durkheim divided the alleged motives for suicide in French society,[12] and one

[11] In the records, no indication is made of who was questioned about the suicide; the investigation is not designed to show motive, but to decide whether the case is one of suicide or murder.

[12] Durkheim, *Le Suicide* (1897), Nouvelle ed. 1930, p. 146.

could hardly say that the structure of the two societies was the same. Durkheim himself discarded the analysis of individual "motives," and showed that suicide rates are determined by extra-individual forces. Let us turn to look at some economic and social factors which affect Gisu suicide.[13]

Sociological studies have related the variations in the incidence of suicide in a particular society to fluctuations in its economy. Durkheim found that dislocation of the economic organization, whether because of a sudden rise or depression, correlated with a rise in the suicide rate.[14]

Henry and Short[15] modified this theory, on evidence from their data that there is a negative correlation between the suicide rate and the business cycle. Both these studies deal with societies where the state of the economy is measurable in terms of a business cycle. In this essay, we are dealing with a society whose economy is, basically, a subsistence one. It is subject to sharp seasonal and local variations, and by its very nature cannot rise above a level which is marked by the greatest productivity of the soil under ideal climatic conditions. The problem is complicated by the fact that Gisu also participate in a money economy. They grow cash crops and buy articles which are the products of industrialized societies using a money economy. One might perhaps use these cash crops as an index of the prosperity of Gisu economy, for they represent a surplus over the basic subsistence needs of the society. However, the cultivation of cash crops has been steadily increasing and has not yet reached its maximum capacity. Fluctuation in the amount of these crops in any series of seasons

[13] Although the following discussion is set forth in terms of the quantities available, the sample is inadequate for the use to which it has been put. However, the conclusions drawn about suicide and economy in Bugisu are based on a general knowledge of the society and not merely on the figures, which are used mainly in illustration. It has, thus, a certain validity in ethnographic observation which it lacks statistically.

[14] Durkheim, *op.cit.*, p. 264.

[15] *Homicide and Suicide*, 1954, p. 23.

is obscured by the fact that there are more and more producers entering the market. Moreover, the income from cash crops is used freely to supplement deficiencies in the food crops. This is made possible by the differing effect of seasonal changes on cash and food crops: one may be affected and not the other.

It is essential to attempt to assess to some degree the nature of the relationship of suicide to economic conditions in order to test the conclusions that have been drawn about their interconnection. Gisu society, like that of industrialized societies, has a status hierarchy that is based on the use of wealth to gain power and prestige. In both types of society, an economic depression involves persons in the hierarchy in loss of status and hence in a situation of anomy. However, the data are such that only tentative conclusions may be drawn.

The quality of the harvests of both food crops and cash crops and the number of suicides for the same year are presented in Table 25.

The total incidence does not seem responsive to changes in the economy. However, if we separate male from female suicide, we can see that economic factors seem to have some significance; the incidence of suicide by males shows more coordination with economic changes. In the post-famine years of 1946 and 1949, and the year following a rapid rise in prosperity in 1952, the numbers of men who committed suicide increased, while those of women do not seem to have been affected. This difference between men and women can be related to their different roles in the economic structure of society, particularly with regard to the opportunity to use economic resources. Food over and above that for consumption and the money from cash crops is in the hands of men. It is the men who own land and cattle and can use these and surplus crops to achieve high status by using these means to create relations of economic interdependence with others or by marrying more wives. A woman, once she has fed her

119

TABLE 25

ECONOMIC CONDITIONS AND SUICIDE IN BUGISU

| Year | Economic Conditions | Total | Suicide | |
			Male	Female
1945	Famine relief necessary. Cotton crop poor	9	4	5
1946	Food still very short. Good coffee crop	9	7	2
1947	Bad year for both food and cash crops though not famine	3	2	1
1948	Bad food harvest. 22 tons of maize imported. Good coffee crop	5	2	3
1949	Food still short	4	3	1
1950	Economy returning to normal	7	6	1
1951	Good year for food and cash crops	5	1	4
1952	Not very good cotton year. Other crops normal	5	2	3
1953	Normal food harvest. Coffee good and prices high	11	8	3
1954	Very good year for both cash crops	0	0	0
1955	Harvest not yet in (suicides for half year)	10	5	5

children and seen that they and she get a fair share of the husband's wealth for buying the necessities of life, has no further interest in wealth. Her position does not depend on wealth, although she gains in prestige if her husband is wealthy. A woman's primary task is to produce children, and her standing in the community depends on her achievement as the mother of many and healthy children.

Interesting results can be obtained from an analysis of suicides by age. Data is not available for all 68 cases; the 44 for which an age is given as summarized in Table 26.

The highest incidence of all suicides is found among the age groups 26-30 and 31-35, a fact which is in striking contrast to findings for other societies in which the tendency to commit suicide increases with age. This has been related to the weakening of the individual's ties to society,[16] and to the fall in prestige which individuals suffer in age.[17] We can relate the difference in the distribution of the Gisu figures to a difference in the position of the aged. Not only are they removed from the struggle for prestige and the necessity to maintain their

TABLE 26

AGE OF GISU SUICIDES

Age	Total Suicides	Women	Men
Up to 15	4	0	4
16-20	3	0	3
21-25	3	2	1
26-30	7	2	5
31-35	7	2	5
36-40	5	4	1
41-45	2	2	0
46-50	2	0	2
51-55	2	2	0
56-60	2	1	1
61-65	2	0	2
66-70	3	0	3
71-75	0	0	0
76+	2	0	2

status, they acquire a positive source of prestige in their age and experience.

In order to explain the peak in suicides between the ages of 26 and 35, one must separate the figures for male and female suicides. Then it becomes apparent that it is the suicide of men that accounts for this rise. Nearly half the male suicides for which data on age are available are under thirty, and two-thirds are under forty. This fact can be related to the structural position of young men in Gisu society. In discussing homicide, we saw that there is tension in the relations between young men and seniors of their own lineage, who

[16] Durkheim, *op.cit.*
[17] Henry and Short, p. 38.

wield authority over them. This inter-personal hostility is a factor in the incidence of suicide as well.

There are two peaks in the suicide figure for men under 35: there are seven suicides of youths under 20,[18] and 10 of young men between the ages of 25 and 35. Each group forms nearly a quarter of the total for all ages.

Boys of the youngest group are not highly integrated into the society. They are of little importance, for they are usually not yet circumcised at this age. They cannot, therefore, take part in the economic or political activities of their elders; they are also cut off from the society of women and young girls who have their own task, in which boys play no part. Boys of this age are not essential to any of the major tasks of the community; those who go to school have little time for additional activities together with other members of the community. They also learn values and acquire knowledge which puts them in a still more isolated position vis-à-vis the rest of the society.

As the youths grow older,[19] circumcision appears as the passport to full participation in the world of men. The position of inferiority in which an uncircumcised youth finds himself appears easily surmountable. In theory, all circumcised men are equal in status; only the uncircumcised are inferior. Circumcision ceremonies involve the whole community and are a powerful force for strengthening the cohesion of groupings at all levels in Gisu society. The novice is the center of attention and is made to feel that it is an integral and essential part of his lineage and of the community. His fortitude during the operation brings him praise and a high standing among his age-mates, with whom he has been made to feel the greatest solidarity. It is noticeable that the suicides of

[18] Three of the under-15 suicides were of boys of 14; the other was a boy of 12.

[19] Circumcision in Bugisu takes place between the ages of 16 and 20.

young men in the immediate post-circumcision years (20-25) drop suddenly from seven to one.

The circumcision ceremonies have the effect of strengthening the solidarity of the lineage group and emphasizing the ties between its members and the common interests, rights, and duties among them. The relation between the newly circumcised men and the fellow lineage members, and particularly seniors in the lineage, do not bear out this ideal. We have seen how the relations between successive generations of males become strained almost to breaking point after the young man has passed through circumcision. The formal inequality of rank which supported the asymmetrical father-son relationship has disappeared. Once the son has acquired a wife and family of his own, which he does soon after circumcision, the social distance between himself and his father is still further diminished. What distinguishes them at this point is that the older man still controls land, cattle and other economic resources that the younger man wants for himself. For the fifteen years after the age of about 25 a Gisu man is more involved in the business of raising his status than at any other time. The traditional status hierarchy was based on wealth; modern conditions have not altered this, but merely offer new opportunities for acquiring wealth.[20] If a young man wants to get ahead, either in the traditional system or in the hierarchy of new jobs, he must do it when still young, before he has growing sons for whom to provide.[21]

The newly-circumcised young man, then, views his elders as frustrating agents, who stand in his way of advancement. Although he is now the formal equal of any man in the society,

[20] See my article on Gisu chiefs in A. I. Richards (editor), *East African Chiefs: a Study of Political Development in some Uganda and Tanganyika Tribes*, London, 1959.

[21] It would be interesting to see if the suicide of the 26-35 age group is more sensitive than others to economic change. Henry and Short (*op.cit.*, p. 29) show that the two age groups 25-34 and 15-24 are the most highly sensitive to changes in the business cycle. Unfortunately, the Gisu data does not make such a close analysis feasible.

his new status does not bring any material advantage of itself. He has to fight for his rights to land and to a wife, to compete with the older members of his lineage for control of economic resources. Land is extremely short in many areas and the prevention of inter-lineage warfare, which provided an outlet for feelings of aggression and a means by which the needs of an expanding lineage for more land might be met, means increasing conflicts between members of the same lineage. The ideals of mutual loyalty and cooperation between members that are the main emphasis of the circumcision ceremonies contrast sharply with the rivalry which characterizes the actual situation.

During their early twenties, many young men leave Gisuland and find work either in Kenya on European farms, or in Buganda on cotton plantations. In this way they can both escape the authority of their elders and hope to earn the money to pay bride-wealth for a wife and buy land, if their fathers refuse to do their duty and provide them with these two essentials. Emigration relieves the situation only temporarily, however. Most of the emigrants go for short periods, and few intend to do other than make money and return to their birthplace. Strong emotional ties bind a Mugisu to his lineage home, the place where he has par excellence a right to land. Title to a piece of land means also a right to citizenship and a place in the society; few Gisu willingly forego it. The return of young men aggravates the situation of conflict in yet another way. Having established themselves as independent, they are less willing than before to submit to the authority of their seniors. They are also, to a certain extent, strangers in the community and their ties with its members are not strong enough to counteract the influence of mutual hostility. Far from relieving the situation, the possibilities of emigration aggravate it.

Among females, there is a difference in the distribution of suicide by age. The figures are not large enough to warrant drawing far-reaching conclusions, but it is significant that the peak occurs at the age at which women are close to the menopause. There are two cases approximately in each of the age categories between 21 and 60, with the exception of the 36-40 age group which contains double that number. We have already said that a woman's position in Gisu society depends on her fulfillment of the role of mother. While she is still capable of bearing children, a woman is of value in the community. Should her marriage break up she will readily find another husband and her family will generally support her in obtaining a divorce if she has no children by her husband. If she reaches the age at which all women stop being able to bear children, without having established herself as the mother of children in a stable marital union, she is liable to be rejected both by her husband and her family. She is no longer an asset to either group.

In the oldest age groups, the suicide of women appears less, in spite of their higher survival rate. This is largely because an elderly woman becomes closely associated with her son's family. She has a vital role as grandmother, whereas men cannot play a similar part in the household of their sons, as is shown by the avoidance between father-in-law and daughter-in-law. Elderly men do suffer some loss of status with the onset of old age, whereas women can achieve a higher status more like that of men. They take an increasing part in ritual affairs. Isolation is greatest for men in old age.

We have said that circumcision ceremonies are a powerful force making for social integration; the effects of this on young men can be seen in the lesser tendency of men to commit suicide in the immediate post-circumcision years. Their influence extends beyond this one category of members of the society. The ceremonies involve all members of the society who take part in the dancing and displays of group solidarity. In spite of this the over-all rates for years in which circumcision took place show little change over other years. Even allowing for a time lag before the effect of the ceremonies makes itself apparent, there is no marked effect.

If however, we separate the suicides by sex some effect is noticeable. In four of the five post-circumcision years, there is a decline in the number of female suicides. No change appears in male suicides, because other factors tend to counteract the integrative effect of the ceremonies on men. The rites mark a crisis for both the youths who are initiated and for their seniors who see a threat to their supremacy in the entrance of more competitors into the male adult world. For women there is no such crisis. The ritual emphasis on lineage solidarity entails no such conflict between ideal and actual behavior as it does for men. Women cannot own or inherit property, so in this respect they are not in competition with other members of their lineage. Their status depends on qualities other than the successful manipulation of the status system; their relations of rivalry are with their co-wives, members of other lineage groups. It is the marital situation which presents conflicts for a woman, and this has no reference in the rituals; a woman takes part as a valued member of her natal family.

In looking at suicide in Gisu society, the marked difference in the factors affecting the suicide of men and women is the most striking feature. It is related to the lesser involvement of women in the economic organization of the society and their status in the hierarchy of prestige-bearing roles. In this, the Gisu material bears out the conclusions of Henry and Short, who found that suicide of females is less sensitive to changes in the business cycle than is that of men, and related this fact to the situation described above for the Gisu, and, to a lesser degree, to the United States. As far as Gisu are concerned, however, the point is not that women have a lower status than men but that their status is based on a different scale of values. They do not enter into competition for prestige as men do. Consequently, they are less sensitive to changes in the economic state of the society and in old age do not suffer the isolation which inability to compete for power imposes on old men. The groups into which women are integrated by periodic rituals, such as those of circumcision, do not contain relationships which make for hostility. The anxieties of women are centered round their role as mother, on the successful performance of which their status depends. Thus, the suicide of women is greatest in those years when they must succeed as wives and mothers in order to establish themselves in a position which will guarantee security in old age and a respected position in the community. For men, membership in a corporate group with ideals of unity that conflict with the necessity to compete with fellow members in a status hierarchy based on wealth, means that they are more influenced by economic factors, less by the integrative force of ritual. Frustration or isolation engendered by the nature of the economic struggle causes men to commit suicide in early maturity.

In attempting to discover if there is any relationship that can be considered meaningful between homicide and suicide in Gisu society, one must again treat the sexes as separate categories. There appears to be a rough inverse correlation between murders and suicides for the years 1945-1955 inclusive. A simple regression test indicates that the correlation is not significant; examination of the two phenomena by sex of the suicides shows clearly that no such correlation is observable.

One must notice, however, that although the absolute number of female suicides and murderers is less than those for men, a far greater proportion of women who commit violent acts kill themselves than kill others. Over a period of ten years, 11 women killed other people, 28 killed themselves: more than twice as many committed suicide as murder. During the same period, 141 men committed murder and only 40 committed suicide. In terms of the theory put forward by Henry and Short, this would seem to indicate that women have higher status than men and that they were also subject to fewer external restraints from a weaker relational system. We have seen that the first implication is not true. Women have lower status than men. However, this lower status does not really fit into the male status hierarchy; it is defined by other non-competitive criteria. I would suggest that it is the involvement of individuals in a competitive status hierarchy rather than the fact of relative status in a hierarchy that is a factor in the situation. This is consistent with the psychological determinants put forward by the same authors: they relate the tendency to commit homicide to the legitimization of other-oriented aggression and a weak internalization of re-straints, consequent on discipline imposed by the father, which consists of corporal punishment rather than mental chastise-ment. This is true for Gisu men.

Aggressive behavior is encouraged for men, discouraged for women. The Gisu boy is disciplined almost exclusively by his father, whose power of inflicting physical punishment reaches its extreme in the circumcision operation, to which the young man must submit in order to be able to take part in the adult world. This adult world into which the young man emerges is one of aggressive competition; the extreme expres-sion of this was found, formerly, in the warfare that broke out sporadically between neighboring groups. A woman's world is entirely different. Brought up by her mother, and discouraged to express her aggressive tendencies, she emerges into a world where her personal achievement depends on her own physical nature.

The second point, that homicide is correlated with strong external restraints from a stronger relational system and sui-cide with weak external restraints and a weak external sys-tem, also holds for the difference in acts of aggression between Gisu men and women. We have seen how men are members of a lineage, a corporate group with a strong hold over its

128

members. The adult male must conform to their expectations of him if he is to achieve full membership and the prestige goods which bring higher status. Rejection from the group is the greatest disaster which can befall him; he loses a right to citizenship and a place in society. Moreover, he takes part in a competitive hierarchy in which the expectations of others play a great part in determining his status. He comes into conflict with those people with whom he is integrated in a corporate group—his lineage mates. A woman is marginal to this group organization. Her membership of the lineage is residual; she has no rights in the corporate group and as such is not subject to their demands to such an extent as her brothers. She forms an integral part, not of a lineage, but of domestic groupings. Her degree of involvement in social or cathectic relationships[22] is far less than that of a man; her status is thus far less determined by conformity or otherwise to the expectations of others.

Gisu society is in a state of change. Contact with Europeans has brought economic development as well as far-reaching social changes. Many of the factors which have been shown to act in determining the expression of aggression can be traced to the influence of these changes. To mention only one: the prevention of warfare, and thus the limitation placed on the area controlled by any one lineage, together with an increase in population, has caused a great change in the nature of relations among members of the land-controlling group, the lineage. It seems tenable, however, that the changes intensify strain at points in the social structure, relationships which by virtue of the type of social organization were always ambivalent.

[22] Henry and Short, *op.cit.*, p. 16.

5

HOMICIDE AND
SUICIDE IN BUNYORO

J. H. M. BEATTIE

BUNYORO is one of the interlacustrine Bantu kingdoms of Uganda. It lies in the west of the Protectorate, and comprises a land area of about 4,700 square miles. Its 110,000 native inhabitants are mostly peasant cultivators who, in addition to subsistence farming, make a small cash income from cotton and tobacco. They live in scattered settlements in the fertile regions of the kingdom; the typical homestead is surrounded by a banana grove and gardens and is rarely more than shouting distance from at least one neighbor. The Nyoro are governed, under the British administration of the Protectorate (represented in Bunyoro by a district commissioner and two or three assistants), by a hereditary king, the Mukama, and a hierarchy of appointed territorial chiefs. There is a system of exogamous totemic clans, membership of which is inherited in the male line; these do not, however, form corporate or territorial units. A man's neighbors and associates ordinarily include a number of unrelated persons as well as kinsmen and affines. Marriage is virilocal, and involves a payment from the groom to the bride's family. When they can afford it Nyoro are polygynous.

In Bunyoro, as elsewhere, people sometimes seek to kill others, and sometimes they seek to kill themselves. The social anthropologist is interested in both kinds of cases, firstly because they may illustrate certain important beliefs and values which determine action in the society under observation, and secondly because they often focus attention on types of social

130

situations in which interpersonal strain reaches a particularly acute level, and so indicate points of stress in the social system.

I begin by discussing homicide, leaving the consideration of suicide to the second part of this essay. First we must decide what kinds of homicides we are to consider. We shall not be interested in killings which are due to accident, whether accompanied by carelessness or not. Our interest is in intentional killings, so we shall also disregard homicides arising from sudden brawls and drunken quarrels, unless it is plain that there was an intention to kill. For it would be unjustifiably arbitrary to take note of those killings where the intention was to hurt and not to kill but where the victim died (though they be technically murder), while disregarding cases identical in all respects except that the victim survived. From our point of view such cases differ in no relevant particular. So in what follows I consider only cases in which there is good reason to suppose that the killer meant to kill. And in considering such cases I shall have regard both to the kinds of social situations in which the intention to kill arises, and to the ideas and values in terms of which Nyoro conceive these situations.

I cannot, of course, hope that this approach will eliminate arbitrariness; assertions about human ideas and motivations are almost always conjectural. Nor can I enter into the difficult problem of psychological abnormality; the question whether a "normal" Nyoro would contemplate homicide in the circumstances of a particular case cannot always, or even often, be clearly answered. But though these methodological dangers must be recognized they cannot be avoided; the anthropologist can only attempt to mitigate them both by using his common sense and by reference to his personal acquaintance with the culture under observation. I shall claim no general validity for my conclusions. I shall suggest merely that they exemplify certain points of stress in the Nyoro social system, and illustrate certain important beliefs and values in Nyoro culture.

Some preliterate peoples believe that when anybody dies this must be due to some other person's malevolence, usually manifested through some sort of supernatural agency. Nyoro notions of causality are a little broader. They believe that sickness and death may be caused by other agencies than living human beings, thus the ghosts of dead persons, and many kinds of non-human spirits, may be responsible. But they know that people do hate one another, a point on which their culture is very articulate, and they hold that since a man who hates another may seek evil medicine in order to destroy him or his children, such hatred does in fact lead to many deaths. It is convenient to use the term "sorcery" to refer to the use of such medicines, even though we should hesitate to describe all the techniques of sorcerers as magical. A common method is the introduction of prepared substances into the victim's food or drink, but there are many techniques, such as the burial of medicated horns in the thatch of the victim's house or in a path where he must pass, which to the European view appear less practical. If a man falls ill and dies, and if it is known that he had an enemy or had recently quarrelled with somebody, it is very likely that the diviners will indicate that person as having been responsible for his death.

So most Nyoro see themselves as living in a community in which very many of the members are actual or potential murderers. Unless a man is himself threatened, this does not bother him very much. But it does have important effects on his attitude to homicide, and it also has significant implications for our enquiry. Thus a Nyoro peasant does not think of homicide as at all a rare event, though violent homicide may be so; for him it is quite an everyday affair, because he knows that people often kill their enemies by sorcery. Though in a particular case this cannot be shown by any kind of scientific demonstration, it can be "proved" quite simply by reference to the diviners. Such homicides, if they occur (and there are some grounds for supposing that some do occur), do not figure in formal judicial enquiries; evidence of a kind which would satisfy a court of law is practically impossible to obtain. The omission of such cases in the material which follows does not, then, mean that there are none, it merely reflects the fact that the court and police records on which this study is based contain no records of them. I cannot give any idea of the incidence of homicides of this nature or, here, of the kinds of medicines and techniques used. It must, however, be said that the detailed figures presented probably do not fully represent the total situation. But of course this does not diminish their value as data for an analysis of cases brought to court. And we shall find that a number of the killings which were the subjects of court cases were acts of revenge for alleged previous homicides by sorcery or poisoning, about which, therefore, something has to be said.

A total of 62 case records of homicides and attempted homicides were examined in the District Court, Coroner's,[1] and Police files of the Bunyoro district. These cases were spread over a twenty-year period ending in 1955, and they include all the cases in the records in which Nyoro were accused of homicide.

A scrutiny of these 62 cases showed that in 28 of them the homicide, if it took place at all, was almost certainly unintentional. In what follows, therefore, we are concerned only with the remaining 34 cases, which are those summarized in the Appendix. Though insufficient to justify any very precise statistical conclusions, they show one or two interesting trends. Let us consider them in terms of our two interests, the kinds of social situations in which the intention to kill predominantly arises, and the ideas and values which are involved.

First, the social situation: who kills whom, and in what

[1] Because a few of the homicides were followed by the suicide of the killer, so that no criminal proceedings could be instigated.

sorts of relationships do killers and killed tend to stand to one another? We may note, to begin with, that the vast majority of killers are men; women rarely kill by violence, and then usually other women. Our 34 cases are summarized in Table 27.

TABLE 27

SEX OF NYORO KILLERS AND VICTIMS

Men killed women	19
Men killed men	12
Women killed women	2
Women killed children	1
Women killed men	–

In 31 out of our 34 cases the killers were men. And in 19 of these 31 cases their victims were women, in only 12 were they men. So it seems that ten times as many men as women kill by violence, and half as many again of their victims are women and not men. Let us look first at the 19 cases in which men killed women.

In 15 out of the 19 cases the victim was related to the killer. Table 28 shows the kinds of relationships involved.

TABLE 28

RELATIONSHIP OF FEMALE VICTIMS TO MALE KILLERS

Wife or ex-wife (including ex-mistress)	8
Wife's mother	2
Mother	2
Father's other wife (not mother)	1
Son's wife	1
Brother's wife	1

What is most immediately striking about these figures is the fact that in two-thirds of the cases the victim was either a wife (or mistress) or a wife's mother of the killer. It is plain, therefore, that the tensions involved in the sexual relationship

134

institutionalized in marriage and concubinage are a major condition of homicide. Let us look a little more closely at these ten cases. In eight of them the killer had been abandoned, or was threatened with abandonment, by his wife or mistress, and avenged himself by killing her (or, in two cases, her mother whom he believed to be aiding and abetting her). In one of the other two cases the husband simply believed that his wife was practicing sorcery against him; in regard to the other no information is available. The case of Mikairi is fairly representative.

Homicide Case No. 1.

Mikairi's wife had a lover and wanted to divorce Mikairi and go to him, but a council of relatives prevailed upon her to stay with her husband and she unwillingly agreed. But one evening she told her husband that she wished to go to her lover's village to say goodbye to him. They went together to his village, where Mikairi had other business, but on the way home they began to quarrel, and Mikairi's wife refused to come any further with him, saying that she would go back to her lover's house. He angrily forbade her to do so, but she continued to defy him, and said that if he came there in search of her, her lover and his brothers would beat him. Then, enraged, Mikairi killed her with an axe.

Isoke's case is also revealing.

Homicide Case No. 2.

At the hearing, Isoke's brother explained that Isoke had had two wives, Matama and Nyantaliya. Matama contracted leprosy and was ill for a number of years, and she believed that her husband neglected her. Eventually her illness became worse and it became plain that she was going to die. Before she died she said to Isoke: "You took me from my parents' home when I was well, but in your house I became a leper, and now you neglect me and enjoy yourself with Nyantaliya. After I die you will see what will happen" (this was a threat that her ghost would punish him). After Matama's death things began to go wrong between Isoke and Nyantaliya, and soon Nyantaliya went home to her parents saying that Isoke and his household were haunted by Matama's ghost and that if she stayed there she would die. But Isoke demanded her return, and her parents agreed that she should go back to him (if she had not, they would have had to repay the bride-wealth), so very much against her will she returned. A few days later her husband killed her and then hung himself, it was supposed because of her continued insistence on leaving him.

It is reasonable to conclude, on the basis of the cases of which these two are examples, that a wife's or mistress's real or anticipated desertion is an important ground of those homicides in which men are the killers and women the victims. Of the cases in our sample in which men killed women 66 per cent fall into this category, and we shall see that a number of cases in which men killed men arose from somewhat similar circumstances.

The other five cases in which men killed female relatives express no very consistent pattern, unless it be the ubiquity of sorcery concepts, which played an important part in three of them. We shall return later to this theme. Of the remaining two cases one concerned a sexual assault in which the victim, who was the murderer's daughter-in-law, resisted and was killed, and the other concerned a drunk young man who, indignant at his mother's attempts to persuade him to leave a beer party, killed her with a spear.

Of the four cases in which men killed women who were not related to them, three were in revenge for supposed acts of sorcery against the killer or his relatives; the other involved the murder of the victim of a sexual assault and is of less sociological interest. Here are brief details of one of the sorcery cases:

Homicide Case No. 3.

Tibagwa, a young man of 23, and his late father's younger brother Bumandwa killed an old lady called Bulimara, whom they believed to have killed Tibagwa's father by sorcery. Bulimara was well known in the neighborhood to have been a sorceress; some years previously an informal village council had ordered her to leave the village on this account, but she had refused. Many witnesses testified that she had killed Tibagwa's father; "She gave him food and afterwards he was sick," it was said. During his illness the deceased man told his brother Bumandwa that if he died the sorceress should be strangled. The two young men said that they had brought a case against Bulimara in the native court but there had not been enough evidence to get a conviction. When they went to kill the old lady she had, so they stated, boasted that she had killed many people and would kill them too. So they strangled her.

I conclude, then, that in Bunyoro men kill women more often than they kill other men, and that the women whom they most often kill are their wives or mistresses. I record also that 8 of these 19 killings, that is 42 per cent, involved magical or sorcery beliefs.

We turn now to consider the twelve cases in which men killed men. The first thing to note is that in the sample the killer and his victim were related in only three cases, that is, in only a quarter of the total as compared with three-quarters of the cases in which men killed women. This is not surprising. For the most part adult women have close intersexual social relationships of kinds in which serious stress may arise only with their husbands and lovers, and to a lesser degree with certain of their kinsmen. Outside of these categories women have few intense social relationships with men, and since there can rarely be incentive to murder a kinswoman, when women are murdered it is usually their present or past husbands or lovers who are the murderers. For men the posi-

137

tion is quite different. A man's social world is far more extensive; he has economic, political and social dealings with many men and women outside his family circle, and we shall see that in many of these relationships stresses sufficiently serious to lead to homicide may arise.

Nevertheless, five of the twelve cases in which men killed men involved women in one way or another. In two the husband found his wife and her lover *in flagrante delicto* and killed his rival on the spot, in one a man killed another whom he believed to have been dancing promiscuously with his wife, in another case two young men resented the sexual success of a rival, and in another the killer believed that his wife's father was using her as a means to injure him by causing her to have numerous miscarriages. Sorcery beliefs played an important part in only two of the twelve cases in which men killed men, a strikingly smaller proportion than we found among those cases in which women were the victims. This is consistent with the pattern of Nyoro culture. Certainly men are thought to practice sorcery against one another, but they also possess other means of harming their enemies. But Nyoro culture provides no charter for physical violence or aggression by women; from women to men, in particular, deference and humility are the proper attitudes. So, Nyoro consider, women tend to be thrown back on sorcery and magic as means to defend themselves or to destroy those they hate.

Of the other cases in this category four are of little interest; in two an argument arose over a debt, in one a man killed a suspected thief, and in the fourth a man shot another in resisting arrest. Two, however, are worth noting: one as expressing the strains which can arise in the father-son relationship, the other as illustrating Nyoro notions of ritual danger and pollution.

138

Homicide Case No. 4

An adult son had been rebuked by his father after he had behaved badly at a beer-drink. His father had told him to stay in the house and not to come back to the party. The young man, "crying with anger" in his own words, took a spear from the house, returned to the party, and killed his father. In court he said that he had "always been badly treated by his father."

Though parricide is rare in Bunyoro, the strain and potential hostility which exists between fathers and sons in this strongly patrilineal society are widely stressed in Nyoro culture.

Homicide Case No. 5.

The killer and his victim had been having a protracted drinking party at the former's house. After a few days drinking, the guest, who was said to have been feeling unwell, defecated in a corner of the house. This, regardless of the intentions of the doer, created a grave state of ritual danger for the householder and his family. The proper course would have been for the culprit to remain within the house until a white sheep, or at least a white chicken, could be procured. The animal should then be killed in the doorway, and the culprit should step over the blood, carrying the excreta, wrapped up in a particular kind of leaves, outside. After that a feast should be prepared at the delinquent's expense, and then the *status quo ante* is restored. Until all this has been done the culprit may not leave the house by the doorway; strictly he should not leave it at all, but if he does a special hole in the wall will have to be made for him to pass through. In the present case the owner of the house went at least three times to the defecator's house to obtain the animal for sacrifice, but each time the culprit's wife made some excuse and refused to provide it. On his final visit the householder, who was an elderly man and a pagan, warned her that if she persisted she might not see her husband alive again. In the end the old man had to let the culprit leave the house himself to search for an animal for sacrifice, but his feelings were too much for him and he followed his one-time friend along the path and speared him fatally in the back. "I killed him because he had spoiled my house," he said in evidence; "this was an evil thing and would kill me and all my family."

We turn now to consider the three cases in which women were the killers. In one case a woman killed her two children and then herself because she believed that her husband was neglecting her in favor of another wife. For our purposes this case is more properly regarded as suicide than homicide. In the other two cases women killed women. It is of interest that both involved accusations of sorcery. In the first a man was accused of sorcery by a classificatory brother and his wife. In the course of a quarrel the accused man's wife and daughter beat the brother's wife so severely that she died. The other case, which also illustrates the stresses which can develop in a polygynous family, is perhaps more interesting. Banyoro are well aware that serious tensions may develop between co-wives of the same husband, and such tensions very often lead to accusations and counter-accusations of sorcery, though less often to overt homicide as in the present case. The circumstances are given in Case No. 6.

Homicide Case No. 6.

Katigi, a woman of about 35, shared her husband with three other wives, with one of whom, Samali, she had a long-standing quarrel, for she believed that Samali was practicing sorcery against her. She had, in fact, made a formal complaint against Samali, which had been heard by her husband and a council of neighbors. The council found that Samali had indeed been practicing sorcery against Katigi, but except for admonishing her they do not seem to have done anything about it. Some weeks later Katigi stole into Samali's house in the middle of the night and stabbed her repeatedly and fatally with a knife.

Katigi's statement in court is worth quoting in full.

"When I was first married into that house," she said, "Samali spoiled my skin. Then she caused me to become sick in my private parts. When I bore a child and he was five years old she caused him to die because I was having male children and she was jealous. Then after I had male twins she went and got medicine and put it in my food and so caused a stoppage in my vaginal passage. She took two of our husband's goats to the man from whom she got the medicine. This was well known to everybody and our husband called a family council to settle the quarrel between her and me, but even after this she did not stop injuring me. Even now I am not all right in going to the latrine; sometimes I spend two days without passing water. I told her that it would be better if she would kill me outright, rather than treat me in so cruel a manner. I am still a young woman, having borne children only twice, and now I cannot have sexual intercourse with any man at all. I begged her to give me medicine to cure my trouble but she refused, hoping that I would die in that way. I have had no menstrual course since the passage was blocked. I am as good as dead: when I begged her to give me medicine and she refused I told her that we should both die. You can do what you like to me."

Katigi's case graphically illustrates the tensions which may grow up between co-wives; when a wife loses her children or becomes ill it is natural to blame a co-wife who has grounds for jealousy. Indeed it would be strange if in the close social confines of a polygynous African homestead ample pretexts for friction did not exist.

This must conclude my brief review of homicide in Bunyoro. My analysis has been based on a very restricted sample, and it has not been possible to follow up all the lines of enquiry which have suggested themselves. But I have elicited a few observations which I believe to be valid in the particular context of Nyoro culture. Thus, for instance, it is plain that men kill more often than women, and that they more often kill women than men. In no less than 14 of the 34 cases, that is, in just over 40 per cent of them, beliefs in sorcery, ghosts, or magic were directly or indirectly concerned. By far the commonest type of killing is the killing of a woman by her husband or lover. And, finally, what we may loosely call sexual crimes (relating directly or indirectly to sexual jealousy or desire) account, also, for just over 40 per cent of the cases.

I said above that the method of selection which circumstances imposed on me may have excluded some killings from the total picture, those, that is, which were achieved by means, including poisoning, which Nyoro classify as sorcery. Our picture may, therefore, be somewhat in error. I have suggested that for our limited purposes this does not matter. It might, however, be suggested that if it were possible to take account of such killings the disproportion between men and women killers might be somewhat smaller. Sorcerers are often believed to be women, and we have noted that women lack recourse to the more overt means of aggression available to men. But this, at the present stage of our knowledge, must remain conjecture.

SUICIDE

I turn now to consider suicide. My analysis is based on a sample of 61 cases which occurred over the ten year period from 1946 to 1955.[2] Most were taken from police or coroner's files, but one or two derive from information gathered in the field.

The first thing to note is that although Nyoro abhor the idea of suicide and express strong moral disapproval of it, its exist-

[2] Before this records are unreliable or non-existent.

ence, and even its necessity, are culturally recognized. For a person to kill himself or herself brings about a grave state of ritual danger from which survivors must be cleansed if danger is to be averted. Thus a tree on which a person has hanged himself must be uprooted and completely burned to ashes, and a house in which a person has hanged himself must be burned and abandoned. If this were not done, the fatal tree or house might cause grave injury to the living. In spite of this the threat of suicide is often made, and many people do kill themselves: according to my records there were twice as many suicides as homicides in half the number of years.[3]

There is, directly at least, only one party to a suicide, so we cannot enquire into the social relationships of the parties to it as we did in the case of homicide. Nonetheless, our interest here is also primarily in the types of social situation in which resort is had to self-destruction. And since we shall find that these types of situation often involve and indeed derive from some social relationships, we shall here, also, be primarily concerned with aspects of the Nyoro social system.

Of the 61 cases I have recorded, 37 involved men, 24 women. In more than 90 per cent of them death was by hanging, either from a beam in a house or from a tree, generally in uncleared ground in the neighborhood of the cultivated plots. Only four men are known to have killed themselves in any other way (two with a spear, two with a knife),[4] and one woman by burning herself in her house. It will be convenient here to do as we did in our discussion of homicide, and to consider male and female suicides separately.

Of the 37 men of whom I have account, 32 hanged themselves, 15 in their houses, one in his separate kitchen, one in a deserted house, one in prison, and 14 on trees. Eighteen, that is, hanged themselves "indoors," as against 14 outside. The

[3] Of course there may, as we have noted, have been undetected and unrecorded homicides. There can be no analogous interest in concealing a suicide.

[4] In one case the method of suicide was not recorded.

significance of this will appear when we come to consider female suicides.

When we turn to the more interesting question of motive, the following position emerges: of 36 male suicides, 8 killed themselves for reasons unknown. Of the remaining 28, 19 killed themselves on account of illness, 7 killed themselves on account of relations with their wives (in three cases after homicide), 2 killed themselves on account of poverty or old age, and 2 killed themselves on account of "shame."

Not much need be said of the majority who killed themselves on account of illness. It is hard for anyone who has not lived in a primitive community to conceive of the despair which painful or chronic illness can induce where medical facilities are few and little used. It has to be remembered, too, that sickness is not considered an accident by Nyoro; if one is ill it is considered that a living person, a ghost, or a spirit has made one so. There is much that Nyoro can do in such cases, but action is not always quickly or even at all effective, and the time when all resources have been tried or at least all money spent may not be long in coming. But for the most part the existence of a painful and protracted illness, such as untreated leprosy or gonorrhea, is sufficient to explain many suicides.

Of the remaining 11 cases, seven arose in a marital context, so it is legitimate to infer that as with homicide so with suicide the stresses associated with the conjugal situation provide its most important social context. This is what we should expect, for the same kinds of strains may lead either to homicide or to suicide depending on such variable factors as the temperaments of the persons concerned. In three, probably four, of these seven cases the husband killed himself because his wife refused to stay with him; in three of these he killed her first. In the other three cases the man killed himself after a quarrel with his wife; in two cases the quarrel was about food, in the other case information is lacking. I need say no more here of the conjugal situation as a source of social strain and tension; typical cases were described in my discussion of homicide, and we shall have more to say about it when I consider female suicides. It is, however, plain that actual or threatened desertion by a wife, whether for another man or not, is a common ground for male suicide, as it was also for homicide. In the two cases in which the explanation given for the suicide was that the husband was aggrieved by his wife's failure to provide him with proper meals, it is reasonable to suspect that there was really a deeper difference involved, most likely a real or implied threat of separation. This, however, is conjecture.

Nothing need be said of the two suicides from poverty and old age. It is still unusual in Bunyoro for an old man to be left poor and completely without relatives to look after him, and if it does happen there is no need to look further for an explanation. Of more interest are the two cases in which I have classified the cause of suicide as "shame."

Suicide Case No. 1.

A youth of fifteen hanged himself after his mother's brother, with whom he was staying, had scolded him for smoking (it was afterwards suggested that he may have beaten him as well, but this was not proved). At the inquest the boy's uncle said: "I saw him take a cigarette out of the pocket of his shorts; he was just going to light it. I had never seen him with cigarettes before so I said to him 'you are only a young boy and it is not good for you to smoke cigarettes. Smoking leads to theft [of money to buy cigarettes with]. You do not smoke in your father's house; if you learn to smoke here your father will blame me. This is your last warning; if I see you with cigarettes again I shall punish you.'" Whether he punished the boy on that occasion is not known, but in any case the dressing-down so rankled that the young man went out and hanged himself on a tree.

Suicide Case No. 2.

A young man of 22 had drunk some beer and was about to assault another youth when his mother attempted to stop him. He turned on her and knocked her down. Enraged and indignant, she said that she would accuse him of assaulting her before the local chief. He went off and hanged himself from a tree in the bush. In Bunyoro it is a very disgraceful thing to assault one's mother or treat her disrespectfully, and no doubt the local chief was correct when he said, "The deceased hanged himself because of shame that he had fought with his mother, and also because he feared that he would be convicted by the court for this shameful action."

In both of these cases there was no doubt a sense of shame and extreme mortification which was unendurable. We should remember that shame, in this context, is not the same thing as guilt (though it may be associated with it); it implies rather the suffering of what is felt as a grave and perhaps irremediable indignity. And suicide, in Bunyoro as elsewhere, may be a weapon of attack as well as of defence: the death which you invoke for yourself will have also its effect upon others, in particular upon those who have injured you.

When we turn to consider female suicide, even plainer patterns emerge. In all but one of the 24 cases of female suicide which we have recorded the victim hanged herself (in the exceptional case she burnt herself in her house). But whereas almost half of the men hanged themselves in their houses, only a quarter of the women did; most women (16 out of 23) hanged themselves from trees in the bush. It would be rash to stress the significance of this too heavily, but the difference is too marked to be accidental, and I believe that it may legitimately be correlated with the relative intensity of the attachment to the homestead (as opposed to its several occupants) of the two sexes. A man occupies and is master of his own house (unless he be very young and still lives in his father's home). Thus being a man and possessing a household imply each other, at least ideally. Accordingly, if a man wishes to destroy himself he may at the same time and by the same act bring destruction upon the house of which he is the head and center, and which is in a sense identified with him. For a woman the position is different. She can never have this intimate identity with a house. Once she is married, as practically all adult women are, she is partly (though by no means wholly) cut off from her parental home; she is no longer fully of her parents' household, for they have received bride-wealth for her. And although she has important rights in her husband's home, it is her husband's property and not hers. Thus there can be no close identity between her and her husband's house of the kind that subsists between a man and the house he has built and the household he has formed. In a virilocal and predominantly patrilineal society it is in men and their male descendants that local stability and permanence are to be found; women change their homes once at least, often in Bunyoro many times more. It may well be, then, that when a woman kills herself in the bush some distance from her house she expresses her separation from and opposition to the household of her husband or father, against one or other of whom her suicide may in many cases be a reaction. Nyoro attitudes to women and to the homestead are, at least, fully consistent with this interpretation.

When we consider the reasons why women kill themselves some even more significant differences between men and women appear, as the following figures, when compared with those for men given above, show.

Of 24 female suicides 3 killed themselves for reasons unknown. Of the remaining 21, 11 killed themselves on grounds deriving from marriage, 7 killed themselves on account of illness, and 3 killed themselves on account of bereavement.

The contrast with the figures for men is striking. More than half of the female suicides in which motives are known derived from the context of marriage, as against only a quarter of the male suicides. This supports the thesis, for which there is already evidence on other grounds, that in a polygynous society like Bunyoro women have a heavier emotional investment in a happy marriage than men have. It is also of interest that whereas nearly 70 per cent of the male suicides were due to illness only a third of the female ones were. I have no record of a woman having committed suicide because of "shame." Again, three women killed themselves because of bereavement, whereas no man did. In two of these three cases the woman had lost a child (a boy in one and probably in both cases), in the other a husband.

I need say no more of the motives of illness and bereavement, but the cases deriving from marriage demand further analysis. They can be subdivided as follows:

Of 11 women who killed themselves for reasons deriving from the context of marriage, 4 were being compelled to go to husbands against their will, 3 were jealous of their husbands' relations with other women (including others of his wives), 3 had quarrelled with their husbands (in one case the husband had accused his wife of having a lover, in another case of being a sorcerer; there is no information in regard to the third case), one was unwilling to be married to her former lover by her older brother whom she hated.

Thus the largest and also the most interesting category of these cases involved young women who were being subjected to pressure to go to husbands whom they did not like. Traditionally in Bunyoro women had little or no say in the matter of their marriages; often their future husbands were chosen when they were still children, sometimes even before they were born. Marriage in Bunyoro was not, and to a large extent still is not, a contract freely entered into by the two spouses, it is rather an arrangement made between two men, the fathers of the prospective spouses. For men this did not greatly matter; a man could always acquire other wives, and in any case a son would rarely be pressed to accept a bride whom he did not want. But for a woman it was different. She was never a contracting party but always rather a negotiable good in a transaction between men and the family groups they stood for. A considerate father would have some regard for his daughter's feelings, but in general few would question his right to dispose of her as he thought best, and the prospect of a wealthy son-in-law, or a long-standing obligation to an old drinking companion, are not considerations easily to be overridden. Nonetheless, it should be said that Nyoro public opinion strongly disapproves cruelty or coercion so violent as to lead to the victim's suicide, and in the cases about to be described many people expressed to me their disapproval of the parents' action.[5]

Brief particulars of two such cases follow.

Suicide Case No. 3.

A sixteen-year-old girl hanged herself on a tree because she did not want to go to the husband to whom her father had married her. Information is lacking as to how old he was, but almost certainly he was considerably older than she. At the inquest her father said: "I had told her that day that she should go to her husband's house" [she had been visiting at her parents' home]. She got angry as she did not want to go back to him, but I continued to press her, pointing out that her hus-

[5] As formerly in Europe, so in contemporary Bunyoro (and of course elsewhere in Africa), young women, like young men, are increasingly taking the matter of their marriages into their own hands. The new ways in which women as well as men can achieve some financial independence, for example by growing and marketing their own plot of cotton, enable the more strong-minded of them to defy their parents and, sometimes, to free themselves from unwanted husbands by returning the bride-wealth paid for them.

band had a right to her since I had 'eaten up' the shillings which he had paid as bride-wealth for her. When I had finished speaking to her she went off into the bush. I did not see her all that night or the next morning, and when I remembered how angry she was when I mentioned her husband's name I thought that perhaps she might have killed herself."

Suicide Case No. 4.

Bihogo, a girl of about 18, had been forced by her father to marry a neighbor called Amedi, a friend of her father's and an elderly man, who already had two other wives. She stayed with him for about a year, but as well as being old he was jealous and possessive and used to beat her, so at the end of the second year she began to run away from him. The first three times she did so her father ordered her to go back to him and she complied, weeping bitterly, my informants said. But on the fourth occasion she refused completely, and instead of returning to her husband she went into the bush and hanged herself on a tree. At that time the girl's mother was away in Buganda, and when she learned that her daughter had killed herself she came back vowing vengeance against her husband, the girl's father, and had she not been prevented by neighbors she would have assaulted him physically. People said that Bihogo's ghost would probably bring misfortune to her father; it would not trouble Amedi (the husband), for it was not he who had compelled her to a marriage she did not want.

Less need be said of the other cases of female suicide arising from domestic quarrels or jealousy within the context of marriage. Two of them are, however, of particular interest. One illustrates the way in which domestic strain may express itself through sorcery beliefs (a theme to which we have already referred).

Suicide Case No. 5.

Marita had an illegitimate male child before she married her husband Makenzi. She had not wanted to marry the child's father, but she left the child with him. One day the boy, who was staying with his paternal grandmother, was severely scalded when a tin of hot water fell from the fire, and he died before his mother could come. A year later Marita bore a fine son to Makenzi, and three years later she bore him another son, but this one suffered from a physical deformity. Thereupon trouble began between Marita and her husband. He denied that he could possibly be the father of a deformed child, and accused Marita of unfaithfulness. Soon Makenzi's repeated accusations became intolerable, and Marita left him and went to her home taking the deformed child with her. After two months the child fell ill, and her family, who were afraid to have a dying child on their hands, sent Marita back to her husband. Meantime Makenzi's older son by Marita became ill and was taken to the hospital. She was not allowed to see the child because Makenzi had been told by the diviners that the illness was due to the ghost of Marita's first child. After a few days the child died. Meantime others in the family had become ill. Makenzi now accused Marita of practicing sorcery against them, an accusation which the other members of the household were very ready to support. Marita, rejected and bereaved, went out into the bush and hanged herself. People say that Makenzi will not marry another wife because of his fear of Marita's ghost.

In the other case the real cause of the suicide was not primarily the conjugal situation but rather the relationship between brother and sister.

Suicide Case No. 6.

Meyi, a young girl who had only just left school, was living with a much older man, Geresomu. She was happy to live with him in an informal liaison, because under this arrangement she could leave him whenever she wanted to, a circumstance which also helped to assure Geresomu's indulgence and consideration. Meyi had, however, two brothers (their father was dead), and the eldest of these, who was his father's heir, decided that Geresomu should marry his sister Meyi, so that he could enjoy the beer, goats, and money which Geresomu would be called upon to pay. Meyi would have much preferred not to have been married to Geresomu at all, but what she resented most was the idea of being married to him by her elder brother, who was called Yobezi. For she hated Yobezi, who was a greedy, domineering man, without affection either for his mother or for his brother and sister. In fact the household had not long before broken up, Yobezi's mother and younger brother moving away from Yobezi's house, after a series of quarrels in the course of which Yobezi had severely beaten his mother. At last, however, Meyi was prevailed upon by the arguments of various relatives to agree to the marriage. On the day of the formal engagement, when the details of the bride-wealth were agreed upon, it could be seen that Meyi was greatly distressed. That day Yobezi said to her: "You used to boast that I would never marry you to Geresomu; now am I not about to 'eat' the marriage payment, and what can you do about it? I shall use the money to buy myself a new bicycle, you'll see!" These words completed Meyi's misery; from that time on she would speak to no one, and after a few days she went into the bush and hanged herself on a tree. Her mother, overcome with grief and resentment against her son Yobezi, died a month later. I conclude the account of this tragedy in the words of my informant: "People say that Yobezi is haunted by the ghosts of his sister and his mother. Yobezi's children are always sick, and some have died, and Yobezi himself is always in poor health. Only a few days ago his eldest son died, and it is believed that the ghost of Meyi who killed herself was responsible for his death."

With this case we must conclude our discussion of suicide in Bunyoro. We have found that most suicides, like most homicides, derive from some aspect of the conjugal situation, especially in a polygynous society like Bunyoro, which is inevitably one of great potential strain. We have noted that while the largest category of male homicides derives from this situation, it gives rise to the greatest number of female suicides, more women than men killing themselves for reasons deriving from marriage. I have suggested some possible reasons for this. We observed, also, that more men than women killed themselves on account of illness, and that while two men but no women killed themselves on account of "shame," three women but no men killed themselves because of bereavement. The evidence tended strongly to suggest, even if it was inadequate conclusively to prove, that there are correlations between the differential homicide and suicide patterns for men and women and the different statuses which the two sexes occupy in Nyoro society. To one or two of these correlations I have drawn attention in the foregoing pages. In the broadest terms, it would seem true to say that for men, in their more extensive social world, no particular kind of social relationship assumes quite such paramount importance as do the marital and also the maternal relationships for women. For women are constrained by traditional Nyoro culture at once to a status subordinate to men and to a social milieu more restricted.

A final word remains to be said. Our twin topics have been melancholy ones, but it would be the grossest of errors to infer from this necessarily one-sided study that Nyoro are a gloomy or degraded people, addicted to suicide, murder and sorcery, and other crimes. Every culture has its seamy side, and I owe it to my Nyoro friends and hosts to say that almost all the Nyoro I know are as law-abiding, cheerful, and considerate as any people I have met.

6

HOMICIDE AND
SUICIDE IN NORTH KAVIRONDO

PAUL BOHANNAN

THE BaLuyia are the congeries of tribes formerly called the
"Bantu Kavirondo." The name means "tribesman" or "clans-
man" and has come into common use within the last fifteen
years or so.[1] This chapter is concerned with the BaLuyia of
North Nyanza (formerly North Kavirondo) District of Nyanza
Province, Kenya. North Nyanza District was—in 1955 when
this study was carried out—divided into 22 "locations," each
dominated by a group of people usually called a "tribe," though
on close examination it is difficult to define a tribe. Certainly
there are more than are recognized by having "locations" assigned to and named for them.

The following are the tribes associated with locations:

Bantu 'tribes':	Kabras	1	location
	Logoli	1	
	Banyala	1	
	Vugusu	3	
	Marach	1	
	BaKhayo	1	
	Wanga	3	
	Buholo*	1	

* There is a large admixture of Luo in this area; comparatively few
BaLuyia realize that BaHolo consider themselves a Bantu stem, highly
Luo-ized.

[1] G. Wagner, *The Bantu of North Kavirondo*, does not record its use.
It is the creation of former students of Makerere College on analogy of
BaGanda. The administrative organization created for purposes of local
government provides the framework of an organization of all the BaLuyia
tribes.

	BaTsotso	1		
	Marama	1		
	Tiriki	1		
	Idakho	1		
	Isukha	1		
	BaNyore	1		
	Kisa	1	= 19	
Nilo-Hamitic				
'tribes':	Itesio	1		
	Elgoni	1		
	Nyangori	1	= 3	= 22

The Bantu tribes above are regarded as "BaLuyia." There is another BaLuyia tribe in Central Nyanza District, the Samia, which is not included in this sample. The Bantu tribes of South Nyanza—the Gusii and the AbaKuria (or Watende)—are different enough from those of North Nyanza that they are not usually considered BaLuyia.

The indigenous social and political organization of the various tribes of North Nyanza before the coming of European government was extremely varied. The Wanga, at one extreme, were characterized by an organization which Europeans easily recognized as a divine kingship. Other tribes were based on ritual associations of clans, and some on rudimentary segmentary lineage systems. The characteristic of all BaLuyia tribes, however, is that the political unit consisted in a knot of clans held together and internally organized in one or another way.

Culturally, the Bantu Kavirondo vary considerably. The variation is, however, regular: those "tribes" on the west resemble the Bantu peoples of Eastern Uganda (see the chapter on BaGisu) and ultimately resemble—or think that they resemble—the BaGanda. Those "tribes" on the east resemble the Nilo-Hamitic tribes, especially the Nandi, whom they bound. There is, thus, a cultural continuum which is more like

Interlacustrine Bantu on the west, taking on more and more "Nilo-Hamitic traits" toward the east.

The small Nilotic and Nilo-Hamitic tribes are enclaves: the Tesio claim a hazy and distant relationship with the Teso of Uganda; the Nyangori (now almost completely gone from Nyangori location, which has been taken over by Logoli) claim to be a sub-division of the Nandi. The Elgoni speak Nandi, but claim to be ancient enemies of the Nandi. There are several small Nilo-Hamitic enclaves not recognized by locations of their own; there are also several Uasin-Gishu Masai colonies in North Nyanza. There is a large admixture of Nilotic Luo in the Southwest of the region.

The official data on which this essay is based consists of records of 114 killings in North Nyanza between 1949 and 1954, both years inclusive. The office of the Resident Magistrate in Kakamega (and from 1953 on, in Bungoma as well) keeps records of all the cases it hears. My clerk and I went through all of the criminal registers for those years and discovered 124 cases. With the help of the Court Clerk, we were able to find more or less complete records for 114 of them. It would probably have been possible to find records of the rest in Nairobi, had I had time to do so. Table 29 sets forth this information. The sample is approximately 92 per cent complete for the

TABLE 29. HOMICIDE CASES, 1949-1954

Year	Number of Cases (Cases not recorded are indicated in brackets)
1949	19 [2]
1950	16 [3]
1951	19 [2]
1952	19
1953	18 [2]
1954	23 [1]
TOTAL	114 [10] [Total, 124]

156

number of killings brought before a magistrate for the six years in question.[2]

The legal disposition of the 114 cases of the sample is shown in Table 30.

TABLE 30. DISPOSITION OF HOMICIDE CASES

Disposition by Magistrate	Numbers	
Released by magistrate—Nol. Pros.		
or justifiable homicide	9	
Inquest by magistrate—no charge	2	
Verdict of suicide	1	
Magistrate refuses to commit on		
advice of public prosecutor	1	
Magistrate sent accused to mental		
hospital for observation	1	
Case withdrawn by police	3	
No records of disposition	3	20
Committed to supreme court for trial:		
Released on legal technicality	1	
Guilty of attempted murder	1	
Acquitted	12	14
Guilty of murder:		
Hanged	12	
Insane	1	
Unrecorded	1	
Guilty of manslaughter	66	80
TOTAL		114

The 80 cases which resulted in convictions for murder or manslaughter are the concern of the greater part of the remainder of this essay.

There is considerable variation in crime from one location of North Nyanza to another. Computations of the rate of homicide per 100,000 persons, by location, is set forth in Table 31.

[2] It is not possible, in local police stations in Kenya, to get figures to approximate the "total crimes known to the police" of the British statistics —at least, it is not possible for before mid-1953. I believe that elaborate and detailed records are kept in Nairobi, but I was unable to visit police headquarters there during the limited stay I could manage in Kenya.

If one maps the various locations, one discovers that the homicide rate rises as one goes eastward, from Bantu to Nilo-Hamitic culture. That *may* be the correct explanation. On the other hand, it may be that the rate rises as one gets closer to police stations. There are five police stations in North Nyanza:

TABLE 31. HOMICIDE RATE, BY LOCATIONS

Tribes, by Location	Population	Murder	Manslaughter	Combined Murder and Manslaughter, Rate per year per 100,000*
Strangers			5	
Not recorded			1	
Bunyala	9,988	–	–	
Marach	23,430	–	–	
Buholo	12,841	–	–	
Bukhayo	24,201	–	1	.69
Wanga	51,997	–	3	.95
BaNyore	41,351	2	2	1.61
Logoli	98,770	4	6	1.68
Marama	33,892	1	3	1.96
Vugusu	111,997	2	12	2.08
BaTsotso	15,781	–	2	2.11
Tiriki	32,863	–	5	2.53
Kabras	27,544	2	3	3.02
Kisa	27,051	1	4	3.05
Isukha	36,152	–	7	3.28
Idakho	30,713	–	7	3.79
Tesio	28,634	1	1	1.16
Elgoni	10,436	1	4	7.90
TOTAL	617,641	14	66	

*[pop x 6 (years)

homicides x 100,000]

Kakamega (Isukha), Vihiga (Logoli), Bungoma (Vugusu), Kimilili (Vugusu), and Broderick Falls (Kabras). All but Bungoma are well to the east of the district. The Southwest, which has the lowest rate, is furthest from a police station. The number of cases amongst the Logoli rose sharply in 1954, the year immediately following the establishment of a police post—although this post certainly, and others probably, were established because the need for them was known. The Elgoni people, who have the highest rate of all, are fairly close to Kimilili police station, but their country, high on Mount Elgon, is not easily accessible from there. The locations with higher rates do not have any different sorts of homicides than those with low rates: the incidence is merely greater.

In examining the weapons used to commit homicide, I have used the complete sample, 114 cases. We find the distribution set forth in Table 32.

TABLE 32. WEAPONS IN BALUYIA HOMICIDES

r	Arson	Striking			Hoe	Cutting		Scythe	Spear	Arrow	Other	
		Axe	Stick	Blow		Panga	Knife					
9	–	2	8	2	–	5	1	–	–	–	1	19
0	1	2	6	–	–	1	–	–	1	–	5	16
1	–	–	8	1	–	–	4	–	3	1	2	19
2	–	–	2	5	2	3	3	–	1	1	2	19
3	1	–	3	3	–	1	5	–	3	–	2	18
4	–	–	4	3	2	1	6	2	3	–	2	23
TAL	2	4	31	14	4	11	19	2	11	2	14	114

The main point of interest in these figures is that in the first three years of the sample, striking instruments are much more commonly used for killing than are cutting instruments. In the last three years of the sample, they are about equally common. I do not know how to account for this change in weapons. It was suggested by Kenya officials that the popularity of the *panga* and cutting instruments among Mau Mau terrorists, and the fact that most BaLuyia kept well informed of Mau Mau developments, might account for the increase. I have no comment to make on this point.

If we limit ourselves to the instruments used by persons convicted either of manslaughter or murder, the situation shown in Table 33 emerges.

TABLE 33. HOMICIDES CONVICTED 1949-1954, BY METHOD
OF KILLING

(murders alone in brackets)

Year	Striking		Cutting		Stabbing	Other	Total	
1949	11	[1]	5	[3]	–	–	16	
1950	4	[1]	1		1	4	10	
1951	9	[1]	3		4	1	17	
1952	7	[1]	4	[1]	1	–	12	
1953	4	[1]	5		2	–	11	
1954	5	[1]	7	[4]	1	1	14	
TOTAL	40	[6]	25	[8]	9	6	80	[14]

Seen in these terms, it seems more sensible to wonder why the number of killings with striking instruments has decreased rather than why those performed with cutting instruments has increased. It would seem more likely that Mau Mau would account more readily for the higher number of sentences given users of cutting instruments than it would account for the number of killings which took place with cutting instruments.

There is no significant correlation between location and the type of instrument used for the killings.

A most interesting situation appears when we examine the 80 convictions for the month in which the crime was committed.

TABLE 34. CONVICTIONS FOR HOMICIDE

(in brackets, all convictions in cases where no alcohol was involved)

January	10	[7]
February	9	[9]
March	2	[1]
April	5	[3]
May	7	[4]
June	6	[4]
July	3	[3]
August	4	[2]
September	5	[3]
October	11	[8]
November	8	[5]
December	8	[4]

There is no correlation between month of the year and the location in which crimes were committed, nor between time of year and weapon. I can, in fact, find no correlations within the sample, with the month of occurrence. March, according to the police, is the low point in all offences. It is also the month during which the most plowing is done.

When I began my study of homicide among BaLuyia, I discussed the whole matter with several people, both Europeans and BaLuyia. The Europeans all told me, "There is no problem, really: they get drunk and do each other in." The BaLuyia said, "There is no problem: all ultimately involve land disputes." Later, after the data were gathered, one of the District Officers expressed amazement at the small number of beer parties; several BaLuyia expressed similar amazement that so few killings concerned land.

Both European and BaLuyia stereotypes are found to be true in a significant number of cases. Neither, however, explains more than a fraction of the sample.

Table 35 shows the number of cases in which alcohol was present.

TABLE 35. HOMICIDE AND ALCOHOL

	Alcohol	No Alcohol	Total
Murder	1	13	14
Manslaughter	26	40	66
TOTAL	27	53	80

Alcohol was, in all instances save one, considered a mitigating factor, and a plea for manslaughter was accepted. Alcohol was present in a third of the killings.

There was a total of 16 cases in which no motive save "accident" in the course of a fight or brawl could be discovered. Of that number, 11 included alcohol—66 per cent. The picture which Europeans draw of the BaLuyia as a brawling people

161

whose fights are sometimes lethal is, in part, true. The following is an example of such a case.

Case No. 1. Licheberere kills his father's brother while under the influence of alcohol. (Kabras Location.)

The deposition of Kulecho gives a full account of the hap-
penings:

On 4 October, Deceased
had brewed beer to wel-
come the Olugongo (a gov-
ernment official) of the region to attend the "after-

Licheberere

Mukhwana   Shiamala   Kulecho
    | (Deceased)
Licheberere
(Accused)

math of the burial ceremony of the deceased's daughter,"
which is "the custom of the Kabras people [and all of BaLuyia]
when an important person visits at such times of sadness."
Olugongo X arrived with his party and his gramophone about
2 P.M. The party sat inside a hut drinking beer from a common pot with reeds. At about 8 P.M. people began to pay in
money "for the music of the gramophone." Before giving, each
person was allowed a short time to boast how important, rich,
or great he was. Accused boasted and praised himself, then
put in a ten-cent piece. The ten-cent piece was rejected by a
tribal policeman attached to the Olugongo, who said the sum
must be at least fifty cents. Accused insisted, suggesting that
he was not getting bribes from the public like an Olugongo's
policeman. Accused was very angry. Olugongo X tried to quiet
him. Deceased was sleeping in the other room of the house.
He overheard what was going on in the beer room, and asked
Accused to leave the house. Deceased then removed the drinking reed of the Accused from the pot and threw it to the
ground. Such an act is a serious insult because the drinking

reed is the symbol of a man's personality and virility. He pushed Accused outside, and returned to bed. Later Accused slipped back into the room where the Deceased was sleeping, and stabbed him with an arrow.

The Deceased was taken to hospital; the arrow was removed by a Medical Officer but Deceased died of ruptured spleen and peritonitis.

The Accused made a plea of manslaughter which was accepted. The judgment included these statements: The parties are agreed that "The Accused and the Deceased quarreled in the course of a drinking party and the Accused stabbed the Deceased with an arrow. . . . The only question which arises for decision is whether the Accused committed murder or manslaughter. The assessors expressed the opinion that the Accused received provocation from the Deceased and that as he had been drinking for several hours, he did not fully realize the nature of his action. . . . If when the Accused was insulted and assaulted by the Deceased he had then and there picked up a weapon and hit back, I would have had no hesitation in finding the Accused guilty of the lesser offence of manslaughter. The difficulty here is that the Accused after being knocked down went to his house which admittedly was close by and picked up an arrow and returning to the house of the Deceased stabbed him with it once while he was lying on his bed. In an ordinary case I would be inclined to think that the conduct of the Accused would be inconsistent with the defence of provocation as his passion would have had time to cool down. In view, however, of the state of intoxication of the Accused it is likely that he did not regain his self-control and was still smarting under the injury that he had received, when he stabbed the Deceased. I would accordingly give the benefit of the doubt to the Accused and find him guilty of the lesser offence of manslaughter."

The BaLuyia notion that killings occur in the course of land disputes has quantitatively a somewhat lesser confirmation. However, 8 of the 80 cases had land disputes somewhere in the background; alcohol was also involved in three of these 8 land cases. That is, land disputes were behind the enmity which flared up at drinking bouts. Two of the cases occurred among the Elgoni tribesmen (both after drinking honey beer); I believe there is no land shortage there, but do not know the area. The rest of the cases occurred in areas in which land shortage is severe to critical: 1 case in Wanga, 1 in Isukha, 1 in Kisa, one in Bunyole, and 2 among Logoli. Murders in which land is involved tend to be among kinsmen: in the Kisa case, the victim was father's brother's son to the Accused; in one Logoli case a man killed his son for trying to take his land; in the other, a man killed his brother's wife and children in a frenzy which arose, in part, out of a land dispute between the brothers. The latter case is the most instructive.

Case No. 2. Joseph Chunguli kills his brother's wife and two children, and a passing clansman. (Maragoli Location.)

Livingstone Mudidi ran a bakery in Majengo, the roadside settlement some two miles or so from the land which he and his brother, Joseph Chunguli, had inherited from their father. Joseph had been in the army.

In February 1949, Joseph, who was very quick tempered, beat a boy whom Livingstone employed on his farms. Livingstone reported him to the Chief, who did nothing, so in March he brought him before the African Court for spoiling his farms, while the boy brought a case at the same time for assault. Three days after the case, Joseph went berserk. He killed Livingstone's wife and two children, set fire to several houses, and killed one of his clansmen who tried to put out the fire and save the occupants of the huts. Livingstone's testimony runs:

"I was at the bakery at Majengo when I saw a fire at Vihiga (where the houses and farms were). I ran there, but when I got to Lotego dispensary near Vihiga, I met John Lango, who was badly cut in the middle of his back. He was being carried. I heard John Lango speaking but did not stop. A little further on I met Joseph and only recognized him when he was very close to me, and he then hit me with a panga without saying anything, he hit me on the head. I hit him with a stick, his panga fell down and he ran away. I ran after him but lost strength and let him go. I went to the dispensary; I was unable to go to the fire."

At the dispensary, John Lango, the wounded man, told him what had happened. After several hours, they managed to get a lorry to collect the bodies of Livingstone's wife and children; he and John Lango and the bodies were taken to Kakamega to the hospital; John Lango died en route.

The extra-judicial confession made by the Accused runs: "We have had trouble in our homestead. My father left a piece of ground for me and my brother, Livingstone Mudidi. When my father died, Mudidi began to quarrel with me about the farm. Mudidi left his share of the garden and came to start digging in mine. . . . I asked the Church elders to settle the quarrel and they told me to wait for a while. Before they decided on the day, my brother sent his laborers out to uproot my bananas and I beat him. After beating him, I reminded the Church elders that they should settle the quarrel. . . . The Church elders did not do what I had asked them. I told them to tell my brother to give me Shs. 143/75, which I had previously lent him. With the money I wished to buy another piece of land. When the Church elders came they tried to settle the quarrel but he would not listen to them."

The Magistrate interrupted here long enough to discover that the elders he referred to were those of the Friends African Mission. When Livingstone began to dig in what he considered his share, "I again went to my brother politely, asking him to give me my money. He told me that he would destroy me because of that farm. I did not argue with him. I went to the Agricultural Department and bought young banana trees and planted a part of the field. I told my brother that if he had any quarrel with me to show it to my clan. Before long I had two summonses from the Tribunal. . . . My brother told me that his tribe had ordered him to destroy me. Chief X was in his Council; he sent a magician to arrest me. In the morning, I went to see my farm, and I met a black hen. Before long it disappeared. I said to myself, 'The magician they sent to destroy Chief X is the one who told my brother Mudidi to bring this hen here.' I lost my temper and did not value anybody. I went to look for my brother and said, 'Either he kills me or I kill him.' I went to his house where I found his wife and I asked her, 'What is this that you did to me?' She told me to ask the Council members and said, 'These are the men who called the magician to drive Chief X from his chieftainship.' I thought, 'Who am I when I think of Chief X, whom they want to destroy?' I took a box of matches and set fire to the house in which my brother's wife was. She cried out bitterly, and I said, 'You shall die and I shall also die!' I went with fire to search for Safan Ndodo, my brother's neighbour who had gone to Mwanza to bring the magician. I called to him to come out, three times: 'Safan! Safan! Safan! Come out with your weapon and let us kill one another!' He did not come out of his house. I set fire to it. His wife cried and told me that Safan was not in. I told her that the house would be burnt down because of what he had done to me. Another neighbour came out of his house. I thought it was Safan. I cut him to pieces. I went to look for my brother Mudidi. I met him on the way at Lotego. I injured him with my panga and he fell down. I thought he was dead. I straight away went to Majengo hoping to set his bakery on fire. I found many people standing round it; I burnt the shops belonging to those people. I went and sat far away among the rocks. I saw many people, among them the

Chief's police and people of my clan intending to kill me. They arrested my wife and took her to the house of the Chief. I asked myself, 'My wife is not at fault, why have they arrested her?'

"Later on I went to burn five houses. I said to myself that I was already in the wrong. The houses belonged to people very closely related to me. I said to myself that I had already sinned and that I must go in person to Kakamega. I left my home at 2 A.M. that morning. I passed my brother-in-law's house and asked him to make food for me, telling him that I was going to Kakamega. After eating I met many people at Milimo's camp. They told me that I was wanted and that I had sinned. I replied that it was all right and that I was going to report to the police. I told them not to beat me and to let it all be the Government. They tied me up and Mr. B of the Agricultural Department brought me to the Police Station. That is the end of my statement."

Joseph Chunguli was found guilty of murder and hanged.

Joseph's case is more or less typical of land cases, though Joseph went much further than most; the case also contains an element of witchcraft, which is rare in BaLuyia cases. In fact, only this one and two others depend upon witchcraft in any wise. In all three of them the notions were not well understood by the magistrates, as the quoted portion above amply illustrates. One of the other two such cases had a highly ironic twist: a woman kept lamenting and complaining to her only son that she had been assured that both of them were being bewitched. He told her to be quiet. After several days his patience grew thin. He shouted at her to shut up and aimed a kick at her buttocks—just as she turned. The kick landed on her enlarged spleen and killed her, thus "proving" that they had indeed been bewitched (although that was not the conclusion drawn by the court, of course).

One other striking pattern attends homicide among BaLuyia:

what might be called "interference." It centers around an act of interfering in a dispute and being killed for one's pains. Eleven cases out of the 80 exhibit this pattern. Beer was present in four of the eleven cases. A comparatively uncomplicated case occurred in South Wanga.

Case No. 3. Rupia kills Oyuga, who stopped him from beating his wife. (October 1951, South Wanga Location.)

The father of the Deceased told the Magistrate: "I live about 50 yards from the Accused's house. On 22nd October, about 6 P.M., Accused was quarreling in his house with his wife, and his wife ran and came to my house; the Accused followed his wife and started beating her in my house. My son and I went to stop him. The Accused struck my son on the head with a stick and he fell down, and a few minutes later he died."

The Accused's statement follows that of the witness closely; his description of the fight is more complete: Musiro "got hold of me and called his son Oyuga (Deceased); they caught me and threw me on the ground and carried me out of the house. When I got out I stood up and hit Oyuga with my hand on the left side of his head and he did not fall down. He walked towards his house, and I took my wife and went to our house. While going to my house I heard Musiro say that he was going to get his arrows and kill this enemy. When I heard this, I went to Malala's house, as I thought they might come and kill me during the night. Malala gave me a room to sleep. At about 5 A.M. the Olugongo Clement came and told me that I had killed a man, and he arrested me and took me to the Chief."

Rupia was given two years imprisonment with hard labour, having been declared guilty of Manslaughter on his own plea.

In investigating patterns of relationships leading to murder, it is desirable to look into the data on who killed whom. Table 36 distinguishes killers and victims by sex.

TABLE 36. SEXES OF KILLERS AND VICTIMS

	Man kills:	*Men kill:*	*Woman kills:*
man	56	2	1
woman	16	–	3
multiple victims	2	–	–

In this sample, there are only two thieves (although the Magistrate released several other persons who had killed thieves caught stealing). Table 37 summarizes the kinship relationships.

TABLE 37. RELATIONSHIP OF VICTIMS TO KILLERS

Thieves	2
No kinship	6
Kinship unknown	35
Agnatic kinship	17
Non-agnatic kin [Mother]	1
Affines	19
TOTAL	80

An analysis of the 37 persons who killed either kinsmen or affines is set forth in Table 38. Of the cases of trouble between spouses in two a man killed his wife's lover: in one the husband caught his wife and her lover *in flagrante delicto*; in the other the wife had spent a night in a "hotel" with her lover. Of the five cases in which wives were victims of their husbands, two concerned adultery. Two others concern sex, but not adultery—one wife refused to sleep with her husband, struck his testicles when he insisted, and he killed her in anger. The other is the case of a couple who had been granted a divorce. They decided to sleep together once more before parting, and did so. Immediately afterwards, the husband picked up an axe and killed his ex-wife. He was the only wife-killer found guilty of murder. In the fifth case, the killer was declared a homicidal maniac. Thus, adultery is involved in BaLuyia homicide, but only in a very small number of cases.

TABLE 38. KINSHIP RELATIONS BETWEEN VICTIM AND KILLER
(*Ego is the killer*)

	Agnates		Affines	
Ascending Generation	Fa	3	BrWiFa	1
	FaBr	3	WiFa	2
	Fa "class"			
	Br	1	FaWi	1
			MoCo-Wi	1
Ego's Generation	Br "Class"	4	Co-Wife	1
	Br or			
	"cousin"	2	Wife	5
	FaBrSo	2	[WiLover]	2
			Br widow Hu	1
			SiHu	1
			BrWi	2
			SoWiFa	1
Descending Generation	Da	1	HuBrDa	1
	Son	1		
TOTAL		17		19

Among the other cases in which people killed affines of their own generation, two men killed their brothers' wives. One of them was Joseph Chunguli whose case is described above: it fits into the land quarrels pattern. The other (which happened in Buholo) was the result of a brother's wife interfering in a quarrel between the Accused and his wife, and fits into the "interference" pattern. In one case in the sample a woman killed her co-wife during a quarrel over their sons' inheritance; in another a man, who considered that he should have inherited his brother's widow, killed the man with whom the widow was living; in another three brothers killed the husband of their sister, who had sent her away; and in still another the fathers of a newly married couple fought over bride-wealth cattle, and one killed the other.

The one case in which an affine of descending generation was killed occurred during a fight between co-wives when the child of one of them got in the way.

Of the five cases in which an affine of an older generation was killed, there were two in which the victim was the wife's father. In both these cases, the "interference" pattern emerges: the wife's father interfered with the husband's beating of his wife. The man who killed his mother's co-wife did so in a scuffle which followed his attempt to interfere in a family squabble which took place at a beer-drink, although the Accused himself had not been drinking. The man who killed his father's wife did so by accident—bringing the cattle in at evening, he threw a hoe at one to head it off, and struck his father's wife. The man who killed his brother's wife's father did so in the course of a fight among brothers: the father-in-law first killed his son-in-law and was in turn killed, in immediate revenge, by the dead man's brother. The official notes on this case are very thin, and the reason for the original quarrel and fight does not emerge.

Among affines, then, we find representative cases of the drinking pattern, several of the interference pattern, but none of the land dispute pattern.

It is among agnates that the land dispute pattern emerges most clearly, although other patterns also occur. The man who killed him son was a Logoli farmer disputing land with his son; he claimed the boy attacked him, but he was found guilty of murdering the son with a pocket knife. (The man who killed his daughter did so by unfortunate accident.)

Four men murdered brothers. One of these cases is an almost classic illustration of tension within the polygynous family: a young man killed his paternal half-brother when the latter assisted their father in beating the mother of the Accused.

It remains an isolated case, however; the Wanga with whom I discussed it saw the justice of the Accused's attack; it would have been difficult to do anything else, they said. This man was given two years at hard labor on his own plea of manslaughter.

A second man killed his brother when he caught him in adultery with his wife. The third case of fratricide involves witchcraft—a man killed his brother because he thought the latter was bewitching his children. Unfortunately there are not enough details for this case to be of value anthropologically. The fourth case was a man who killed his full brother; the motivation never emerged in the evidence.

There are three more cases in which men killed more distant classificatory "brothers." It is a pity that most Kenya magistrates, when recording their findings, translate kinship terms into English terms such as "cousin," making it impossible to tell what the relationship is. One killing occurred when a man beat his "cousin" (enough information was given in the evidence to indicate that it was an agnatic "cousin") for carrying on a dispute about land cases with the wife of the Accused. One man killed his father's brother's son (either real or classificatory) in a scuffle about the outcome of a land case. Another killed a "cousin" when both were drunk and fighting over a blanket.

When we come to those cases in which persons killed agnates of the ascending generation, we find three patricides, and with them another recurring pattern: all three were counterattacks against the father. One man struck his father a single blow in self-protection. The father was drunk at the time and had not been on good terms with his son for some time because he claimed that the son did not "help" him. Another man, given 8 years at hard labor on his own plea of manslaughter, killed his father when the latter attacked him and threatened to withhold his bride-wealth cattle. The third case is one of a Logoli who drove his son summarily out of the house after telling him that he was his *pater* only, and that he had been begotten by the *pater's* brother. The youngster, in heat, took the stick away from the old man and killed him with it.

One case, again obscured by translation of the kinship terms into English, was that of a man who killed his "uncle" for reprimanding him for chasing a group of girls which included his "sister." (The "uncle" was almost surely an agnatic kinsman, for a mother's brother would not, in all probability, behave in this way, and the mother's brother's agnates would not be "sisters" of the boy.) Three men killed fathers' brothers: one man killed his father's weak-witted brother (whom European doctors would not, however, certify) when the latter did not answer a challenge at night; we have already investigated, above, the case of Licheberere who killed his father's brother in the course of a beer-drink. The third case was a man who killed that father's brother who had inherited his mother; he said it was because the father's brother had "spoiled his name." Intent was proved in the last case; the murderer was condemned and hanged.

The above cases show five repeating patterns which end in homicide—there would probably be more were our data fuller. These were (1) the drinking pattern, (2) the land dispute pattern, (3) the "interference" pattern, (4) the adultery pattern, and (5) the counterattack against the father.

I cannot, within the scope of this chapter, go into indigenous BaLuyia means for countering homicide once it has been committed. They formerly had a system of blood-wealth but it has been inoperative for many years, except in cases of juvenile offenders; they still perform some ritual, but it will be reported in another place. I am limiting this chapter to circumstances leading to homicide, not what is done once homicide is committed.

It is, however, very much to the point to examine BaLuyia classifications of killing. The LuLuyia word meaning "to kill" is *okhuira*; words both for killer and victim are formed from it, but it is not (in Wanga dialect at least) a word to which any emotive value is attached. The emotive aspects all cluster about the word *eshilominda*. Amongst the Wanga and Marama, *eshilominda* refers to murder, abducting a married woman, and serious theft. In Tiriki dialect[3] it means only murder, but specifically excludes killing one's wife's lover, killing in battle, or killing in revenge those people who have murdered one's clansmen. *Eshilominda* is a category of secular anti-social acts, not a single type of "crime."

In Tiriki dialect, *eshilominda* is distinguished definitely from another concept, *maraba*, which is not found among the speakers of Wanga. *Maraba*, in Tiriki, means killing or injuring a person by accident. It differs from manslaughter in that death need not result, and that it has comparatively little to do with intent, but is defined by the notion of "bad luck" (*ihabi idamanu*). Other distinctions may well exist in other dialects of LuLuyia.

It is also possible to distinguish several types of killing by use of adverbial descriptions meaning approximately "accidentally," "acting while bewitched," "acting in hot blood," and "acting without purpose or motivation." These distinctions did not, however, affect payment of blood-wealth, or ritual; the distinction between *eshilominda* and *maraba* did not affect the payment of blood-wealth, but it did affect the type of ritual which followed. These distinctions are, today, being assimilated to those which BaLuyia are learning from Europeans; the *eshilominda-maraba* distinction is becoming a translation of the murder-manslaughter distinction, even though its original meaning was somewhat different.

SUICIDE

Suicide among the Bantu Kavirondo is much more difficult to study than is homicide, mainly because the official records are much less rigorously kept. Comparatively few suicides are

[3] For information about Tiriki I am indebted to Dr. Walter Sangree, who was of great help in my understanding these matters.

reported to the police, and permanent records of them in police stations have been kept for only a very short time. In order to study suicide, I found it necessary to rely upon histories collected from the Wanga; Dr. Sangree had to do the same among Tiriki.

Both Wanga and Tiriki believe that they are not prone, as a people, to suicide. Tiriki say that the suicides which do take place are always performed by hanging; one of my Wanga informants, who spoke very good English, confused "suicide" with hanging: he told me that most people who killed themselves did it by committing suicide [hanging], but a few killed themselves in other ways as well—he noted that women sometimes drown themselves. All BaLuyia with whom Sangree or I talked said that no person can have enough courage to stab himself (although I collected two cases, both women, in which stabbing was in fact the suicide method) and they express a combination of admiration and horror at the European method of committing suicide with firearms (the means used by all save one of those European suicides whom they have known—the other drank poison).

Wagner noted, in passing, that an unhappy marriage often led to suicide by women; he was referring particularly to Logoli.[4] Sangree did not find this to be the case in Tiriki, where his informants either could or would not recall any cases of this sort. Amongst Wanga, however, the pattern definitely holds. I collected a total of 15 cases from several groups of informants. I asked for no specific instances other than (at the close of a session) the question whether they had heard of suicides by means other than hanging. Of the 15 cases, seven are suicides of women. Except for one, in which a woman resolved that her daughter of about twenty should not pre-decease her, all of these women were involved in unhappy marriages. My informants told of one instance of a man who beat his wife severely and often; when she ran to her father's home,

---

[4] Gunther Wagner, *The Bantu of North Kavirondo*, pp. 380, 408-9.

he refused to refund the cattle of her bride-wealth. She finally hanged herself from a tree just outside her husband's hut. Another case was the suicide of a woman whose husband preferred his other wife. Her husband would not eat her food or sleep in her hut, sometimes for weeks at a time, but always went to the other wife. This woman drowned herself.

The eight suicides of Wanga males in my sample show a somewhat wider range of motive; although the theme of unhappy domestic relations recurs in three of them, the idea of shame is also present. One young Wanga committed suicide in 1929 (my informants dated it) when accused of stealing; he was a man with a family. They also told of the suicide of Nawanga, who heard his associates trying to convince his sweetheart that he was a bad lot, and that she would do well to have nothing further to do with him. Petero committed suicide some years ago because (it is said today) his friends had teased him for having impregnated such a short, ugly girl.

Dr. Sangree's informants amongst the Tiriki told him of a case in which a man made his biological daughter pregnant, and committed suicide when she reported the matter to the chief. There is more than shame involved in this case; it is connected with notions of ritual impurity (*luswa*)[5] which are thought to affect the entire community.

There are other patterns as well: one old man committed suicide when his last surviving child died, and two murderers committed suicide before they could be arrested. These four patterns—domestic difficulties, shame, loneliness of the aged, and suicide following murder—cover all of the suicides which I collected amongst Wanga, those which Mr. Sangree collected amongst Tiriki, and four which we found in inquest files in Kakamega. They do not adequately explain them all, however; BaLuyia say that persons can be made to commit suicide by means of witchcraft and, in fact, one or two of these persons

[5] See Wagner, *op.cit.*, p. 107.

(who had other reasons) were considered to have been bewitched: witchcraft seems to account for the state of mind which makes suicide for other motives possible.

If we use Durkheim's classification of suicide, all these cases must be considered "egoistic suicide." There is no altruistic and as yet little anomic suicide amongst BaLuyia. M. D. W. Jeffreys has drawn attention to another type of suicide, which he calls "Samsonic suicide"—killing oneself to avenge oneself on others.[6] He shows this form to be widespread in Africa; it is found among BaLuyia. They hesitate to refer to any specific suicide as having been motivated by revenge, but they do believe that the ghost of a suicide can be particularly potent in bringing trouble and difficulty, and that there undoubtedly are people who commit suicide in order that their ghosts may trouble the husbands, fathers, or other persons who forced them into impossible situations. The "Samsonic" interpretation is, therefore, sometimes emphasized and sometimes not, in any specific case.

Once a suicide has occurred, the efforts of BaLuyia are turned toward rendering it harmless to the community. The person who discovers the suicide goes away quietly and reports the matter to the next of kin of the dead person. It is considered dangerous to discover the body of a suicide, as it renders one especially subject to the ghost of the deceased. The discoverer must be given a goat by the kin of the dead man; the body of the suicide is removed and buried in the ordinary manner; the tree or hut is destroyed and burned, together with the rope with which the hanging was done, and a sheep is sacrificed on the spot and eaten by the discoverer and those persons connected with the deceased. Some BaLuyia deny that cutting down the tree has anything to do with the ghost of the deceased, but say that if the tree were not destroyed, others would commit suicide on it. The ghost of the

[6] M. D. W. Jeffreys, "Samsonic Suicide or Suicide of Revenge Amongst Africans," *African Studies*, Vol. xi, No. 3, 1952, pp. 118-122.

deceased is sometimes feared by the discoverer, but usually mainly by the intimates of the deceased, who have reason to believe that the suicide may have taken place in order to take revenge on them. There are elaborate ritual precautions for avoiding such contact.

7

HOMICIDE AND SUICIDE
AMONG THE JOLUO OF KENYA

G. M. WILSON

THE Luo ("Jaluo," singular; "Joluo," plural) are unique in that they are the only Nilotic speaking people in Kenya. Their place of origin is the Nile Valley; through the centuries by gradual expansion by war and peaceful penetration, they migrated up the Nile Valley, through Uganda, into Kenya, along the shores of Lake Victoria. The term Luo means "swamp" and Joluo "the people of the swamp." Through their migrations they have left behind other Nilotic groups in Uganda and in the Sudan.

The Joluo are chiefly concentrated in Central Nyanza where over half a million of them are found today. There are, however, Luo pockets in North Nyanza and also in South Nyanza. The Luo of Central Nyanza are divided into twelve tribal groups. Each tribal group, with a Government-appointed chief, today forms an administrative unit, a "Location," within the District of Central Nyanza. These administrative units, laid down in the early twenties, coincide fairly accurately with the former tribal boundaries and are accepted by the people.

Each Luo tribe can be described as a society of agnatic parallel lineages or clans, each tracing either real or mythical descent from a common eponym or descent through an adopted or affiliated family to the eponym.

The original form of the clan and lineage structure remains today in comparative purity. The Joluo people—although on the surface they have accepted Christianity—still retain the ceremonial, religious, and ritual aspects of their culture to a

179

very large degree. Their family system remains strong and largely unimpaired by the impact of Western civilization. The patriarch of the extended family unit, the *jokakwaro*, remains the local authority. Because a series of family groups together form a territorial unit, the sub-clan, the strength and solidity of the Luo family and lineage structure remain supreme. Obviously there have been changes. Basically, however, the changes are superficial.

The role of women in Luo society is a subordinate one. Indigenously they play no part in the major ceremonies or rituals and have never had political authority. They do not organize in age groups or societies as in other cultures, and remain primarily the property of their father and his lineage or, on marriage, the property of their husband and his clan.

Polygyny is still the ideal and goal of the majority of Luo men. A recent village survey showed that taking a sample of 744 homesteads, which varied between a simple monogamous family and the very large unit of the extended polygamous family, 55 per cent were monogamous units, of which 9 per cent had a leviratic wife or wives, thus making them socially polygamous units; 45 per cent were polygamous homesteads, of which 11 per cent had a leviratic wife or wives. Only 27 per cent of the total sample were found to be simple monogamous households, that is one in four of the family type associated with Western culture: a man, his wife and children. The remainder were either polygamous or had leviratic wives or were of the extended family type. Of this 27 per cent, moreover, it was the ideal of the vast majority to become polygamous later.

Education among the Joluo has increased rapidly in recent years, and it was found in our sample that 63 per cent of the boys of school age were either at school or had been to school for more than one year. The figure was 30 per cent for the girls. Of the adult males, however, only 26 per cent had been to school, and of the married females, only 7 per cent. The standard attained, moreover, was not high. More than half the male group had less than three years' education and over half of the female group had less than two years' education. This pattern, however, as already indicated, is changing rapidly. The majority of the Joluo are nominally Christians, although half of those who called themselves Christians were polygamists. Historically, of course, all of the schools in Luo were Mission schools and therefore those who go to school tend to call themselves "Christians," and most of them in fact have a basic understanding of the Christian religion.

One aspect of Joluo life which has changed considerably is the tremendous increase in spatial mobility. Prior to European ascendancy, the Joluo did not move among the tribal units because of the continual wars between them. Moreover, banishment from the tribe usually meant death at the hands of the neighboring Nandi, Kipsigis, or Masai. Lately, however, the village census established that most Luo males had been out of their district and well over half had been to Nairobi or beyond. At any given point in time nearly one half of the adult male population is engaged in employment away from the tribal area. Nearly one half of the Joluo adult women in the sample, 40 per cent, had been outside of their district, although only 11 per cent had been to Nairobi or beyond. It is the custom, therefore, for married men to migrate for labor and to leave their wives and families in their family locations to cultivate the gardens.[1]

HOMICIDE AMONG JOLUO

The Nilotic Joluo regard violence as an unnecessary loss of control, or at best a calculated necessary last resort to secure

---

[1] Professor E. E. Evans-Pritchard has written a study of the Luo in his "Luo Tribes and Clans" (*Rhodes-Livingstone Journal,* No. 7), and description of the marriage customs of the Luo in his "Marriage Customs of the Luo of Kenya" (*Africa,* Vol. xx, No. 1, 1950). Dr. A. Southall has published a memorandum entitled "Lineage Formation among the Luo," Memorandum xxvi, International African Institute, London, 1952. My own work among the Luo, *Law and Custom of the Joluo People of Kenya,* is forthcoming.

goals which have been carefully weighed and assessed as to the possible supernatural and social consequences. The Joluo believe that a goal does not justify the means if the means require violence, unless all methods of arbitration, conciliation, appeal to authority, both temporal and supernatural, have been tried and proved to be unsuccessful or inadequate.

Violence requires cleansing—physical and spiritual cleansing of the most exacting nature—to avoid the supernatural consequences (*chira*) which violence may bring in its wake. One case has been recorded which contains an excellent description of the ceremonial and ritual cleansing thought to be essential after a murder. This particular murder was planned and executed by a group which, after years of thought and effort to resolve the conflict without violence, finally resorted to murder. Obviously, with the coming of the European, other factors were involved to escape detection for an act which in the old days would have given the group high status within its own community and which would have created feuds or precipitated a war that ultimately would have been resolved by blood compensation or schism of the political unit and migration by the weakest group.

Violence which arises immediately and unpremeditatively from quarrels, drinking, infidelity, sex, marital tensions, or family differences, and which results in a death, is not regarded in the same way as predetermined action decided upon as a last resort. Ceremonial cleansing is still necessary but does not take the extreme form because these acts are regarded by the Luo as bringing consequences which affect the individual only, that is *kwer*, and not *chira*, which affects the group, clan, or tribe as a whole. Fortunately British law makes a similar distinction: that between murder and manslaughter. It will be found therefore that the majority of cases involving Joluo which have come before the courts of Kenya as murder cases are resolved and punished as cases of manslaughter. The Joluo do not, however, understand why many of those convicted under the head of manslaughter should be punished at all. They feel that a person who makes the mistake of killing in anger is or has been or will eventually be punished by the ancestors, God, the elements, by illness, bad luck, misfortune, or the like, in the inevitable nature of things.

It is believed that cold-blooded, premeditated murder brings *chira* to the group and is therefore punished by the tribe or by the segment affected. The group or the individual who took what they regarded as this calculated risk was eventually banished from the tribe or if large and strong enough to dominate the political unit to which the deceased belonged could force his supporters, usually his segment of the clan, to break away and leave the area. Luo kinship describes all members of the clan in the same genealogical generation as brothers; fratricide, therefore, has a very wide range.

Luo clans occupy and are identified with a geographical area. The clan and the area it occupies are usually called after the eponym of the tribe. Those living within a clan or tribal area who are not members of the clan or tribe are regarded as squatters (*jodak*) with limited rights. They may be unrelated squatters, but most often are found to be affines of legitimate clan members. Murder committed by such persons invokes immediate counteraction on the part of those who belong to the land by virtue of descent, *jogweng*. Cattle could be taken by force, the culprit banished or killed, and/or a woman from that group married by a member of the dead man's minimal lineage, his *jokakwaro*, to raise seed unto the dead man's name. This woman would be regarded as the wife of the dead man, her children would placate his ghost as father (*wuoro*), the physical father would merely serve as genitor.

One major clan, *Kakia*, of a powerful tribe, the Seme of Central Nyanza, descended from a woman of this type—but then not exactly of this type: what happened was as follows. A *jadak*, living in the clan area of Seme, killed the son of an important elder of the tribe. He fled to his own tribal land to avoid the immediate consequences and as a result war broke out between the people of Seme and the people of his tribe, Ugenya. After many years of intermittent and bitter warfare the elders of both tribes met to settle the dispute. Their solution was as follows: because the elder who lost his son did not have an unmarried son to take a woman of the killer's clan, and because the killer's minimal lineage did not have a suitable daughter to give in marriage, it was decided that the killer should marry the daughter of the deceased's father, and through her raise seed to the dead man. The killer, contrary to custom but as part of the settlement, was forced to live at the home of his bride and was subsequently adopted into the clan of the deceased. It is interesting, however, that the eponym of the clan which today traces descent from this couple is the bride, Kia, and not the killer or the deceased. It is, to my knowledge, the only clan in Luo which has a woman as an eponym, but then she was apparently regarded as a male by her contemporaries.

This background was given to provide the reader with some idea of the Joluo attitude to homicide. Deeply ingrained is the notion that life goes on after death on earth—that ancestors in the spirit world are able to influence the lives, conduct, fortunes, for good or evil, of their descendants. Ghosts are more likely to be benevolent if they can count numerous descendants on earth and extremely malevolent if life on earth was cut short by violence or unnatural death by war, accident, or suicide. The ghosts of the latter are believed to be more difficult to deal with than those of ordinary spirits of old men or women. The more descendants a ghost has, the higher its status in the afterworld, and therefore the greater its pleasure and benevolence.

The Joluo had developed several devices to deal with cases of homicide. A wife could be married in the name of a murdered youth to raise seed to his name, to placate his spirit and to continue his line for posterity. A young adolescent woman who died was deflowered by a stranger (*jokawiny*)

because a ghost of a virgin who has reached puberty was regarded as extremely dangerous. The defloration, still practiced
in parts of Luo today, was regarded as satisfying her natural
desire to bear children.

The spirits of warriors killed in battle were placated by the
tribe as a whole in ceremonial and ritual held at the borders
of the tribal land (*thim*) by *poro bilo* and *tero buru*, where
sacrifices were made and the tribal ancestors placated to welcome the ghost of the hero. The affair became a tribal responsibility, whereas normally death is regarded as a responsibility
of the family or minor lineage segment.

A person who found the body of a man or of a woman would
commence wailing as a closely related mourner. If the body
turned out to be that of a person among whose clan the finder
could marry, then a wife or husband was found for the finder
in the belief that the spirit of the deceased planned and directed the discovery of the body to the end that the group of
the finder should be united in marriage with that of the deceased.

Witches, if caught in the act of "running about at night,"
were killed instantly and with equanimity. The body of a person killed as a witch was mutilated by driving a stake into the
rectum after which the body would be thrown into its village.
An old custom still associated with this is the insistence of the
relatives of a woman who died suddenly, or inexplicably, to
examine her body for signs of having been a witch. Female
witches are believed to be trained by their husbands to run
at night with them and, because they are weaker, are frequently caught and killed. Bride-wealth may not be reclaimed
or, if not finally paid, must be completed by her husband if
a woman is killed under these circumstances.

Accidental deaths are regarded as having been inspired by
the ancestors, and therefore require placation of the spirit of
the ancestor divined as having been responsible. Deaths from
sickness are believed to come from many causes, the chief of

which is the infidelity of the spouse of the deceased; in the case of a child, by the adultery of its mother. Ritual cleansing of the members of the minor lineage is therefore necessary, as for *kwer*.

I mentioned above a classical case of homicide which illustrates what the Joluo regard as a calculated risk of the consequences. It deserves fuller analysis.

Case No. 1.

This case involved a group of nine related men. Only one of them was convicted, and he eventually was acquitted on appeal through lack of corroborative evidence.

A quarrel began between members of two major clans of the same tribe over the appointment of an assistant chief. The clan from which the assistant chief was appointed—we shall call it Jokoth—is alleged to have taken advantage of the clan—which we shall call Jokech—which was unsuccessful. The clans feuded in every way, over land, cattle grazing and so on, until the elders of Jokech decided, as a warning in the ancestral way, that they should burn the hut of a leading elder of Jokoth. This was done. The assistant chief arrested a member of clan Jokech, a person with whom he is alleged to have had a personal grievance, and this man was convicted of the burning and sentenced to a term of imprisonment. His sons fought hard and long to have him released on grounds of ill health and, when finally successful, took him home only to have him die shortly after. On his death bed, he made his sons swear to avenge his death.

Diviners and medicine men were consulted, and many methods were tried unsuccessfully for several years to bring clan Jokoth to its knees and to bring about the death of the assistant chief who had by now retired.

All was not well with the affairs of Jokech clan. Each new catastrophe was taken as evidence of the malevolence of the ghost of the deceased because his death remained unavenged.

Finally, in desperation, his sons and a group of his *jokakwaro* consulted the head diviner, *jabilo*, to choose an auspicious day for the killing of the ex-chief and to collect the animals and materials necessary for cleansing after the deed had been accomplished.

The ex-chief was found and stabbed to death at the place named by the *jabilo* and his body was hidden in a nearby river. It was found several days later, and a witness was found who alleged that he came upon the group on the day of the murder in the act of disposing of the body.

Those who had had actual physical contact with the blood of the murdered man were cleansed as soon as they arrived home by the leading *jabilo* of the clan. He used a grey ash from burning the sacred *buombwe* vine. The minimal lineage, *jokakwaro*, assembled at the village of the senior son, who was the head of the lineage segment, and who had struck the fatal blow. There the following cleansing ritual was performed: at about two o'clock the following afternoon, a black sheep and red chicken were slaughtered by the head of the lineage. The sheep and chicken were first prepared by the *jabilo*, who placed his medicines in the mouth of the sheep and of the chicken before the sacrifice. The *jabilo* cut strips of skin from the animal and wrapped them around the spear and knives used in the murder. The spear had to be destroyed at sundown because the victim was related to the spear clan of the tribe. The meat was divided on the lineage principle and consumed ceremonially. The meat of the chicken was eaten only by those who actually struck blows.

The purpose of these sacrifices was stated by the *jabilo* to "keep the spirit of the murdered man from doing evil to the clan." It also cleansed the bodies of those who drew blood so that they could now eat with their families and once more participate in the activities of the village and clan.

After the meat was eaten, those present held a meeting to decide which old woman should act as a wife to the ghost of the murdered man, to mourn his death, to placate his spirit, and to retain the grey ash medicine left over from the first cleansing to be used when necessary to remove the danger of his ghost returning to harm members of the clan. An old woman past child bearing, *pim*, was selected and agreed to perform these functions. She was given animals for this service and a hut was built for her outside the village, where she placated the spirit of the dead man.

Most Joluo will agree that when a witch is killed, the dead man's relatives do not take legal action but try to cover up the incident. This is not difficult in Luo society. One case did, however, occur during the period of this study which could not be hidden from the authorities.

Case No. 2.

A youth of seventeen was escorting his sister from a marriage ceremony back to their village some miles away. It was late at night or early in the morning, time could not accurately be assessed, when suddenly an apparition appeared in the path of the couple. It was a naked man—swerving, jumping, screaming, and brandishing fire which glowed red as he waved his arms. The night was very dark and to the young couple the apparition appeared as a ghost. The woman fled the way she had come but the youth in his frantic effort to escape stumbled and fell. The "ghost" was on top of him instantly, clawing at his face and throat. The youth had a sheath knife in his belt and frantically struck out blindly several times as he managed to struggle free. He fled back to the village from which he came. A party of youths and men armed themselves and set out to search for and kill the witch but were unable to find the exact spot in the darkness.

Next morning a body was found, naked, and with several stab wounds on it. The man was identified, and the finder, ignorant of the previous night's events, notified the police. Thus the story was out.

The Joluo were concerned that the youth should have been arrested and charged with murder. He was acquitted after trial on the grounds of self-defense, but the opinion remained that he should have had praise and not have suffered the indignity of being held in custody which, to the unsophisticated, was punishment and prison.

The Joluo discipline wives and children, when it is thought necessary, by beating and kicking. One or two cases each year come to the courts as a result of excessive force resulting in the death of a victim of discipline. Out of 46 cases between 1949 and 1954, 10 were of this type.

The largest number of murder cases today arises from drunken quarrels during beer parties. Native beer does not have a high alcoholic content, but a beer-drink often begins at mid-morning and continues well into the night and, on special occasions, until the next day. The quantity consumed therefore frequently produces an acute state of drunkenness. Of the 46 cases, no fewer than 12 can be classified as the result of excessive beer drinking. These cases, without exception, were finally treated by the courts as manslaughter.

Family quarrels, often over bride-wealth payments, account for a few cases every year. A typical case of this type is as follows.

Case No. 3.

In 1949, the Accused caught his wife in the act of adultery with an acquaintance. The wife returned to her father's village, as is the custom in such cases, and made several efforts to elope with her lover. On each occasion, her brothers forcefully restrained her and threatened her lover with a severe beating or death, should he attempt to elope with their sister. After several weeks of argument and numerous meetings of the elders of the clans involved in the case, the husband went to the village of his wife and took ten head of cattle by force from her father's herd. This action is approved in customary law after the elders have met and discussed the matter and are unable to resolve it by any other method.

Naturally the brothers of the girl were extremely angry that their sister should have behaved in this way that meant the loss of animals which they, no doubt, had planned to use for their own bride-wealth. The girl remained unrepentant and troublesome. She stated that she was determined to return to her former husband's village to collect her clothes, and that she would leave her brothers and her former husband in order to join her lover. Her brothers followed her to the village of her former husband and there began to quarrel. Her former husband joined the group, and the three decided to teach this woman a lesson. They beat her with sticks until she was dead.

The court took a lenient view and decided that their intention was not to kill the woman but merely to discipline her, and each of the Accused was sentenced to six months hard labor for manslaughter.

The next case also arose out of bride-wealth.

Case No. 4.

In 1949, a woman left her husband to live with her lover. Her husband tried through indigenous and legal channels to get his bride-wealth returned. The woman's father, however, had used the animals and could not return them, although he was sympathetic. The husband, therefore, was left with only one course, to demand the return of his wife. To this end, he went to the village of her lover and threatened him. They began to quarrel and to fight. Each was armed, the lover with a spear and the Accused, the husband, with a *panga* and a knife. The lover was killed and the husband charged with murder.

In this case, the court decided that this was manslaughter,

and the Accused was sentenced to three years' hard labor. The sequel to the case is that the wife was repentant and returned to the village of her husband and was there to welcome him on his return from prison.

Polygamy is the desired goal in marriage in Luo society. The word for co-wife in the Luo language is *nyieko*, which also means jealousy of an intense kind. The jealousy between co-wives occasionally ends in quarrels which result in the murder of one or the other.

Case No. 5.

A quarrel developed between the senior and most junior wife, when the latter accused the former of trying to poison her child. Her child was an adopted child, being a child of the deceased second wife of their common husband. When a woman dies, it is customary for the husband to decide which of his wives should act as foster mother to her children. This quarrel began because the senior wife had demanded custody of the child but the husband decided to place the child in the care of the junior wife, who had no sons. The argument went on for years. The child became ill and the junior wife was convinced that he was poisoned by the senior wife. A quarrel developed and the junior wife, who had just returned from the fields with a *panga* in her hands, struck the senior wife, killing her instantly.

Again the court decided that this was a case of manslaughter, and the accused was sentenced to four years' hard labor.

The Joluo people have a custom at marriages of "pulling the girl" to the village of the groom. Traditionally, the brothers and friends of the girl should resist this "capture." In fact, however, the marriage has been arranged by them and both parties are fully aware that this is a mock battle. On occasion these fights become a spirited and serious "free for all." From time to time, therefore, one or more of the party is seriously injured and not infrequently death results. Indigenously the method of resolving this situation is to cancel the arrangements of the wedding which was to have taken place and to continue these arrangements to marry a girl to the dead man. If the dead man is from the party of the prospective groom, the girl is married to his name. If the death has occurred among the relatives or friends of the girl, then a bride is chosen from the relatives of her prospective husband to marry in the name of the dead man. Whenever possible, this custom is followed today. The authorities, however, naturally prosecute in cases of this kind. The result is usually manslaughter, and the sentence is a light one.

There are cases in which it is difficult to determine whether the death was caused intentionally or accidentally. For example: a food which is now becoming increasingly used is the cassava root, and raw cassava contains cyanogenic glucoside which, when acidified by gastric fluid, forms hydrogen cyanide and is therefore a virulent poison in this form. Adequate cooking destroys this poisonous principle, and most Luo women clearly understand this. Therefore, when the death occurred of a child who had consumed cassava which had been prepared and given by a co-wife, its mother's suspicion was immediately aroused. She accused the co-wife of giving the poison intentionally. It is very difficult, however, to prove, as in the case mentioned, that death was caused intentionally and not accidentally by the ignorance of the co-wife. The case was dismissed by the court.

The sequel, however, was that the husband did not accept the explanation of ignorance and divorced the woman because, as he stated, "there would never be peace in my village. It is obvious what this witch has done and although she has been a good wife to me, she has broken my village and killed my child. I therefore will divorce her and get my cattle back to marry some woman who is not a witch."

SUICIDE AMONG JOLUO

We have discussed the Luo attitude toward death at some length in our description of homicide. These attitudes apply equally to suicide, except that they are extended to an association of the idea of death and its concomitant link with the supernatural to self-destruction, as an assurance or determination on the part of the individual to hasten the day when supernatural forces can be made to bear on the frustrations which led up to the act of suicide. The motives for suicide are thought to be to avenge the deed by the malevolent supernatural forces which at death become allied to the dead, who are able to use them against those on earth to solve problems which they found beyond human solution.

Throughout childhood there is constant reference to suicide, and in adolescence, early marriage, and old age the threat of suicide is an effective technique used by the Joluo to achieve goals or to avoid distasteful consequences. Threats are not often put into practice because they are used only when their effectiveness is relatively assured.

Unfortunately for the student, suicides are not usually reported to the authorities, although legally they should be. Therefore, few cases are recorded as in advanced countries in the coroner's court. The Joluo believe that suicide brings *chira* to a large segment of the clan of the suicide, and it is therefore kept as quiet as possible and dealt with immediately by the clan elders and clan medicine men, *jobilo*. The family of the suicide are forced to perform cleansing rituals and ceremonies before they may again participate in the social life of the clan. Data are for these reasons hard to collect. The few cases which were brought to the attention of the authorities were only those suspected of having been cases of murder which were made to look like suicide.

During a two-year tour among the Joluo tribes of Central Nyanza, I was able to collect 220 cases from informants. Of this number, 90 were male suicides and 130 female. I have selected for the purpose of this chapter 10 male cases and 13 female cases as typical, and these were investigated in more detail to provide examples. Considerable time was spent among the villagers in each case, and full discussions were held with the elders in an attempt to determine the motive and the events which led up to the suicide. For obvious reasons, I shall not use correct names when describing these cases.

MALE SUICIDES.

Male suicides in Luo usually follow loss of status. Seven of the ten cases can be so classified. The first five are of the type which involved intense emotional feelings of shame, loss of honor and status within the framework of the indigenous culture. Following these are two case histories of suicides which involved loss of status in the acquired or modern sense. Two cases will be described which involved the loss of status through poverty and the loss of traditional respect of sons, and finally one case which resulted from social ostracism.

The first suicide concerned a man whose younger brother married before he did. In Joluo society, men of the extended family marry in strict order of status, that is, the senior son of the senior wife must marry first. It may happen that he is younger in chronological age than, perhaps, a son of a more junior wife, but even in this circumstance, the younger son in years, who is senior in status, is technically married before his brother—that is, the payment of the first animals for a young girl allow the senior son to marry.

Suicide Case No. 1.

A young man who was the senior son of a senior wife was chronologically the oldest of all the sons in the village. His father and mother were both dead and, although he would eventually become head of the homestead, until he married he was regarded as a juvenile. The homestead was supervised by the levir of his father's second wife. The young man desperately wanted to marry. His stepmother, however, had spread the rumor that he had had syphilis. Therefore none of the eligible girls would have him. He went to a medical dispensary off and on for several months but treatment was not successful.

While he was away, a half brother, the son of the senior living wife of the village, married without his knowledge. The young man obviously had been under intense emotional strain caused by the rumors and gossip associated with the fact that he had a venereal disease. He was the senior son by Luo customary law and on marriage would be the head of the village. His half brother had taken a wife. This added to the humiliation and shame and would bring ridicule upon him whenever he met with his contemporaries for the rest of his life. This was too much. He went to the *thim*, the no man's land surrounding his clan grazing area and the place where the ancestors are normally placated, and there hanged himself from a tree.

His brothers and relatives were concerned about his absence and suspected what he had done. He was found by one of them after many days and his family and minimal lineage group completely destroyed the tree, including the roots, and there on the spot buried him and performed his funeral rites. The family was cleansed by the *jabilo* and the ancestors placated to receive his spirit by the sacrifice of a white cockerel and a black sheep.

The first son to be born to his brother's marriage was named after him to placate his spirit and to continue his name in the lineage genealogies.

Naming a child for a relative who had died is used by the Joluo in many ways, but only after consultation with the *jabilo*. It is obvious therefore that any misfortune which occurred to the family or to the lineage segment after this suicide was attributed to it. The fact that the first child born after the suicide was given his name reveals their attempt to avoid the consequences of his act.

The second case arises from a breach of customary law which in the old days would have meant banishment but which today brings social ostracism.

Suicide Case No. 2.

The suicide was caught in the act of intercourse with his full brother's wife. The Luo believe that such an act involving members of the same *Jokamio* (that is, those descended from the same mother or grandmother) brings *chira* to the whole clan. The security and solidarity of family relationships are threatened by the act because it involves quarrels which may lead to violence within the primary segment of the clan. In this case the brother did not tell the elders of the clan but merely threatened to do so. The guilty man returned to his own homestead and hanged himself in his hut. The house was destroyed and members of the extended family were cleansed by the *jabilo*. The cleansing ceremony took the same form as in the first case, with the addition that the village was sprinkled with medicine in order that it might continue to be used by the dead man's family.

In the next case there are two clear motives which led to the suicide. The first, perhaps the most important, lies in indigenous beliefs and attitudes, while the second lies in more modern attitudes.

Suicide Case No. 3.

This Luo was about 30 years old and had been employed as a driver for the Government for many years. Drivers in Kenya receive a relatively high salary, and in addition some take advantage of their position and make extra money by illegally charging people for transportation. Through these activities, he became a relatively rich man and was able to marry a total of five wives at his comparatively young age. He was also wealthy

in cattle, and had a permanent modern house at his homestead where four of his wives cultivated large gardens. His
fifth wife lived with him at his place of employment. At the
time of his suicide he was in the process of marrying a sixth
wife when, during one of the marriage ceremonies at her village, a brother of the bride objected to her becoming his wife.
He charged that the man had already too many wives and
could not look after them. As proof, he offered the evidence
that his most recent wife, the fifth one, was no more than a
prostitute and that he, himself, had used her on several occasions. This caused a fight in the village and quarrels which
led to the exchange of many curses between the two groups,
and therefore the wedding could never take place. The driver
returned to his homestead to confront the wife named in the
incident with the accusation and, in typical Luo fashion, she
calmly admitted her guilt, chiding him to do something about
it. He beat her severely and she ran from her house and spent
the night in the bush. He brooded all night on what had happened and on the shame his wife had brought him. Moreover,
he knew that he was shortly to be accused of fraudulent con-
version of funds by the Government and would lose his job,
if he did not end up in prison: neither of which were considered really serious. However, in his emotional state, these
must be considered as contributory causes. He could see his
whole world collapsing around him.

The next morning he sent his servant, a young lad, to the
butcher's shop for meat in order to get him out of the way. He
then hanged himself from the ceiling of his hut.

My Luo informants state with confidence that the prime
cause of this suicide was the behavior of his wife, which had
brought shame to a proud and successful man, so that he could
no longer face his friends. The fact that the Government was
interested in recovering a large sum of money which he was
alleged to have used for his own purposes is, in my opinion
however, a contributory factor.

Suicide Case No. 4.

A young lad aged about 23 years was being married to a girl from a neighboring location. He had paid a portion of bride-wealth and many of the early ceremonies had been performed. His bride had returned to her home as is the custom until he had paid the remainder of the bride-wealth. He went to his father-in-law to discuss the last and final payment, with his *jagam* as witness, and the father-in-law agreed that a milch cow would complete the payment. He returned in high spirits to the home of his father and asked for the cow, stating that this was all the father-in-law demanded. His father told him that if he had not paid enough, then the father-in-law must be a bad man and the girl was not worth having. The father and the son quarreled, and during the quarrel the son threatened suicide if he did not get the animal. The next day the son took a cow by force, while his father was absent, and sent it off to his father-in-law by a group of herd boys. When the father returned, he was furious at what his son had done and went after the cow himself. He caught up with the boys and brought the cow back to the village.

The son had warned his father that, if he should take this course, he would hang himself, and, as he saw the father returning in the distance, he hanged himself from a tree which stood just outside his father's village. This tree, as is the custom, was completely uprooted and destroyed.

The next cases are two which were due to modern circumstances but which in a sense involve the loss of status and therefore brought shame to the individual.

Suicide Case No. 5.

A young man eloped with the wife of a Kikuyu in Nairobi, far from his homeland. Whereas in Luo customary law to run off with the wife of another man is not considered to be particularly serious, in Kikuyu customary law it is regarded as a criminal offense. He was caught, and the Court fined him a relatively large sum of money and gave him thirty days in which to pay. He became very depressed and, after unsuccessful attempts to raise the money, he hanged himself.

Suicide Case No. 6.

The man involved was in his early thirties, and was in a position of trust with a Local Government body in Nyanza Province. He was alleged to have abused his position of trust by embezzling a considerable sum of money. The auditors had come across this defalcation in the books and brought it to his attention, but before he was arrested he killed himself by falling on a knife. Both the cause and the method can be said to be modern.

Case numbers seven and eight involve a loss of status, but on the other hand are attributable to poverty.

Suicide Case No. 7.

An old man whose wives had all died had to depend on his sons for support. The sons supported the old man while in his village but, after a quarrel, built a new village of their own and refused to build a house for him. As he had no one to support him and as he felt that he was ostracized by his sons, he had, to quote the Luo elders, "No other recourse than to commit suicide. His sons killed him and will suffer." He hanged himself on a thick tree which grew by a river, where he was found by an ex-chief. The Luo elders were quick to point out that he achieved his revenge, because the descendants of his sons were already few in number and mostly girls. "The line will die out because they killed him."

Suicide Case No. 8.

The man in this case was a widower living with his only son, who gave him food, but could not afford to maintain the appropriate prestige of beer parties and entertainment of his father's friends. On the day of the suicide, a group of the father's friends arrived at the village and the father asked his son's wife to prepare food and drink for them. This she refused to do, so that night he burned himself in his house, which the Luo believe brought ruin to the lineage and particularly to his son.

The next case is an interesting one because it illustrates an inherent Luo trait: the profound jealousy of anyone who is successful.

Suicide Case No. 9.

The man who died was the brother of the suicide in case number 2, and took the latter's wives as leviratic wives. He also inherited his gardens. Shortly after this, he began to prosper phenomenally. The elders state that his cattle produced mostly heifers and some produced twin heifers. His crops were better than his neighbors, so they began soon to suspect him of witchcraft. In the space of a few years as his prosperity increased, he was more and more ostracized from the activities of the community. The final blow came when his own *libamba*, minimal lineage group, denied him entrance to a lineage sacrifice on the grounds that he was a witch. Ten years after his brother's suicide, almost to a day, he hanged himself.

When the elders were questioned as to whether or not this man was a witch, they replied that he could not possibly have been a witch, because he had committed suicide. If he were a witch, his medicine would have been so powerful that the effect of being ostracized by the community would not have bothered him at all, let alone driven him to suicide.

The Luo believe that those most likely to commit suicide are those who have descended from a lineage in which there has been a history of suicide. Case number 2 was the brother of case number 9, and case number 5 the son of case number

9. This example is used time and time again by the Luo to prove the point that the tendency to commit suicide is inherited or caused by ancestors.

I was able to follow one particular series of events in connection with Luo marriage laws and customs over three years, which began with the elopement of a girl and her lover, and ended in suicide only a month before this chapter was written.

Marriage in Luo is traditionally arranged by the family of the boy and the family of the girl. Not infrequently, because of debt or close friendship, a father may promise his daughter in marriage to a friend or creditor while the girl is still very young. He obtains the animals to which he is entitled (*dho i keny'*) approximately one half of the final bride-wealth, at that time and the girl is known as *nyar kiseke*, "the wife of the beer reed," as this arrangement is usually contracted and finalized at a beer party. So it was in the case we are about to describe.

Suicide Case No. 10.

The girl in this case had been promised by her father when she was but three years of age to a friend of his own age group. The father, Opio[2], was a well educated Jaluo, and by the time his daughter, Akech, was ready to be taken in marriage, at the age of 18, he was employed as the headmaster of an intermediate school administered by a local mission. He had insisted that his daughter be educated to enhance the final payment (*dho miluhini*) of her bride-wealth. She was, for an African woman, a well educated girl. She had received a secondary school education where, in this particular segment of the Joluo tribe, fewer than 1 per cent of the girls have had as much education.

Akech had been prepared for this event all her life. She knew her future husband and from a child, each time he visited

[2] All names are fictitious, but common Joluo names.

the village, she would be teased and chided pleasantly about the fact that he was her future husband. Perhaps she would have been married sooner, had her future husband, Opala, not been employed in a city many hundreds of miles away. He returned on his long leave to consummate the marriage at the time when the girl had just finished her secondary education and was about 18 years of age.

While at school, however, Akech had fallen in love with a teacher, Okare, in a neighboring technical school and he was determined to marry her. He went to her father and pleaded to be allowed to repay the bride-wealth animals her father had received years before and to complete the bride-wealth payments to marry the girl by Luo law and custom. Opio adamantly refused, and her brothers threatened Okare with physical violence if he should try to see the girl again. Okare was heartbroken and returned to his place of employment. Akech, however, had other ideas. When she was told that the date of her wedding had been fixed, she pleaded and tried every traditional way of breaking the marriage, but was unsuccessful. Her father and her prospective husband remained adamant.[3]

The night before the wedding, she ran away from home to join Okare at his place of employment. Both knew that they would be pursued by the girl's brothers and by her father, so they hired a car and fled to the boy's village in a distant Luo tribe, some 200 miles away. Her father, brothers and future husband pursued the lovers to Okare's village where the father had him arrested for taking Akech from his custody. Okare's brothers, however, took the girl to Nairobi to hide her pending the result of the case. One of the brothers was then arrested for aiding and abetting the elopement.

Now the essence of this case goes to show that the father

[3] By tradition, a girl may run off to the home of a "bride," thus to marry will produce sterility. She may climb a tree *bondo*, an *euphorbia*, which is believed to be closely associated with the ancestors. There are several other ways, all of which would cancel an ordinary wedding, but none is effective in the case of *nyar kiseke*.

wanted the best of two worlds. Traditionally, elopement (*por*) is justified and is legal, albeit more difficult in cases of *nyar kiseke*, providing that the young man has stated his willingness to pay bride-wealth and has been refused. Moreover, it is the last remaining traditional way by which a young woman, forced to marry against her will, is able to break the arrangement. To-day, however, because there are so many illegal unions, the African courts take a serious view of young men and women running off to the towns without the slightest intention of paying bride-wealth.

While Okare and his brother were retained in gaol, pending the case, the girl's father and her brothers went to Nairobi, where they found the girl after some difficulty and took her back to her village by force. There they married her to Opala and he, with two of her brothers, took her by force to the place of his employment which was in another territory nearly 700 miles away.

Opio, who was an influential man in his district, then pro-ceeded with the case against Okare and his brother. The Court decided in favor of Opio, ordered compensation for the ex-penses he had incurred securing the return of his daughter. Okare and his brother were heavily fined for having taken the girl from the protection of her father. The compensation and the fine amounted to a very large sum of money and the boy appealed to the District Officer's Court. Pending the Appeal, he went to search for new employment at Nairobi. Akech, in the meantime, had arrived at the home of her husband in the far away city, only to find that he was already married and that his first wife, as a Christian, refused to have her in her home. Quarrels and arguments began in earnest, with the re-sult that Opala had no alternative but to send the girl back to her father and to demand a divorce. Akech, however, did not go home but returned to Nairobi to Okare.

The father heard what had happened and, in the shame and humiliation, hanged himself in a classroom at the school where he was headmaster. His final act was to write to all those involved in this series of incidents, which had taken nearly three years, to the effect that his daughter had killed him, that shame was brought to his clan and lineage, and that the liaison she had formed with Okare would end in disaster. He swore he would return in spirit to ensure that the marriage would end in failure.

It can be seen from this case that the difficult transition faced by even the most educated Christian Jaluo is complicated by the intense residual customary law and the attitudes of the people regarding the authority of a father and the duty of his daughter to this authority. The father in his case was a well educated, highly respected, important person in his district. The daughter, by her behavior, had humiliated him and he took recourse in indigenous rules and beliefs to solve his problems. They were initially successful. In the end, however, the threat to his status as a Christian of the fact that he had married his daughter by force to a Christian who was already married and therefore a bigamist in the eyes of the Church, brought shame and disaster to his social position as a Christian headmaster. His final act, however, was typically an indigenous one. He would not face the shame and humiliation brought to him by the course of events, so he took refuge in traditional recourse to suicide as a curse to the future happiness of those whom he thought had caused his grievance. To the end, therefore, he struggled to obtain the best of two worlds.

FEMALE SUICIDES

The most common cause of suicide among females is domestic quarrels and, coupled with that, the fear of physical violence from their husbands. Secondly, jealousy between co-wives; thirdly, the result of extreme grief, and finally, illness.

In the first category, out of the thirteen cases recorded from our sample, seven were of the domestic quarrel type. Of these, one was complicated by a curse from the husband, another from the fear of consequences arising from the behavior of her son and, in two cases, there was a suspicion that the women did not in fact commit suicide, but were murdered by their husbands in such a way that it looked as if they had committed suicide.

Suicide Case No. 11.

A young woman was accused by her husband at a beer party of having slipped quietly out for intercourse with a man from the village. To prove that she was innocent, she hanged herself on a tree which was near the homestead. If she had been guilty, the Joluo argue, "she could have been cleansed, but she could not be cleansed for having done nothing."

Suicide Case No. 12.

A young wife, newly married, had offended her husband in some way and he refused to eat her food. (This is a customary curse and is a very severe punishment to a wife.) She threatened to kill herself if he did not eat it. He then took the food to the senior wife, who ate it, adding insult to the injury already done. The young wife went to her hut where she stood on her grinding stone and hanged herself from the roof.

The elders were quick to point out in this instance that since her death the village had been abandoned and many children of the lineage had died. All this, they believe, was caused by the ghost of the abused wife.

The third case involved a young girl who committed suicide because she did not wish to marry the person chosen for her by her parents.

Suicide Case No. 13.

A very young girl, little more than a child, objected in the traditional way to the union which her parents had arranged.

The parents insisted that she be sent or "dragged" to her husband. On the night of the ceremonial defloration she committed suicide by hanging. This act is said to have brought a curse, not only to the prospective groom's homestead, but also on her own minimal lineage. Her mother was so struck by grief that she committed suicide later. The mother's case will be discussed below as case number 21.

The next two cases are those where foul play was suspected.

Suicide Case No. 14.

A woman was found hanging by a rope at night by her husband. He dug her grave and had buried her in the morning. In evidence given at the preliminary inquiry witnesses testified to the fact that she and her husband quarrelled some hours before her death, as the result of a beer party, and that she had left early for her own village. The body showed signs of having been beaten, but her husband argued that he had beaten her after she had hanged herself, as is the custom of the Joluo.

The case was not tried for lack of evidence, and the husband's family believed that she did in fact commit suicide, whereas her family believed that she was murdered.

It is significant to note that the husband did not claim the return of bride-wealth, as he would likely have done had it been a clear case of suicide. Neither did her family offer to repay the bride-wealth, or to give another girl in lieu of bride-wealth, as they might have done had the husband been clear of blame.

Suicide Case No. 15.

A woman had quarrelled with her husband because she alleged that he would not give her her proper share of sexual pleasure. The argument involved other wives and they told this woman that her husband hated her and that she would be better dead. The next morning she was found on her bed, having been killed by a knife or having inflicted a fatal wound on herself with a knife.

As in the previous case, the woman's family believed that she was murdered and the man's family believed that she committed suicide. It is difficult to say which version is true. It is extremely unusual, however, for a woman to kill herself with a knife, and I have not recorded another case. There was one case among the men, Number 6, but this was a modern "intellectual," who lived in a Council house with a plastered ceiling, which was hardly suitable for hanging in the traditional way.

The next case is the one mentioned earlier involving a woman's fear of the consequences of her son's behavior.

Suicide Case No. 16.

The woman in this case was the wife of a squatter who was a servant to an important Chief. The Chief helped him to get married to this woman, a local girl who was in fact related in some way to the Chief. After his establishment as an affine of the Chief, the *jadak* became very wealthy and built his own village on a place allocated by the Chief. He married a second wife after the building of his village and, just before the case we are discussing, married a third wife. The first wife had many children, most of whom were daughters. At the time of her suicide, all but one had married and her house was very wealthy. The houses of the other two wives were therefore extremely jealous.

One day during the short rainy season, the owner of the village, the husband, wished to make a present of *sim-sim* to his Chief and benefactor in order that he might pay the tax which at that time was calculated on the number of wives and also to pay the traditional tribute to the Chief. The woman's son at about that time invited a large number of guests to his village and demanded that his mother give him *sim-sim* with which to entertain them. She refused because she knew her husband intended to use the entire crop. The son disobeyed his mother and took the *sim-sim* by stealth. When the husband came to collect it for the Chief, he found that a large portion of it had disappeared. This caused a bitter quarrel between him and the boy's mother.

In fear of the consequences of what her son had done, the woman placed a rope, which was used for tying up one of her cows for milking, in a small basket and went out of the village as if to collect vegetables. She went to one of the largest trees in a nearby valley which was hidden from sight by thick bush and there hanged herself. My informant then described the scene as follows: "The first person who found the body caned it very hard and, after having cut the rope, started mourning. The place was soon filled with people and some were asked to bring hoes, axes, and *pangas* to destroy the tree. There and then people of the village and her lineage started their work and within a day the tree was completely destroyed and all the roots dug up from the ground and burned."

"When I asked why the tree was being destroyed," the informant went on, "the elders told me that it was being done to stop more people from hanging from it, for we Luo believe that hanging is inherited by different people in different clans. If a clan had not had a person hang himself before, it is difficult for one in that clan to hang himself or herself. If a tree on which someone had hanged himself was allowed to remain, it would drag other people to it for the same purpose."

The next case involves a curse as well as domestic trouble.

Suicide Case No. 17.

The husband of this suicide had been having considerable trouble with his cattle and many were dying from disease. The beginning of the illness coincided with the elopement of her daughter with a young man who had neither paid bride-wealth nor seemed likely to pay it. Her husband blamed his misfortunes on this incident and his suspicions were confirmed by the local prophet (*jabilo*). When he returned to the village from his visit to the *jabilo*, he cursed his wife as follows: "I wish the disease which killed my heifers would kill you, my wife, for your daughter is a whore who has brought the disease of her womb to my cattle." From the evidence, the woman seemed to have planned her death carefully. She made her daughters swear that they would not be married to anyone who would ever give her husband cattle. She distributed all of her belongings to them and placed a curse on the village to the effect that her husband should never be able to marry another wife. She then entered her house and hanged herself.

Since that time, the Luo pointed out, his daughters have all eloped with persons who have not paid bride-wealth and no other woman has ever consented to marry him or to live with him.

The next case is typical of many which involve jealousy at the taking of a second wife, especially without the first wife's permission, or as in this case, expressly against her wishes. My informant was living near the village when the suicide took place and his mother became involved in it. The story was told to me in his mother's presence and she helped with the details.

Suicide Case No. 18.

A man, Okech, who was happily married, invited his wife's sister, Apolo, to come to live at his homestead to act as a nursemaid for their first child.[4]

---

[4] This is common practice among the Joluo and often the "nurse" (*japidi*) is later married by her brother-in-law, especially if the sisters cooperate and agree to be happy together. Frequently the *japidi* will form a strong attachment to her brother-in-law, and marriage becomes desirable or even necessary. If a man marries a *japidi*, she becomes known as *nyar siweho*, the wife of the same blood, and the children of both wives share the same hut and trace descent through the elder sister. The term *siweho* is also used to describe a girl given to replace a sister who was unable to bear her husband a son; it therefore does have a slight connotation of stigma.

Okech decided to marry the nursemaid but his wife adamantly refused to agree. Okech beat her severely and she ran home to her parents where she remained for several weeks. Her sister, Apolo, continued to live in the village and by now cohabited openly with the husband as if they were man and wife. The wife eventually returned and made an effort to accept the situation as it existed. The husband built Apolo her own house as the second wife (*nyachira*) in the customary place in the homestead, but had not paid bride-wealth. In fact, he had not completed (*riso*) bride-wealth of the first wife, which added tension to the situation.

All appeared to go well until one night Okech returned from a beer party and abused his wife. What was more serious, he went to the hut of Apolo to sleep although it was the customary period of the month when he should have gone to the house of his first wife.

Early the next morning, the wife visited the mother of my informant and insisted that she accept as a gift her cooking pot and other household utensils. Her excuse was that she had bought new ones. She returned to her house where she packed the utensils and sent Apolo to carry them to my friend's mother. Meanwhile, Okech was sleeping.

She then hanged herself from a rafter in her hut. The noise of her strangulation awakened Okech, who cut the rope and made frantic efforts to revive her with water and to cane the body in the customary Luo manner. His wailing brought his brothers and relatives from their homesteads nearby.

When Apolo returned she was confronted by the irate brothers of Okech who accused her of being a witch who had brought *chira* to the village and to the lineage. They beat both Okech and Apolo and drove them from the homestead. The hut in which the woman had hanged herself was then immediately destroyed.

Apolo was not allowed to enter the homestead of her father who, with his sons, drove her from the clan area by thrashing her with canes. She never returned to the district. In time Okech was forgiven and returned to his homestead. He never remarried, but now lives with two leviratic wives.

Suicide Case No. 19.

This suicide was the junior wife of a very wealthy man. Although he was wealthy, he did not provide the modern luxuries for his wives which are now becoming customary and which carry high status among women. This woman decided that she would take matters into her own hands and killed a goat belonging to herself in order to sell the meat at the market to get money and millet, so that she could get the things that she desired. When her co-wives saw what she had done, they took part of the millet and some of the money. The woman appealed to her husband, but he sided with his other wives. That evening she went into the bush near the village and hanged herself.

Suicide Case No. 20.

This woman was the second wife (*nyachira*) of a wealthy man who preferred his first and third wives to her. This preferential treatment gave them courage to abuse her often and to show her that they were the only wives of the husband. On one occasion, when she was quarrelling with the husband, the other two wives joined in and beat her and abused her. The husband looked on in amusement. Shortly after, he took hold of her son and began to cane him, saying that he was as bad as his mother. His mother tried to interfere, but was prevented from doing so by her co-wives, who continued to beat her. As soon as it got dark that night, she disappeared. Her son had run away to her mother's home. The people from the village and her relatives searched for her for three days, and at the end of the third day, her people began to mourn as if she were dead. The head of a goat was buried in front of her house to represent her body, for they were certain that she was dead and her body devoured by wild animals.

The elders claim that her life was a tragic one, and that her sister had hanged herself a few years before and had returned for her.

The next case is the one mentioned earlier in connection with case number 13 involving the mother of a girl who had committed suicide after her mother had forced her to marry against her wishes.

Suicide Case No. 21.

This mother realized that her daughter's death was due to her action. She therefore tried to commit suicide by hanging shortly after she heard the news, but was prevented from doing so by her husband and his children. A week later, she tried to hang herself on a tree by the river but she had been followed by her co-wives, who cut her down in time. Finally, a month later she hanged herself from the roof of her hut and, although she was cut down while still alive by her watchful co-wives, she died shortly afterwards from a broken neck.

Profound grief lay behind the next case. It was related to me by an informant who was present at the time.

Suicide Case No. 22.

A man in the prime of life died suddenly. His death came as a shock to all his friends and relatives, among whom he was regarded very highly. This man had two wives and a mistress (*nyas gogo*). The latter was away at the time of his death visiting her family, and she had been cursed there by her father because she refused to return to the family into which she had been legally married. Her father refused to return the bride-wealth, or to accept bride-wealth from her lover, with whom she was living. When she returned to the village of her lover, she heard the wailing of the women and knew that her lover was dead. On such occasions it is customary to run into the village straight to the hut which houses the body and to fall prostrate on it, wailing and crying. However, on this occasion, the woman walked very slowly into the village as if in a daze and without crying and without wailing and without saying a word to anyone. She entered her house and locked the door. Those in the village immediately became suspicious and broke the door down but within those five minutes she was found dead from hanging. The villagers told me that she believed the curse of her father had killed the man she loved, so she went to join him.

Suicide Case No. 23.

An elderly woman, whose husband had died, depended on her children for sustenance. In her old age she contracted a disease similar to leprosy. Her son, as is customary on such occasions, destroyed her house in the compound and built one for her outside of the homestead. One morning they found that she had hanged herself because, they stated, of the pain and trouble she experienced through her illness and because she was so unhappy that she could not take her grandchildren to teach and love as was her role in life as a grandmother. Her illness barred her from all of the village activities, and she felt that she was no longer part of the family. Her ghost was not considered to be any more dangerous than that of a person who died a normal death because she was old and her suicide was from old age and weariness. She held no grudge against anyone.

8

HOMICIDE AND
SUICIDE AMONG THE ALUR

A. W. SOUTHALL

GENERAL accounts of the background to Alur society have already been given in several places,[1] therefore it is desirable to
be brief. The Alur live in northwest Uganda and the neighboring part of the Belgian Congo, but we are here concerned with
those of Uganda only. They are Nilotes of the Lwoo group.[2]

Both social organization and countryside show marked contrasts. Alur territory in Uganda can conveniently be divided
into lowland, midland and highland zones, stretching up west-
wards from the Albert Nile, 2,000 feet above the sea, to high,
hilly plateaux at an average level of 5,000 feet. The highlands
and midlands are now included in one administrative county,
called Okoro after its major chiefdom. The lowlands constitute
another county, called Jonam, which means river-dwellers. The
modern administrative chiefs of the counties are called *sultans*,
those of subcounties *wakils*.

Jonam contains a number of traditionally autonomous chiefdoms, all very small, but Ragem, which is larger than the rest,
aspires to dominate them. The midland zone traditionally consisted of numerous petty chiefdoms, ritually or even politically

---

[1] A. W. Southall, *Alur Society*, Cambridge, 1956, pp. 3-6 and 10-24.
A. I. Richards (editor), *Economic Development and Tribal Change*,
Cambridge, 1953. A. I. Richards (editor), *East African Chiefs: a Study
of Political Development in Some Uganda and Tanganyika Tribes*, London, Faber & Faber, 1959.

[2] See A. Butt, *The Nilotes of the Anglo-Egyptian Sudan and Uganda*,
International African Institute, London, 1952; J. P. Crazzolara, *The
Lwoo*, Part I, Verona, 1950.

214

dependent on the much larger chiefdoms of the highlands, and especially on Okoro itself, which was the largest of them all. The chiefdoms of Jonam were heavily influenced by Bunyoro in culture, while the highland chiefdoms were more independent in this respect.

The Alur usually held that no death was natural, in the sense that non-material, ritual, or supernatural causes accompanied the material circumstances of death, however self-explanatory these might seem. The non-material causes were sought out by divination, and might take the form of involuntary witches or malicious sorcerers, sometimes belonging to potentially hostile local groups such as the in-laws, or even the victim's own group as in the case of old, jealous, or barren women and solitary or non-conformist men. Or the causes might be the spirits of unassuaged ancestors, or other supernatural beings dwelling in springs, hills, rocks, caves, and trees.

While Alur have a term for illness, or disease (*twoo*), the word for death (*tho*) is commonly used instead. The terms for witchdoctor (*ajuoga*) and witch (*jajok*) are related to the concept of *jok*, or spiritual power, which is also used of the supernatural entity addressed in ancestor worship. *Ni nego* is to kill, *nek* is killing, and *ja-nek* a killer. Murder and manslaughter are not terminologically distinguished.

The Alur social system is characterized by a high degree of localization of patrilineages and also by the presence of embryonic forms of politically specialized chiefship. These two characteristics are relevant to the study of homicide. The solidarity of local lineage segments was very great. They were exogamous and potentially hostile to one another. The idea of homicide within these groups evokes great horror and was certainly rare. However, the reaction to it in such rare cases varied, like most elements of Alur culture, from one part of the country to another. Such homicide usually required ritual expiation, involving the slaughter of an animal by the killer's group for a feast of reconciliation. It might also require payment of a fine to the chief for the infringement of his exclusive powers of life and death over the subjects within his jurisdiction. The wilfulness and provocation of the deed also affected the reaction to it. Reaction to homicide occurring between local groups, instead of within them, depended on the degree of their relationship, that is, from the recognition of remote common clanship, to that of only common tribal membership or allegiance to the same chief, to the lack of any recognized common bonds between members of different neighboring tribes having no common political allegiance. In the latter case, the usual reaction was feuding and revenge with little chance for the payment of compensation in lieu. Homicide in these latter circumstances was therefore a very different offence from homicide occurring either within the same local kin group or even the same political jurisdiction. Contemporary Alur behavior suggests that this distinction persists, and that they have different moral feelings about violence committed on and among strangers, when they are away from home, from those they have about violence among their own kin or fellow tribesmen. This seems to be the most important influence of Alur traditional life on contemporary homicide.[3]

What net difference the imposition of colonial government on tribal political systems has made it is difficult to guess. Inter-tribal warfare, and perhaps more important, intra-tribal feuding, has been stopped. The capital powers of chiefs have been withdrawn and the killing of witches prohibited, though it occasionally happens still as a result of popular frenzy. The

---

[3] See *Alur Society*, pp. 121-125 and 136-142, where the sociological implications of Alur jural processes and, in particular, of the treatment of homicide, are dealt with. The question of homicide within a local descent group, and especially of fratricide, has been further explored by Schapera ("The Sin of Cain," *Journal of the Royal Anthropological Institute*, Vol. 85), who points out that the reaction to fratricide of the Biblical Hebrews depended "not so much upon fixed legal rules, as upon the size and momentary composition of the family, the domestic balance of power, the circumstances of the killing, the personal feelings of the people involved, and other factors of the same general kind."

projection of violence outside the local group is therefore more difficult than in the past. Acts of violence which the people still tend to regard in the same way as Western nations regard war casualties, have now become internal crimes against the state. On the other hand, modern war casualties cannot be comprehended by many unsophisticated Alur within their world of ideas. Alur deaths in the First World War led to the emergence of a new spirit cult. The political relativity of the concept of homicide is obviously of great importance in transitional situations.

ANALYSIS OF ALUR HOMICIDE

Inspection of all the case files for the ten-year period from 1945 to 1954, inclusive, revealed records of 51 cases of homicide involving Alur as defendants. Of these it was possible to analyze 47, the others being deficient or impossible to trace. These cases in fact involved 77 defendants, of whom 8 were not Alur. Of the 47 victims of homicide or attempted homicide, only 23 were Alur, 9 of the others being Ganda and 3 Ankole. Only 2 of the defendants were women, 1 of them jointly with her husband. Eight of the victims were women, including 1 baby girl. Thirty-four of the 77 defendants were not convicted, and in 17 out of the 47 cases there was no conviction. A *nolle prosequi* was entered in relation to 17 of these 34; 12 of them were acquitted, 1 was discharged, 1 committed suicide, and 1 entered a mental hospital. Of the remaining 2 cases, 1 was remitted to the District Court and no further record of it traced, while the other file was deficient on a number of points.

The incidence of homicide among the Alur is an approximately average one in relation to other Uganda tribes. This being so, coupled with the fact that the Alur are not one of the largest tribes, and that only half their population is in Uganda, meant that cases of Alur homicide were rather few for purposes of this analysis. This influenced me in including all cases coming up to the High Court during the ten-year period, whether they resulted in conviction or not. But there is also a more logical reason for inclusion. These cases were undoubted instances of homicide or attempted homicide. The reason why prosecutions may not result in conviction is usually lack of incontrovertible evidence, in a country where the forces of law and order are still comparatively primitive by Western standards and where formidable difficulties of communication arise from differences in language and culture. To exclude them would have been to omit a particular category of cases which are in certain respects characteristic. Ten of these 17 cases in which there is no conviction occurred outside West Nile, the home District of the Uganda Alur. Naturally, it is these cases in particular which involve non-Alur. They constitute a high proportion of the total of 26 cases which occurred outside West Nile District, and they accounted for 4 of the total of 8 non-Alur accomplices and 9 of the total of 24 non-Alur victims.

If there is one general deduction to be drawn from the Alur material it is that life in the migrant labor situation, in a rural community where immigrants of many tribes are mixed, is more conducive to homicide than life in a relatively unmixed tribal area. The question at once arises as to whether this might be due to homicide being chiefly committed by young men and the proportion of young men away from home being as high as the proportion of homicide committed away from home. Data on the age of defendants is probably unreliable and in any case deficient, its having been secured for only 50 per cent of the cases. For these, however, the average age was 30.9 years, with a wide range including two of 50 years and four others of 40 years or over.

A further difficulty arises from the fact that the census of 1948 treated the Alur and Jonam as different tribes. The result is that the latter are too small to enter the list of tribal totals for the Protectorate as a whole, and no estimate can be made of their numbers outside their home District. It is possible that

Jonam living in Buganda usually returned themselves as Alur in the census, but this is uncertain.

However, on the conservative supposition that the figure of 12,558 Alur males in Uganda outside West Nile does not include Jonam, the rate of homicide among Alur away from their home District is 1.75 per annum per hundred males. If Jonam were included as well, the rate would be 2.07. Both these are very high figures, and if for conservative reasons the lower one is taken the argument is not affected.

Whereas the rate for highland Alur at home is 0.385 (19 cases) and for lowland Alur at home 0.905 (13 cases), for highland Alur abroad it is 1.75 (22 cases involving 32). Of tribal rates in Uganda, only the Teso (2.87) and the Sebei (2.38) equal this.

It can therefore be stated that the most significant factor in Alur homicide appears to be life in the conditions which obtain in those areas to which Alur emigrate. In the remarks which follow, the four cases of homicide committed by Jonam outside West Nile are included. In this total of 26 cases, 22 occurred in Buganda, including two in the Kampala area. The others were in Bunyoro and Teso. In 12 of these cases the drinking of native beer or illicit spirit seems to have been a contributory factor. Many of these cases occurred in the context of a crowd of people of many different tribes who were happy to fall out with one another. Four of the cases involved theft, which was not a factor in any of the West Nile cases.

The homicide cases from within West Nile District express various interesting aspects of Alur culture and society. In one case a suspected witch was kicked and beaten while she was collecting herbs as antidote to the "death" which she was supposed to have put upon the dying wife of a kinsman of the man who attacked her. She was herself an old woman of about 60 and died of internal haemorrhage. In another case a man killed his wife in jealousy of a half-brother, with whom his wife had bathed at a spirit-possession seance. These are not orgies, but it is recognized that the ordinary canons of social relationship are to some extent in abeyance, and retribution after a seance for what would in ordinary life be regarded as misconduct is not considered right. In one of the two cases in which women were involved as homicides, a woman stabbed the co-wife whom her husband had inherited from his brother. The offense occurred in the heat of a quarrel which had arisen over discriminatory treatment of the two women's children. A man who had provided his son with two wives, from neither of whom had the son got any offspring, was said to taunt and abuse his son for thus wasting their patrimony. On one occasion when the two men were walking along, the son became so incensed at these taunts that he speared his father to death. In another case, strong antagonism had arisen between a young man and the older kinsman who had inherited his mother and so become his stepfather. A quarrel flared up over trivial articles belonging to the woman. After being thrown in wrestling the older man threw a spear at his stepson and killed him.

Several other homicides resulted from communal quarrels at dances involving rival clans or lineages. Two cases concerned the celebrated dynastic dispute which has rent Jonam County for fifty years. The traditional chief of Ragem was also Sultan of Jonam County as his father had been before him. He was assassinated in the presence of a government officer on tour, by the heir of the main rival chiefdom in Jonam County. The killer had been *Wakil* of his subcounty, but was dismissed because of a loss of government cash. This assassination fulfilled a prophecy that the Chief of Ragem would not maintain his position as Sultan of Jonam County unless he made a human sacrifice. He was succeeded as Sultan by his brother. The latter was subsequently sentenced to death by the High Court of Uganda for conducting a human sacrifice to consolidate his position. However, the Court of Appeal for Eastern Africa quashed this sentence. It was held that dynastic disputes of this sort, in largely illiterate communities, involved too great a risk of false evidence, given either in conspiracy or in fear of supernatural or political pressure, to permit that degree of certainty necessary for a conviction.

ALL CASES, IN AND OUT OF WEST NILE DISTRICT

A number of cases (19 out of 47) contain the suggestion or the open admission of drunkenness as a factor in the commission of violence. This is certainly a common idea among the general public, which is actually shared by the judges. It is therefore worth considering with a little more precision. As already remarked, 12 of the 19 cases occurred outside West Nile, one of them being a traffic accident. In no case could drunkenness be considered the sole cause of the offence, although in one or two instances the bone of contention between drunkards was exceedingly trivial. In general, the factor of beer drinking, and in one case of *waragi* (illicit spirit) drinking, seems to represent a lowering of inhibitions, which permits violence to result from pre-existing differences not otherwise sufficient to cause it. The cases show men falling out with one another, when drunk, over idle boasting, mutual insults, and abuse about women, or trivial disputes over property, in one case while gambling. Three of the cases in West Nile took place at dances. A certain amount of drinking always accompanies a dance. More important, perhaps, in the condition of Alur society, dances take place between different kin groups which always see one another in terms of rivalry. But it must be stressed here too that most of the cases which can in part be attributed to drunkenness took place away from home in the context of beer parties of the modern commercial type, where the brewer sells beer to all comers. Formerly, the Alur never drank beer in this way. As in most other tribes, beer was either drunk quietly by members of the family in the home of the brewer, or in recompense for cultivation by groups of kinsmen, neighbors and friends, or at various ritual occasions the solemnity of which precluded quarreling, or at certain stages of betrothal and marriage where again the etiquette of the situation ensured harmony, or at dances and certain other ceremonies. It is only in the latter (dance) context that drinking could justifiably be considered a potential incitement to violence, because of the presence of rival groups. Here too, modern changes have increased this danger. In the past, dances were of two types. They were either part of the funeral mourning, and were in fact referred to as mourning (*ywak*) and not dancing (*myel*) by the Alur, or they were a kind of ritual meeting between neighboring groups. On both types of occasion there were strong sanctions against violence. Dancing accompanied the funerals of great men only; funerals were a time of amnesty, when hostile feelings, if any, would be focussed against those absent persons held to be responsible for causing the death, usually by supernatural means. At these funeral dances, also, many chiefs and elders would be present, and strong action would be taken at once against the unruly. For the dances which were not a part of mourning, elaborate ritual precautions, occupying several days, were taken precisely to ensure that no persons should attend the dance with evil designs and that peace and harmony should prevail. In the context of the profound consensus in beliefs and morals, characteristic of traditional tribal society, such non-material sanctions were highly effective.

Consideration of the place of drunkenness as an incitement to homicide leads on to the further conclusion that Alur homicide never seems to be premeditated. Often it may be the unintentional outcome of a quarrel, as is indicated by the proportion of manslaughter charges in relation to those of murder. Even when convincing motives are apparent in the situation of the parties, these motives only lead to the commission of violence and homicide in moments of sudden and unforeseen excitement or release from normal inhibitions.

Abuse and obscenity about women is the commonest factor which raises a simple quarrel on the basis of underlying tensions to the pitch of violence. It was specifically mentioned in eight cases. It is a traditionally patterned theme in Alur culture. The stereotyped modes of abuse are to dare a man to copulate with his mother or to accuse him of doing so, and to accuse a man or woman of having red genitals or of sucking them (an admittedly impossible feat). To these are added the modern taunt of being a prostitute or of having a wife who is one. All these taunts can be exchanged with impunity by those who stand to one another in a culturally recognized joking relationship, such as that of mother's brother and sister's son. But if applied to anyone else it is recognized as a serious offense, causing extreme anger and probably violence.

The point already made about lack of premeditation is reinforced by consideration of the weapons used. Most frequent was a stick, club, or pestle (the heavy wooden pole used for pounding foodstuffs). These may normally be regarded as the instruments of attack most ready at hand, and not very dangerous ones at that. They were used in 22 cases. Judges usually rule out the charge of murder and reduce it to manslaughter where the instruments used were not likely to cause death. Knives or *pangas* were used in eleven cases and spears in five. Hoes were twice used, two other cases were of strangling, and two more were traffic accidents. One involved wrongful use of a hypodermic syringe (but the evidence was defective), one simply involved wrestling, and another contained no evidence of instrument.

GENERAL CLASSIFICATION

What has been said already extracts what appear to be the most meaningful conclusions from this material. The factors which have been treated so far are not mutually exclusive, and several of them may be combined as contributory to the same case. It is not easy to make a valid exclusive classification based on the predominant cause or motive of each offense, though it is desirable to attempt this for comparative purposes.

Motives have to be deduced from the total body of recorded information; they are hardly ever clearly stated at trial or at any stage of judicial investigation. As I have already stated, Alur homicide seems to be especially characterized by lack of premeditation and clear motive, and to be attributable in the largest number of instances to the conditions of life away from home in which few sanctions apply effectively. But of this general underlying cause the Alur concerned can hardly be expected to be aware. The judgments show that in many instances homicide was probably not intended.

The most numerous category, comprising 29 cases, can only be characterized as that of the mere quarrel. This includes 13 beer party cases and 2 more at dances. Two of the cases, occurring between rival kin groups, had former abductions as a stimulus. Four more of these cases occurred between close kin, that is brothers, near patrilineal kinsmen, stepfather and stepson, and father and son. Next come the 5 marital cases, 4 of which were between husband and wife and one between co-wives. Four concerned theft, two concerned chiefship, two arose from rape, though one of them was unsubstantiated, two were traffic accidents, one concerned a suspected witch, one took the form of brutal treatment of a prisoner by jailers, and one was a suspected case of illegal injection.

SUICIDE

When we come to the question of Alur suicide, other problems face us. One of the general points of interest attaching to this comparative study will doubtless be whether or not the incidence of homicide and suicide in a particular social system can be related in any consistent manner to other factors. It seems that certain factors lead to a high incidence of violence both against the self and others, as in the case of Busoga. But the Alur situation is not of this type. The apparent rarity of Alur suicide, coupled with the serious deficiencies of the records, inevitably make the following quantitative analysis unsatisfactory.

The coroners' records were searched for the whole period from 1936 up to and including 1955. For the years 1937, 1939, 1943, 1944, 1948, and 1949 records were totally lacking. For the years 1945, 1947, 1954, and 1955 they were so incomplete as to be for most purposes unusable. This leaves the ten haphazardly spaced years 1936, 1938, 1940, 1941, 1942, 1946, 1950, 1951, 1952, and 1953 for analysis. During these years there were only 3 cases of Alur suicide. Even granting the great difference in population size, there remains a striking contrast with the Soga, among whom Dr. Fallers recorded 85 suicides over a period of only 3 years.

Though the records of 1955, the most recent year for which they were available, had to be rejected because only 23 out of 46 death reports could be traced, these 23 included 3 cases of Alur suicide. While this year cannot be included in any reckoning of the incidence of Alur suicide over time, or in relation to other tribes, it is permissible to include these 3 cases in considering the general characteristics of Alur suicide. Even so, we have only six cases for analysis. To this a seventh can be added, which was found accidentally among the homicide records, belonging to the year 1948, for which the other death reports could not be found.

THE SEVEN INSTANCES OF ALUR SUICIDE

1. An adult hanged himself after hitting his mother on the head with a blunt instrument, as a result of which she died.

2. A married woman hanged herself after suffering for twelve years from an infirmity in her knee.

3. An adult male, a clerk in the African Local Government, hanged himself, apparently in distress at the fact that his wife, his grown daughter, and two small children had all died.

4. A man stabbed an unrelated neighbor after a quarrel in which insults were exchanged, he then committed suicide while in custody.

5. A man hanged himself immediately after the sudden ill-

ness and death of his two children. It was alleged that he feared the accusation of witchcraft.

6. A woman hanged herself after a very long illness in the course of which, it was claimed, she had already died and subsequently come to life.

7. A woman hanged herself to avoid a leviratic marriage with the brother of her husband who had been killed in the King's African Rifles.

From the above, it will be noted that of the 7 instances 4 concerned males and 3 concerned females. With the exception of the case which occurred in custody, for which further details were missing, all the suicides hanged themselves from trees. Only one of these cases concerned a highland Alur, 2 were from the midlands and 4 from the lowlands, one of the latter derived from a group of Madi incorporated with the lowland Alur.[4]

Remorse for violence, desperation in the face of chronic disease, escape from an unwanted match, and distress at the loss of wives and children, with its special importance in a social system which stresses agnatic growth, are all recognizable themes in suicide. Can the larger political unit of the highlands be linked with the lower incidence of suicide there than in the midlands and lowlands? Or are the relevant factors to be sought in ecological and economic contrasts between the backward, cattlekeeping, labor-exporting highlands, and the cotton-growing midlands with their greater cash wealth, and the disease-ridden lowlands with fishing as well as cotton-growing opportunities?

Nothing certain can be said on the basis of such inadequate data. The hypothesis which they suggest may, perhaps, be tested against the comparative material from other tribes included in this study. I have not yet been able to interview any members of the families of Alur suicides. In general, Alur

---

[4] For more detail on the ecological and sociological significance of these divisions, see *Alur Society*, pp. 10-13 and 218-19.

profess horror and disapproval, but do not suggest that suicides are denied burial rites, or the treatment appropriate to their status in the ancestor cult.[5] This lack of specialized attitudes is reflected in Alur speech, which has no term for suicide and can therefore only refer to it as *ni nego gire* (to kill oneself).

THE ALUR AND OTHER UGANDA TRIBES

Uganda lies at the cross-roads of most of the major linguistic groups of Africa, having Bantu, Nilotes, Nilo-Hamites, and Sudanics all within its borders. Languages have no established connection with social systems of those who speak them, but these major divisions are a sign of historical movements, and great contrasts in social structure are in fact associated with them. However, these do not appear to be associated in any straightforward way with the varying incidence of homicide, and the same is probably true of suicide.

Table 39 shows, for each of the main tribes, the average number of homicide cases per year, for the period 1945-1954 per 100,000 population, coming before the High Court of Uganda. Table 40 shows in the same way homicide cases occurring within home Districts in relation to the male population of tribes in their home Districts.

The implications of these tables are obviously inconclusive. Remarkable contrasts occur between the various tribes, indicating how meaningless it can be to talk of "Uganda Africans" in general, still less of Africans as such. But these contrasts certainly do not relate consistently to the tribal classification which is based on language. It is, indeed, interesting that the Nilo-Hamitic Teso, Sebei, and Kumam[6] stand out above all other tribes for the high rate of homicide among them. The Karamojong are also Nilo-Hamites, yet show a very different incidence. However, Karamoja District is unique in the Uganda Protec-

[5] *Op.cit.*, Chapter v.
[6] The Kumam are now, strictly speaking, Nilotic in speech, but are usually considered to be of Nilo-Hamitic origin.

TABLE 39. HOMICIDE IN UGANDA TRIBES

Average Annual Incidence per 100,000 population for the 10-year period
1945-1954

Sebei	11.6	Padhola	4.8
Teso	10.8	Lugbara	4.6
Kumam	8.6	Rwanda	4.5
Gisu	8.2	Karamojong	4.3
Rundi	7.5	Lango	4.3
Gwere	6.4	Soga	4.3
Ganda	5.9	Nkole	4.1
Acholi	5.9	Madi	4.1
Toro	5.6	Kiga	2.8
Nyole	5.6	Konjo	1.2
Nyoro	5.5	Amba	1.1
Alur	5.0		

torate for its insulation from the outside world. While the continuance of tribal raiding there might lead one to expect a high rate of homicide, these raids are of very irregular occurrence and, in any case, may not be reflected fully in the High Court figures.

Interlacustrine tribes, such as the Nyoro, Ganda, Toro, Soga and Ankole, show a fairly near incidence to one another. The very closely related Acholi and Alur are alike in the simple index of homicide per head, and very similar to the Interlacus-

TABLE 40. NUMBER OF DEFENDANTS INVOLVED IN HOMICIDE CASES

in Home District per Year per 1,000 Male Population
in Home District, 1945-1954

Teso	2.87	Soga	.89
Sebei	2.38	Madi	.86
Kumam	1.59	Karamojong	.85
Gisu	1.51	Lango	.81
Nyoro	1.38	Nkole	.79
Ganda	1.22	Lugbara	.65
Gwere	1.14	Alur	.54
Nyole	1.06	Kakwa	.51
Acholi	1.035	Kiga	.41
Toro	.96	Konjo	.14
Padhola (Dama)	.92	Amba	.08

trine Bantu, but they diverge sharply in the index of homicide to population in home District and differ again from the Nilotic Padhola. The Gisu and Kiga, both Bantu tribes outside the spheres of the Interlacustrine kingdoms, show no similarity, the Kiga having less homicide than any other tribes except the Konjo and Amba, whose populations are probably too small for their data to have significance, while the Gisu have the highest rate next to the Nilo-Hamitic peoples already mentioned, the Sebei being in fact their neighbors.

The conventional ethnographic classifications are, therefore, of little use. The contrast already demonstrated between small sections of the Alur tribe shows that only the most detailed and painstaking analysis of multiple factors has any chance of revealing significant correlations. Documented cases of homicide and suicide must be sufficiently numerous to be related to the relevant sex and age groups both in the tribal home District and abroad, at least to the extent of distinguishing male and female adults and children. Centralized and non-centralized traditional political systems must be distinguished, together with the implications for them of modern local government organization, and, over and above all this, that whole crucial complex of factors which centers about descent groups, localization, and marital stability. If all these factors could be isolated, the comparative study of homicide and suicide might shed great light on the significance of ethnic origins and of different types of social structure in relation to cultural values.

9

PATTERNS OF MURDER AND SUICIDE

PAUL BOHANNAN

THE contributors to this book, in part because of the free hand given them, have put forth several ideas that must be checked with other material, both in this book and from other sources. Bringing their information and ideas together into a comparative framework, related to other studies of homicide and suicide, necessitates first of all a classification of homicides. Three general classes of homicide appear in our data.

In a number of the societies studied, some homicide occurs in dangerous but not illegal institutions in which people participate at their more or less consciously acknowledged risk. Homicide occurs with some regularity in the course of action associated with such institutions, but is "accidental" and not necessarily part of that institution. Members of the society are aware that the institution is dangerous, and that participation in it may lead to such accidents. Our own society institutionalizes automobile racing, which is admittedly dangerous. Even automobile riding demands a certain calculated risk. In all instances save those which involve gross negligence, homicide which occurs in such an institution is classed as non-culpable.

A second type of homicide is also non-culpable, but whereas the first type occurs as a fairly regular but accidental or unfortunate event and is outside the recognized and intended course of events of any institution, this second type is institutionalized. Here homicide which is classed as non-culpable actually occurs as an institutionalized, recognized activity.

230

Omitting genocide (which Africans do not practice) and infanticide (which they no longer practice), there are two areas in which a society may institutionalize non-culpable homicide: the jural area and the ritual area. Institutionalized homicide in jural institutions is found in the Western world as execution of convicted perpetrators of specific crimes. It is carried out by officials of the state. In the societies examined here, "execution" is performed by other agents, but is still considered non-culpable and an institutionalized jural necessity.

Ritual killing, which is also a form of institutionalized homicide, is rare in this sample. It is suggested, and two or three cases of it appeared, among the Tiv, who, under certain conditions, consider it non-culpable. One Alur case is mentioned.[1]

We shall examine our material and these two types of non-culpable homicide before proceeding to those instances which are considered culpable in the societies in which they occurred.

Three of the seven societies represented here recognize institutions which are dangerous in that their activities increase the likelihood of homicide. Among the Tiv, the communal hunt with poisoned arrows is admitted to be extremely dangerous. Over 17 per cent of the Tiv homicides recorded occurred within this institution. The Luo of Kenya practice ritual wife-capture at marriage. They recognize it as a dangerous institution. They take both ritual and practical precautions to see that it does not end in "real" violence and in killing, but when it does so they make (or, in the indigenous system, made) ritual and domestic adjustments, not predominantly jural ones. The percentage of Luo homicides which fall into this dangerous institution pattern is much lower than that for Tiv, but it is nevertheless culturally significant. The Alur also have their "dangerous institution": dances which are attended by rival groups. The danger of these dances was recognized, and several days' ritual

[1] Details of this case are to be found in Aidan W. Southall, *Alur Society*, Cambridge, pp. 198-199.

precautions were taken to guard against untoward incidents arising from them. Although these "immaterial sanctions," as Southall has called them, were highly effective, some homicides did indeed occur at these dances. Such non-culpable homicides were unsanctioned and were usually unpunished.

In most African societies either today or in the recent past, some forms of homicide are positively sanctioned: this sort can be compared to execution. It is the duty—at least the right—of a person to kill some people in some situations. One such situation is the ritual of sacrifice. In some areas, such as nineteenth century Dahomey and Ashanti, human sacrifice was generally used as a means of executing criminals, although slaves might also be sacrificed. Many African peoples acknowledge—or in the recent past acknowledged—the necessity for human sacrifices in specific religious institutions. Occasionally newly institutionalized homicide, definitely extra-societal, such as Mau Mau killings or the Diretlo murders of Basutoland, springs up in Africa even today. Insofar as these institutions are acknowledged by the peoples of the tribes where they are found, homicides occurring in connection with them must be considered as ritual, non-culpable homicide. They are branded criminal by the British-dominated law in all cases, and by "native law and custom" in many, but not in all.

Tiv, even though they are extremely upset when such killings are believed to have occurred, acknowledge the right of the "league of witches" or *mbatsav* to make certain human sacrifices. It is difficult to draw an objective line between those cases which a people such as the Tiv consider legitimate and those they consider criminal because the view of different individuals may vary depending on relationship to the victim and other factors. Because most of the "victims" are "killed by witchcraft"—death considered by Europeans to be from normal causes—these cases do not enter the criminal records. Ritual homicide is rare in Africa, by European definitions. If we accept African definitions, it is much more frequent.

Much less equivocal is the non-culpable homicide that occurs within jural institutions. In Western society, most cases in which policemen kill in the course of their duties are dismissed as excusable or justifiable homicide. Cases in which the victim of homicide was involved in commission of a felony at the time of his death are often dismissed by coroners' courts or otherwise excused as justifiable. The difference between excusable and justifiable homicide in interpreting African data would be mere pedantry. But examining the sort of victim and the situation found in non-culpable homicide elicits African patterns which are comparable with, though notably different from, those found in other societies.

First of all, thieves either now are or in the past have been the victims of non-culpable homicide in most of the tribes examined here (the point was not mentioned for the Luo or Nyoro). Among the Soga, thieves were formerly subject to execution by their victims, though today Soga concur that such killing is felonious in spite of the fact that 15 per cent of Soga killings are classified as "self-help justice." There are examples of thief-killing for the Tiv, Alur, Gisu, and Luyia. Among Tiv, they accounted for over 6 per cent of the homicides for which records existed, of Alur, 4.2 per cent. Killing thieves has, of course, been universally proclaimed culpable homicide by the British governments. However, judges tend to be lenient to this type of killer.

Witches were or still are "fair game" in many African societies, and killing a witch was sometimes considered not only non-culpable but justifiable. The witch-killing pattern emerges unequivocally for the Luo, the Alur,[2] the Gisu, and the Nyoro. Luyia, with one example of a woman killing a female witch, shows the pattern, but in only a very small number of cases. Usually the witch is killed because he or she was bewitching the killer's kinsman. Among the Nyoro particularly, the witch is likely to be female. The Tiv situation of witch killing is more

[2] *Alur Society*, pp. 142-143.

equivocal. Killing a witch may be a jural act. Much more common, however, is killing a person thought to be killing one for ritual purposes. Instead of a jural or ritual act, this is an example of self-defense when the legal or ritual force of the community is directed against one. By their act of choosing a victim, the rationale goes, the community has placed him outside the pale of the law—he may fight with any weapons available to him. In all such homicides, which appear as a form of self-defense, the British judges tend to be lenient.

Killing an adulterer, although it is of course everywhere considered a felony under British law, was not considered by Gisu, Alur, or Luyia to be culpable. British judges, unless premeditation can be proved, usually consider adultery a mitigating circumstance in homicide cases, sufficient to reduce the charge to manslaughter.

Other non-culpable homicide patterns were mentioned for the Gisu, the Soga, and the Luyia: the Gisu claim that provocation by certain insults makes resultant homicide non-culpable; Soga (and probably all the others) defend their right to kill in self-defense; Luyia claim that killing in revenge for killing is not wrong, though they realize that it is today considered a crime under British law.

Finally, we must note the different attitudes that exist depending on tribal membership of the offender and the victim. Southall notes in some detail the differential attitude Alur have toward killing tribesmen and foreigners: Alur not only kill non-tribesmen more readily, but they claim that killing a non-Alur is less heinous. Although it is not recorded in the Tiv essay, I have on several occasions been told the same thing by Tiv—one man who had just been released after serving three years of a sentence for manslaughter of a non-Tiv thought his sentence grossly unjust because he had killed a mere stranger.

Africans tend to evaluate the culpability of homicide not only in over-all terms of the institutions with which it is associated,

234

but also by the relationship between the offender and the victim. The Fallers noted that Soga sometimes give the relationship between killer and victim as the reason for homicide. Even we, of course, recognize some degree of differential moral turpitude depending on the relationship. This problem becomes of major concern in analysis of culpable homicide.

By far the most homicides in our samples are culpable: homicide that is branded as wrong in the society in which it occurs and that indicates the anomic state of the institution with which it is connected. The most important single factor to keep in mind in a comparative study of criminal homicide is that it, like any other culture trait, must be studied firmly within its social and cultural setting. To lift a homicide out of its social context for comparison with a homicide in some other society or at some other time is to rob it of its significance and meaning. For homicide in a society does have meaning: after eliminating non-culpable homicide, we have a series of situations with which at least some people in the society could deal only by killing. Repetition of these situations indicates weak points, or points of stress, within the social organization of the group concerned.

Several factors are to be noted in studying the repetitive situations of homicide typical of various societies. First is the relationship between the criminal and his victim. Criminologists have only recently become interested in this relationship and, as we shall see, have not yet faced the task of interpreting the place of this relationship in a more general social and cultural setting. Wolfgang[3] has shown that some concern for the matter goes back as far as Tarde, but the only major source of theory on which he could draw for his Philadelphia material was Hans von Hentig's book, *The Criminal and his Victim*. We shall in turn interpret our data in connection with Wolfgang's Philadelphia study, since it is by far the most advanced and thoughtful analysis of the subject.

[3] *Op.cit.*, pp. 218, 246.

Hentig's and Wolfgang's books have shown that kinship and family relationships between homicide offenders and victims in Western society are comparatively simple—compared, that is, to Africa. Obviously this is a function of a simpler kinship system and of the reduced range of family relationships in modern Western life. Here I shall examine the African material on the basis of sex distinctions, comparing it with some material from modern Europe and America. Then I will proceed to a fuller comparison of the relationships themselves, first kinship relationships and then others.

Wolfgang has shown the necessity for keeping the offender and the victim figures separate when discussing homicide. In Philadelphia during 1948-1952, the time covered by his study, Negroes were 73 per cent of the victims and 75 per cent of the offenders; males were 76 per cent of the victims but 82 per cent of the offenders. Table 41 shows the rates per 100,000 in Philadelphia.

TABLE 41. HOMICIDE RATES IN PHILADELPHIA,
PER 100,000 POPULATION

	Victim	Offender
Negro:		
male	36.9	41.7
female	9.6	9.3
White:		
male	2.9	3.4
female	1.0	.4
Both:		
male	9.0	10.2
female	2.6	2.0

We cannot present data strictly comparable with Wolfgang's because the population counts and homicide records with which we worked in Africa are vastly inferior to those with which he worked in Philadelphia. However, two significant factors do emerge. First, it is obvious that homicide rates among American Negroes are several times as high as those among

African Negroes. Material from British East Africa (where the records are best and the police systems efficient in most areas) allows the comparisons made in Table 42.

TABLE 42. ANNUAL HOMICIDE RATE OF OFFENDERS
PER 100,000 POPULATION

Soga	4.0
Luyia: from	.7
to	7.9
Uganda Tribes: from Amba	1.1
to Sebei	11.6
Philadelphia Negroes, 1948-1952	24.6

If it needed stressing, here is overwhelming evidence that it is cultural and not biological factors which make for a high homicide rate among American Negroes. More homicides may go unreported in East Africa than in Philadelphia, but the difference would still be significant.

It is, of course, not our purpose to analyze the anomic position of the American Negro. But we note that insofar as homicide is indicative, his position is more grave than is that of socially dislocated African Negroes.

Second, African rates tend not only to be lower than American Negro rates, but lower than American rates for the general population, and strictly comparable with rates from Europe, as well as with other primitive societies where the information is available.

Differences between males and females both as victims and offenders have been of primary concern in most studies of homicide because the difference is so startlingly significant. In his Philadelphia study, Wolfgang found that 76 per cent of the victims and 82 per cent of the offenders were male, while only 48 per cent of the population of Philadelphia were males. Taking both Negro and white races, the male rate per 100,000 was 9.0 for victims and 10.2 for offenders, whereas for females it was only 2.6 and 2.0. Wolfgang's summary of the literature on

TABLE 43. ANNUAL HOMICIDE RATE OF OFFENDERS
PER 100,000 POPULATION

18 American cities, 1948-1952:[a]	
from Milwaukee	2.3
to Miami	15.1
Uganda Tribes: from Amba	1.1
to Sebei	11.6
U.S., 1946	6.3
Britain[b]	.5
Bison-Horn Maria[c]	6.9
Ceylon[b]: from Muslims	2.5
to Sinhalese	7.4

[a] Wolfgang, *op.cit.*, pp. 25.
[b] Strauss and Strauss, *op.cit.*
[c] Elwin, *op.cit.*

this subject[4] showed his figures approximately representative for America: most of the studies he cites found that between 70 and 80 per cent of the offenders were male; a few studies found an even higher proportion of males. In some European countries, he found, the proportion of females is very much higher: in England between 1900-1948, the proportion of females was 57 per cent of victims and 32 per cent of offenders, showing a ratio among offenders of 2 males to 1 female, compared with the Philadelphia rate of 5 males to 1 female. Pollak noted[5] that in Italy during the late part of the last century, the rate was 63 female offenders per 100 male offenders, that is, almost 40 per cent of offenders were women.

The proportion of female offenders in the African societies studied here is even smaller than it is in most Western communities. The highest proportion of female offenders, 9 per cent, was found in three tribes—Gisu, Nyoro, and Luo—while in all other cases the proportion was well below 9 per cent. The Philadelphia figure for female homicide offenders is 17.6 per cent. However, this figure is made up of two subcultures— Negro and white—which show very different homicide pat-

[4] *Op.cit.*, pp. 46ff.
[5] Pollak, Otto, *The Criminality of Women*, Philadelphia, University of Pennsylvania Press, 1950, p. 81.

terns. Of all Negro offenders, women are 20 per cent in the Philadelphia sample; of all white offenders, women are only 10 per cent. The African data, thus, indicate not only that Negro women are offenders in Africa even less often than Negro women in Philadelphia, but even less often than white women are offenders in Philadelphia. It may be argued, but is difficult to prove, that African women use poison and "get away with murder." However, this charge is brought against women everywhere in face of overwhelming lack of evidence.[6]

It is among victims that the greatest differences appear in the African societies. The number of female victims of homicide runs from 17 to 25 per cent among five of the tribes studied here (Table 45). This figure compares with 23.6 per cent in the Philadelphia sample (24 per cent for whites, 22 per cent for Negroes). In two of the African tribes, however, the proportion of female victims soars. Among Nyoro they reach 62 per cent of intentional killings, and among Soga 45 per cent of the total homicide victims. This high incidence of female victims occurs among the only two tribes of Interlacustrine Bantu represented here, suggesting that the position of women in those tribes is a focal point for difficulty. Both Beattie and the Fallers have in fact indicated in their essays that such is the case. Yet, there are two other tribes in our sample—the Gisu and the Luyia—who have been influenced by the Interlacustrine Bantu, particularly the Baganda. In neither case have the domestic institutions—if that is indeed what the high female homicide victim rate illustrates—been seriously affected by Interlacustrine patterns or attitudes.

When we consider the sex both of victim and of offender, as is set forth in Table 45, we find that for most of the tribes (the exception is Nyoro) the majority of cases are male victims of male killers. This figure runs from 55 per cent of cases among the Soga to over 75 per cent of cases among the Tiv. Only the Nyoro have the maximum in another area—56 per

[6] *Ibid.,* pp. 16-19.

TABLE 44. PROPORTION OF FEMALE OFFENDERS AND
VICTIMS OF HOMICIDE

	Total Cases	Female Offenders	Per Cent Total Offenders	Female Victims	Per Cent Total Victims
Tiv (accidents omitted)	122	5	4.0	22	18.0
Gisu	99	9	9.0	17	17.0
Nyoro (intentional killings only)	34	3	9.0	21	62.0
Soga	100	2	2.0	45	45.0
Luyia (those found guilty of murder or manslaughter)	80	4	5.0	19	24.0
Luo	47	4	9.0	12	25.0
Alur	47	2	4.0	8	17.0
Philadelphia			18.0		24.0
Britain			32.0		57.0

cent of cases are men killing women, whereas only 35 per cent
are men killing men. This fact may be accounted for by the
fact that the Nyoro sample takes only cases in which intent was
proved; the Alur sample shows 39 per cent of cases with female victims also show intent, whereas 61 per cent do not.

TABLE 45. SEX OF KILLERS AND THEIR VICTIMS

	Tiv	Luo	Nyoro	Gisu	Luyia	Soga	Alur
♂ kills ♂	75.4%	71.7	35.4	69.5	70.0	55.0	47.6
♂ kills ♀	16.4	21.7	55.8	15.1	20.0	43.0	14.3
♀ kills ♀	1.6	2.2	5.8	2.2	3.8	1.0	2.4
♀ kills ♂	1.6	2.2	—	7.7	1.2	1.0	—
Multiple victims or offenders	5.0	2.2	3.0	5.5	5.0	—	35.7

Veli Verkko has, on the basis of Scandinavian and some comparative data,[7] put forward some hypotheses about the proportion of female participation in homicide. Reduced to its simplest terms, he has postulated that the percentage of female

[7] Verkko, Veli, *Homicides and Suicides in Finland and their Dependence on National Character*, København, 1951, especially pp. 51-55.

participants (both victims and offenders) is high in areas where homicide is of low frequency, and low in those areas of high frequency. In other words, according to his hypothesis, homicide by female offenders is fairly constant, and the variation in rates found in various societies and at different times is accounted for by male offenders.

Among Philadelphia killers, Wolfgang found Verkko's hypothesis verified, but he rejected Verkko's explanation that the fact can be accounted for by biological qualities of the sexes.[8] Murderousness can no more be assigned as an attribute of one sex over the other than it can be assigned to one race over another, unless all other possibilities have been exhausted. Preliminary questions lie in the area of the adjustment of women to the roles that they play in their societies.

The African data do not verify Verkko's hypothesis. In all the societies we have considered, the homicide rate can be considered to be low, by Verkko's definitions. The range of female offenders is also low in all cases, while the proportion of female victims ranges from 17 to 62 per cent.

Although Verkko's hypothesis about female homicide rates is not valid for Africa, it would seem to be possible to formulate an hypothesis under which both Verkko's results and our own may be admissible: it may be that, in the vast majority of societies, men kill in the same situations and similar patterns as do women—and in some others besides. Save in situations of serious and widespread domestic stress, it is the "some besides" which most affects the rates and the changes of rates. This hypothesis makes two assumptions: that woman's primary concern is in the domestic institutions, that men must in addition adjust to other institutions. Although women may be better adjusted to the institutions in which they participate, their range of participation is in most societies narrower. The second assumption is that the homicide rate is composed chiefly of anomic homicide.

[8] Wolfgang, *op.cit.*, pp. 61-64.

There is, however, more to the study of offender-victim relationships than differential sex rates. Criminologists themselves
have done some further work in this regard, but for many of
them statistics and rates become an end instead of a means.

The first step that faces any student of the relationship between offenders and victims in homicide cases is how to classify
them. There is no "natural" classification; rather, the classification must vary with the society of analysis. How, then, do we
compare the various societies and their typical classifications?
I have worked in an *ad hoc* way, beginning with Wolfgang's
categories, which he derived from police files in Philadelphia,
and have added whatever categories I have needed to get three
African societies and a Danish sample sensibly onto Table 46.
This process has meant subdividing the categories almost every
time a new society is added. If the categories are broad enough
to be comparable, they are also more or less meaningless in
specific instances. Obviously, "family relationships" will not
work as a category in tribal society on the same basis as it will
work in modern Western societies. I have changed this category to "kinsmen (including affines)"—whereupon most of the
material other than spouses and parents from Western society
has to be put in a category called "other," for it is hopelessly
miscellaneous. Less obvious—but more difficult—is the notion
of "close friends" and "acquaintances" as cross-cultural categories. Friendship lacks the biophysical basis of comparison
that is evident in kinship. It also lacks any full-fledged cross-
cultural analysis that can be used as a background for classification. There is not, so far as I know, a cross-cultural study of
friendship.

However, when the data is forced onto a chart, to give us
at least primary comparability, several points do emerge. When
Tiv kill kinsmen, they kill agnates; when Soga and Philadelphia
Negroes kill kinsmen, they kill spouses; when Danes kill kinsmen they kill their children; when the Gisu kill kinsmen they
kill parents and spouses—theirs is, in fact, the only high in-

TABLE 46. VICTIM–OFFENDER RELATIONSHIPS

	Alur	Tiv	Gisu	Soga	Philadelphia Negroes	172 Danish Killers
Kinsmen						
Spouses	8.9	8.8	11.0	37.0	19.5	12.2
Other affines	–	5.5	5.0	8.0		
Parents	2.2	–	11.0	–		4.0
Children	4.4					33.1
Agnates	6.7	24.4		5.0		
Others	–	5.5	11.0	6.0	4.4	7.5
Sex partner or rival						
Paramour, mistress, or prostitute	–	2.2	–	2.0	10.0	8.7
Paramour of mate	–	7.7	3.0	–	3.0	
Rival	–			5.0	5.0	
Homosexual partner	–				.5	1.7
TOTAL	22.2	54.1	41.0	63.0	42.4	67.2
Close friend [same village or lineage]	–		17.0	6.0	31.0	4.0
Acquaintances	46.7	14.4			14.0	21.0
Stranger	8.9			10.0	8.0	7.6
Enemy	15.5				3.0	
Felon or officer	4.4	8.8	17.0	1.0	.5	
Innocent bystander	2.2				1.0	
TOTAL	75.7	25.2	34.0	11.0	57.5	32.6
Relationship unknown	–	23.3	24.0	20.0	–	–

cidence of killing parents. It also indicates that Philadelphia Negroes have much higher incidences of killing mistresses, sex rivals, or mates' paramours than do Danes or Africans. It shows that killing of felons is very much higher among Tiv and Gisu than among Soga or Philadelphia Negroes. These indications have to be explained.

First, however, we must examine in greater detail the patterns for killing kinsmen. Comparison is difficult because kinship systems and kinship institutions vary so greatly from one culture to another. For example, Svalastoga uses, for Danish material, the categories spouse, children, parents, secondary relatives.[9] As anthropologists are all aware, not a single one of these categories is unequivocal in the African situation—not even the first. "Parents" is likely to include mothers' sisters and fathers' brothers in many African societies. "Children" often includes all one's clansmen younger than oneself. And "secondary relatives" may be a satisfactory catch-all in European studies but, when applied to Africa, hides the most important aspects of the problem. Even when the precise biological relationship can be traced between an offender and a victim, it must still be evaluated in the kinship nomenclature and system of the society in which it occurs, else it will be without meaning. I have therefore tabulated the relationships first in general categories (Table 46) and then in Descriptive Categories (Table 47). Several interesting correlations emerge from this classification. We shall first list them before going more deeply into the institutional patterns of the societies in which they occur.

Only two kinship relationships between killer and victim were found in all tribes of our sample: in all tribes, wives were killed and brothers were killed. No other relationship between killer and victim is found in them all. Killing the father, fairly common among the Gisu and present among the other Bantu tribes, was absent among Tiv and Luo. However, killing fathers' brothers was of extremely high frequency among the Tiv, present among the Gisu, but not noteworthy elsewhere. Tiv and Luo are also the only tribes that show no examples of killing parents-in-law.

Although all tribes showed uxoricide—some of them very high rates of uxoricide—only two (Gisu and Tiv) showed any examples of killing a husband. In the one Tiv case, there was no intent—which leaves the Gisu as the only tribe in which husband-killing is present to any appreciable degree (4 per

[9] Kaare Svalastoga, "Homicide and Social Contact in Denmark," *American Journal of Sociology*, LXII, No. 1, pp. 37-41.

TABLE 47. KINSMAN VICTIMS

	Gisu	Tiv	Luo	Luyia	Nyoro	Soga	Alur
Kinsmen							
Ascending Generation							
Father	7	0	0	3	1	1	1
Class. father (inc. FaBr)	4	5	0	4	0	0	0
Mother	4	2	0	0	1	0	0
Class. mother	1	0	0	0	1	0	0
Mother's brother	1	1	0	0	0	0	0
Other	0	2	0	0	0	0	0
Ego's Generation							
Brother	5	7	1	4	1	1	2
FaBrSon	0	1	0	2	0	0	0
Sister	0	0	1	0	0	0	0
Other	0	1	0	2	0	2	0
Descending Generation							
Brother's Son	0	4	0	0	0	1	0
Child	0	1	0	0	1	0	0
Son	0	0	0	1	0	0	0
Daughter	0	1	0	1	0	0	2
FaBrSoSo	0	1	0	0	0	0	0
FaBrDaSo	0	1	0	0	0	0	0
Affines							
Ascending Generation							
Father-in-law	2	0	0	2	1	0	0
Mother-in-law	1	0	0	0	2	0	0
Father's Wife	0	1	0	2	1	0	0
BrWiFa	0	0	0	1	0	0	0
Other	0	1	0	0	0	1	0
Ego's Generation							
Wife	7	8	6	5	8	39	2
Husband	4	1	0	0	0	0	0
Brother-in-law	2	1	0	1	0	0	0
Brother's Wife	0	1	1	1	1	0	0
Co-wife	0	0	1	1	1	0	1
Son's Wife's Fa	0	0	0	1	0	0	0
HuBrWi	0	0	0	0	1	0	0
BrWidow's Hu	0	0	0	1	0	0	0
Other	0	0	0	0	0	6	0
Descending Generation							
Mistress' Da	0	1	0	0	0	0	0
Co-wife's Da	0	0	1	0	0	0	0
HuBrDa	0	0	0	1	0	0	0
Son's wife	0	0	0	0	1	0	0
Other	0	0	0	0	0	1	1

cent of the total cases, 4 of the 9 cases of female offenders).
Killing of the wife's brother occurs in three of six societies
(twice in one; once in each of two others); and killing the
brother's wife occurs once in each of four societies. Two Nyoro killed mothers-in-law because they claimed that these old
women encouraged their wives to break up their marriages.
The only other mother-in-law victim was among the Gisu.

TABLE 48. SUMMARY OF KINSMAN VICTIMS, BY GENERATION

	Ascending Generation			Killer's Generation			Descending Generation		
	Kin	Aff.	Total	Kin	Aff.	Total	Kin	Aff.	Total
Gisu	17	3	20	5	13	18	–	–	–
Tiv	10	2	12	9	11	20	8	1	9
Luo	–	–	–	2	8	10	–	1	1
Luyia	7	5	12	8	10	18	2	1	3
Nyoro	3	4	7	1	11	12	1	1	2
Soga	1	2	3	3	45	48	1	1	2

When generation is considered, still other patterns emerge.
Gisu is the only tribe in which there are more victims in the
ascending generation than in the killer's generation—LaFontaine's explanation of tense intergenerational conflict is borne
out: in tribes such as Luo and Soga, the intergenerational conflict is at a minimum; conflict centers in ego's generation—in
both cases, in the marriage relationship. The Nyoro are interesting for the fact that the marriage relationship is the pivot of
conflict, but it extends into both the ascending and descending
generations.

With one exception, the tribes represented here do not kill
kinsmen of the descending generation. There are no cases at
all among the Gisu, and only negligible numbers of cases
among the other tribes—save the Tiv, in which almost a quarter of the victims are in the descending generation from the
killer.

Another factor which lends itself to ready comparison—and

the meaning of which must also be explained—is differential use of weapons for homicide in various societies. It has been repeatedly stressed by criminologists that killers commit homicide with whatever weapon may be handy. The implication is that the weapons used are no more than a reflection of patterns of cultural activity in the society concerned. The fact remains, however, that some societies stab, others beat, and still others shoot. The African situation, from the tribes represented here, is summed up in Table 49.

Africans are not allowed, under colonial government, to have rifled guns without a license (though some may have clean-bore, muzzle-loading guns without one). The number of small arms or rifled firearms is small in African societies. The rarity

TABLE 49. WEAPONS USED IN HOMICIDES

Weapon	Tiv 87	Gisu 99	Luo 44	Nyoro 34	Soga 100	Luyia 114	Alur	Philadelphia
Piercing and Cutting:								
Arrows	30.0	2.0	–	–	–	1.8	0	
Spear	3.5	12.1	11.2	29.4	3.0	9.5	10.6	
Axe and Adze	5.6	1.0	4.9	5.9	5.0	3.5	0	
Knives (including matchet and *panga*)	33.3	23.2	38.4	26.5	22.0	26.3	23.4	
	71.4	38.3	54.5	61.8	30.0	41.1	34.0	39.0
Striking:								
Hoe and scythe	–	4.0	0	–	–	5.3	4.2	
Sticks	17.2	27.3	9.8	11.8	21.0	27.2	⎰ 40.4	
Blows		9.1	24.5	–	3.0	12.3	⎱	
Pestles and other household implements	–	6.1	–	–	2.0	–	6.4	
	17.2	46.5	34.3	11.8	32.0	44.8	51.0	22.0
Arson	–	–	–	8.8	–	1.8	–	
Firearms	1.1	–	–	2.9	–	–	–	33.0
Strangling	–	–	–	8.8	3.0	–	4.2	
Misc. or unknown	10.3	15.2	11.2	5.9	35.0	12.3	10.6	6.0
TOTAL	100%	100	100	100	100	100	100	100

is reflected in the fact that firearms as a means of homicide occur only in two tribes—the Tiv and the Nyoro. When accidents are omitted, only one case in each is recorded. Both are atypical. Since firearms are the most commonly used weapons in most Western societies (Philadelphia is atypical of America in this regard), the percentages of killings by means of cutting or striking implements is naturally higher in African societies than in our own. In only two of the societies represented here is there a significant difference between the two methods—again, they are Nyoro and Tiv. Both societies stab. Or, more accurately, both societies, but especially the Nyoro, avoid striking and beating.

These facts, like those of offender-victim relationships, must be explained in terms of the culture of the social groups in which they occur before they can be compared meaningfully.

Another mode of explanation followed by some criminologists has been in terms of motive. Wolfgang traced this practice in criminology back to Tarde.[10] Several contributors to this book have found motive a useful tool for exposition. However, I have found it useful for comparison only in a rough sort of way, because motive is even more difficult to comprehend cross-culturally than are kinship relationships. In order to illustrate the difficulties involved, I have taken the two contributions to this book which give the fullest analyses in terms of motives, and have compared them, in Table 50, with Wolfgang's analysis of motive for Philadelphia offenders (both Negro and white).

The most obvious fact about Table 50—at least, it was obvious in constructing it—is that the motives assigned by various writers to homicide in various societies are not comparable. To determine whether this lack of comparability is a factor in analysis or one in data, it is essential to look at the method of analysis and the definitions used by the various writers. Wolfgang has had space to be specific in this matter. His statement of the difficulties is worth quoting at length:

[10] Wolfgang, *op.cit.*, p. 185.

Patterns of Murder and Suicide

TABLE 50. MOTIVES FOR HOMICIDE

	Philadelphia	Gisu	Soga
Altercation of relatively trivial origin (insult, curse, jostling, etc.)	36.5		
Resentment of authority		5	
Property rights (including beer distribution)		12	
Drunken brawl		10	12.0
Response to provocation		10	
Domestic quarrel	13.4		
Marital disputes		10	48.0
Quarrel over bride-wealth		2	
Control of women		5	
Quarrel with in-law			3.0
Quarrel with agnatic kinsman			4.0
Jealousy	11.1		
Altercation over money	10.3		
Altercation over land		3	
Robbery	7.9		
Killing in connection with another crime			3.0
Revenge	4.8	4	
Accidents	4.5		8.0
Intervention in quarrel		2	
Self-defense	1.3		
Halting a felon	1.1	17	15.0
Escaping arrest	1.0		
Other and unknown	8.1	19	7.0
	100%		100%
	(621 cases)	(99 cases)	(100 cases)

"The present analysis of motives is necessarily rudimentary and relies upon terminology used by the police to describe those factors which prompt one individual to take the life of another. The Homicide Squad uses the term "motive" in descriptive summaries, but it is well aware of the fact that most underlying "causes" and unconscious motivations usually lie beyond the realm of necessary police investigation. The term used in the present analysis refers to the ostensible and police-recorded motive."[11]

[11] Wolfgang, op.cit., p. 187.

The major difficulty lies in Wolfgang's word "ostensible." An "ostensible motive" must be so in terms of some set of cultural valuations. He himself (to give him the benefit of any possible doubt) uses the culture of the members of the Philadelphia Homicide Squad. Therefore the "motive" classification which he gives (and which is duplicated in Table 50) is a part of the ethnographic data of the total situation. Our own contributors, likewise, have been led, in their recording of motive, to use the classifications of the societies concerned insofar as members of those societies explained them or as the contributors from intensive first-hand ethnographic knowledge understood them. Even so, as LaFontaine has pointed out, "a study of individual motive gives only the pattern of precipitating causes."

No better proof of the relativity of "ostensible" motive could be asked than that provided under the listing "domestic quarrel" in Table 50. In American culture, "domestic quarrel" means a quarrel between spouses. In the two African cultures it need not, and the authors have had to make finer subdivisions to accord with the facts of domestic grouping in those societies. In the same way, Wolfgang, who is writing of Americans for Americans, can use the word "altercations" and note that many seem of relatively trivial origin. The reporters of African societies, faced with a translation problem, have had to be more specific.

For a fuller evaluation of "motive" classifications we must be a little more specific about what we mean by "motive." A careful look at the categories that are to be found in Table 50 (all of which are used by one or more of the investigators),[12] shows several uses of the word "motive." Some motives are no more than situations of homicide (domestic quarrel, robbery); others are evaluations made by survivors (jealousy, resentment of authority). A domestic quarrel may be a situation in which

[12] I have, for the two African societies, combined thieves, adulterers, and sorcerers, and put them under Wolfgang's heading "halting a felon."

homicide recurs, but it is not a "motive" for homicide. Calling it so is to fall into the same sort of logical error that the Fallers report for the Soga—confusion of a relationship with a cause for killing.

The word "motive" has been used with three meanings probably none of which is adequate in the light of dictionary definitions: (1) a psychic state that leads to an act (which MacDougall divided into emotion and intention); (2) an evaluation by survivors of an act of killing (which is, of course, not "motive" at all); and (3) a social situation in which homicide occurs, also not really a "motive." It is the last two of these points that are important here.

Assignment of "motive" by the survivors of a crime or a suicide is relative, without any doubt, to the cultural values; therefore, it varies in greater or less degree from one culture to another. These cultural evaluations of motive, as LaFontaine noted for the Gisu, may be "not entirely irrelevant in deciding the course of events after a murder took place." In the Gisu case, a man's lineage will support him in homicides with some motives, that is, their evaluation of his intentions; it will not support him with others. Evaluations, in this sense, are social facts whatever else they may be—they affect social action. In the three societies dealt with in Table 50, we have sets of social facts as they are perceived and acted upon by Philadelphia policemen and by informants in two African societies. In all these societies, the domestic situation is recognized as touchy, and marital or domestic disputes are recognized as a possible source of homicide. American ideas reflected here are that homicide is a very grave offense and is sometimes—relatively often—mysteriously committed for what appear to be minor motives or none. Furthermore, money is one of the basic values of Philadelphia society, and hence a motive. But altercation over money as a "motive" (incentive) for murder does not occur in the African societies. In Africa, rather, the recognized motives are fear of witches or revenge upon them, and land disputes in areas which are both dependent upon subsistence farming and short of land.

Thus "motive" becomes a social fact when it is made overt by the people of the society concerned, and when their regard for it affects the actions they perform after a homicide. However, studying homicide in terms of "motive" is often only a shorthand for studying social situations in which homicide occurs. Motives need explanation as much as rates among various relationships need it.

It has been the battle cry of anthropologists for over half a century that the procedure of lifting social or cultural facts out of context and comparing them with other facts also lifted out of context is inadmissible procedure. Until now, that battle cry has never been directed toward criminologists, who are still lifting crimes from context by comparing crime rates in general or rates of specific crimes—like homicide—in particular, or occasionally of classifying crimes by "motive."

The differential rates among the sexes are interesting social facts, but they need explaining. The differences in motive assigned by different peoples to homicide are interesting, but they too need explaining. The explanations of these differences and others must be begun by an analysis in terms of basic, functionally defined institutions. The institution comprehends the social relationships and social structures, the culture and the values which are represented in those situations in which homicide is recurrent.

We started this analysis of classification of homicides by pointing out that homicide occurs accidentally in dangerous institutions in some cases, and as an accident intermittently in others; that it may be institutionalized in jural and ritual institutions. In our discussion of culpable homicide we left the institutional frame of reference, and we must now return to it.

The most apparent institution to be involved with homicide —and, as we shall see, with suicide—is the domestic institution. Perhaps the most interesting thing about murder in domestic institutions is that the patterns displayed by men and by women vary comparatively little, whereas they vary almost wholly in nearly all the other institutions. It is nothing new to note that when women kill, they kill "within the family" —usually within the household. Yet, the patterns within the family vary greatly. Who the victim may be, and the means of killing are extremely variable.

First of all, except for the Gisu, killing the husband scarcely occurs in our sample. Rather, in Africa women kill their children, usually in a state of emotional stress following break-up of the family or contravention of important norms. This pattern is found among Tiv and Nyoro, and is almost precisely similar to one presented in a book of case histories by Wertham.[13] These murders of children are often followed by suicide or attempts at it. African women also kill co-wives in some of the tribes recorded here (Nyoro and Luyia). If the term co-wife includes the wives of the husband's close kinsmen, as in most African languages, the Tiv can be added.

When men kill women in domestic institutions, it is overwhelmingly their wives who are their victims—and in extended households this is not a redundant statement as it would be among ourselves. Uxoricide occurs in all our societies—indeed, it probably occurs in *all* societies. The pattern is clearest among the Soga, who have the highest rate, and the Nyoro, where men kill the wives they fear will desert them, thus breaking up the domestic group. In the latter tribe, two-thirds of the female victims of men are deserting wives or long-term mistresses. The Nyoro even extend this pattern to the wife's mother, who is thought to be in league with the absconding wife.

Yet, what appears to be the same pattern in wife-killing can be given vastly different expressions. Among the Luo, for example, uxoricide is not associated particularly with absconding wives, but rather with the disciplining of wives, leading to

[13] Frederick Wertham, *A Show of Violence*, Garden City, pp. 25ff.

what are usually considered (at least by the murderous husbands) accidental deaths. In the Luo sample, 10 of 46 cases were of this domestic discipline type. The Luo are unusual in that a woman's brothers may join her husband in administering the discipline. This particular pattern does not occur in homicide cases elsewhere, even in the other East African societies in which bride-wealth is paid in cattle, and where presumably the desire of both husbands and brothers to keep the marriage going is to be found to the same extent.

Among the Soga, the large number of uxoricides (that is, high when compared to total homicides) usually takes place during domestic quarrels, giving still another pattern, though one possibly related to either or both of the above.

In some African groups, men kill men within domestic institutions. This factor is, of course, dependent on the shape and size of the domestic institution. The Tiv are the most pronounced in this regard—there we found men killing their senior kinsmen because they fear they are being bewitched, and their junior kinsmen whom they are bewitching or from whom they fear "counterattack." This pattern was discussed above under jural institutions, because it is undeniably a jural response, and because of the fact that it is likely to occur not only within the domestic group itself but also among kinsmen who live near one another but who do not actually form a single homestead. Tiv do not themselves consider this a domestic matter, but rather one associated with the lineage. This overlapping of the jural and domestic institutions also occurs among the Nyoro—when sorceresses are killed it is usually by a kinsman of their victims, so that the killer's act can sometimes be seen as an act within an anomic household.

One of the most interesting facts is the rarity of patricide. Only among the Luyia has it become a recognizable pattern: there it is usually some form of counterattack, for generally it occurs when the father becomes violent with his grown son. The Gisu show this pattern, but to a much lesser extent—it is, further, usually to the classificatory father, and especially the substitute father, that Gisu react. Father's brothers are more commonly killed in some of our societies than are fathers —the reasoning may be correct that they occupy the disciplinary and authoritarian roles of the father untempered by the kindly, instructive roles of the true father. The Tiv pattern of reaction against witches who are one's agnates can be seen as turning on the father-substitute who is in authority but is without paternal love and the emotional desire to protect.

Matricide is, compared to patricide, almost common insofar as the number of clear-cut cases is concerned. Among Tiv, matricide accounts for 2 of 16 female victims. Both cases showed a context of witchcraft. Among the Gisu, matricide accounted for 4 of 18 female victims, and among the Luyia, for one of 29 female victims.

It would seem, then, that when women kill or when men kill women, the family and household institutions are the ones in which the strain is severe. For women, there tend to be few other relationships in which the strain is sufficient to lead to killing. In our sample, a Gisu woman on one occasion killed a thief (it is rare that women participate quite so actively in this jural institution); there are a couple of examples in which women killed sexual assailants, thus getting into the pattern of killing in connection with a crime. These instances are rare. We can safely say that when women are concerned in homicide, the situation is likely to be domestic.

Aside from domestic institutions, accidents, and killing of witches and thieves in jural institutions, only a single theme occurs in which women are involved: in both Gisu and Tiv there are examples of killing an enemy's daughter, presumably to do him both psychical harm and to deprive him of a source of bride-wealth.

There remain the situations in which only males are involved. The most important factors here are economic and political.

It is, in most parts of Africa, pedantic to separate family

institutions from economic institutions. This fact brings the land dispute cases recorded here into a somewhat equivocal position. The Luyia are the most important example because land dispute cases account for almost 10 per cent of Luyia killings. The disputes are usually—but not always—between kinsmen. However, they are most often between kinsmen who no longer actually live in the same homestead, and hence they are not domestic in the strict sense of the word. Certainly they occur in terms of economic institutions.

The land-dispute killing occurs in the East African areas of land shortage. It does not occur among the West African Tiv, although land disputes are rife there, and in some areas land is extremely short. Land has, however, become a rallying cry in parts of East Africa, and is one of the major points of strain in the society. This fact emerges clearly not only for the Luyia but for the Gisu as well—and it must be kept in mind that land was one of the ostensible sources of strain that led to Mau Mau.

Aside from the land dispute pattern, the remarkable fact seems to be how *little* homicide occurs in economic institutions, or with an economic motivation. This factor is, of course, partly accounted for by the lack of institutions that are specifically economic—there are few production firms or institutions and only comparatively crude distributional institutions. But so-called "economic motives" are singularly rare in Africa. Undoubtedly this fact is a reflection of another, that is, in a subsistence-dominated economic system, it is not possible for an individual to enjoy the gains of his crimes any more than it is for him to enjoy any other sort of gains. He must share them. In the case of crime, however, his sharing his economic gains would also involve sharing his guilt. The community of sharers seems to act as a sanction against crime—or at least homicide—for gain. One case in Tivland did occur: a foreign trader was murdered for his goods, which were discovered a few days later, distributed among the offenders' kinsmen.

Among the Gisu, 12 per cent of the cases involved "quarrels

over property rights other than land, including distribution of beer," and two cases involved sharing of bride-wealth. The latter situation is also equivocal—quarrels over bride-wealth are in a sense domestic, but usually occur between people who are members of different domestic groups. Cases involving quarrels over property that are certainly within domestic institutions or jural institutions can also be found in other tribes. The pattern is not one, however, which is dominant in any of the material.

It would be impossible not to comment here on alcohol as an element in patterns of homicide in African societies, even though its importance seems to be less than is commonly believed, even by Africans. Alur, Luyia and Gisu show "drunken brawl" as a pattern of killing. Southall, LaFontaine and I maintain, however, that this statement usually indicates inadequate reporting or interrogation and hence poor records. Killings that occur at drinking parties are seldom random. Seldom, when the information is complete, is a victim a stranger to his killer. The relationship of killer to victim is too often not given in the records of such cases—we think because the stereotype of killing wantonly in a drunken brawl is so commonly held by European officials that it is deemed sufficient explanation. At least some tribes know this and may take advantage of it. The entire problem of alcohol in Africa and its relation to crime (as well as to many other types of activity) awaits analysis. It would seem, however, to be as a catalytic agent rather than as a cause that alcohol appears in situations of homicide.

What becomes clear from consideration of killings connected with alcohol is that the tensions of one institution may erupt when the members participate in another institution. Killings that occur at beer-drinks among the Luyia and the Gisu tend to be part of a cycle not of beer-drinks, but of domestic or production institutions. The Luyia murders which fall wholly within the institution of the beer-drink are very few. Yet beer-drinks are neighborhood affairs, not domestic affairs. A pattern may, therefore, overlap two institutions: the tensions created in one may erupt in the course of activity in another.

There are, finally, two more patterns which should be mentioned but which seem to be confined to one or two tribes. The Soga seem to be unique in that a "shame" pattern of homicide emerges among them. "Shame" is given by several of our peoples as a recognized motive for suicide, but appears in homicide context in only this instance. The "interference" pattern is to be found among Luyia and, to a lesser degree, among their neighbors, the Gisu. These patterns defy institutional classification, for either "shame" or "interference" may be recognizable in several institutions. The pattern here, like that of the pattern of killing while drunk, forms an example of institutional linkage by common personnel.

It is interesting to compare the patterns we have discovered here with a series of patterns found among executed English murderers between 1949 and 1954.[14] The British sample, including only executed murderers instead of all homicides, would not be strictly comparable to our African samples if statistical means were to be employed or if we were trying to discover all the patterns of homicide in Britain. However, as a source for patterns which do occur, and to underline the narrow range of patterns in Africa, it is useful. In the 85 cases of murder in which offenders were hanged in Britain, two overwhelming patterns emerge, both of which are absent or very rare in Africa. The first of these patterns (25 cases out of 85) involves the murder of a mistress or girl friend. This is very much higher than is wife-murder, though of course our sample here may indicate only that wife murderers are not executed while murderers of mistresses are. The other pattern (16 out of 85) is the murder committed in the course of another crime. This factor occurs in Africa (the Soga material shows 3 out of 100), but it is relatively rare. The English sample also shows

[14] Vigil, "Patterns of Murder," a pamphlet published by the *Observer*, London, 1956.

an interesting absence of parricide: among those executed there was one case of a man who killed his parents and three cases in which victims were affines. This fact may mean no more than that the English tend to declare anyone who kills a kinsman to be insane—a feature that we have found to be so in the Colonies: killing a kinsman would seem to English colonial judges to be proof par excellence of madness.

We have, throughout this discussion of homicide, emphasized the fact that homicide is a social relationship and that, to be understood, the social relationship between killer and victim must be seen in its institutional setting, with regularities and patterns noted. It would have been equally possible to make this analysis from the standpoint of role: the institutional and societal role of victim or offender or both—to ask what roles in society are homicidogenic. We did not do so because the relationship itself allows a more direct and simple analysis—if there were no other reason, it allows a single classification instead of demanding two, one for offenders and another for victims.

When we come to discuss suicide, role situations seem to offer a better analytical framework than relationships. That is to say, suicide occurs in institutionalized situations as much as does homicide. But the act of suicide is not *per se* a social relationship in the same sense that homicide is. Thus the act of suicide, in which victim and offender is one, is best considered in terms of role, whereas the act of homicide, in which victim and offenders are different, is at best two roles in a relationship. The comparable units therefore are the suicide role on the one hand and the homicide relationship on the other.

So far as I am aware, no study of suicide in terms of role has as yet been made—a peculiar oversight in view of the wide acceptance of the role concept. It may sometimes be difficult to say that a suicide occurred in the course of an individual's playing a single given role, for obviously his death is reflected in all of the institutions in which he played roles. But it may be that certain combinations of roles are suicidogenic in one or more cultures, whereas each role alone is not.

The information at our disposal does not allow us to make an exhaustive analysis of the roles and social settings of suicides. The main lines are clear, however. The major division is between suicide as a counteraction or correction and suicide as a breach of norm. Suicide may follow homicide or some other serious offense and be considered "jural" in nature. It has been estimated that as many as 34 per cent of homicide offenders in Britain take their own lives.[15] The figure for the United States is much smaller: Wolfgang found in Philadedphia that only 4 per cent of persons charged with homicide also killed themselves, and that the percentage discovered by other investigators in America ranged from 2 per cent to 9 per cent. Wolfgang also found that "although whites are one-fourth of all offenders, they make up half of the homicide-suicides."[16] Thus, suicide following homicide marks the white group just as suicide in any other situation marks the white group rather than the Negro group. An analysis of the 10 cases of homicide-suicide for which Wolfgang gives details shows that in 8 of the 10, the homicide victim was a spouse or mistress, in one a man killed his daughter (age unrecorded), and in the last a mother killed her three-year-old son and herself. Wolfgang notes that it would seem that more persons who commit murder in the first degree ultimately kill themselves than are legally executed—even in Philadelphia. In Britain the difference is between 34 per cent of homicides who commit suicide and 15 per cent who are executed.[17]

The African material on homicide-suicide is variable. In the case of the Soga and the Nyoro, it would seem to be good. The Fallers found among the Soga that 15 per cent of recorded sui-

---

[15] Vigil, *op.cit.*

[16] Wolfgang, *op.cit.*, Chapter xv.

[17] Vigil notes that 28 per cent are declared insane at some stage of the proceeding, leaving 23 per cent who are apparently either imprisoned, reprieved, or disposed of in some other way.

cides occurred after an attack on the spouse or on an affine—an attack which sometimes did and sometimes did not lead to the death of the victim. At the other extreme, among the Tiv, successful homicide-suicides would not have reached the files from which the data were gathered: even there, however, four suicide attempts by homicide offenders were noted. Suicide following another crime, usually homicide, is found in all our societies. But the percentage of these "jural" suicides is not large.

By far the greatest number of suicides in our samples occurred in domestic institutions. That is to say, a large proportion of women committed suicide *as wives*; a smaller but sizeable number of men committed suicide *as husbands*. There were a few other kinship roles mentioned—son, mother, father, co-wife.

In order to investigate the material in this light, we shall first look at the sex rates of suicide where they can reasonably be inferred, and then look to differences which occur in them in the light of domestic and "other" institutions.

TABLE 51. SEX OF SUICIDES

	Luo	Nyoro	Gisu	Soga
Male	41%	61%	59%	69%
Female	59	39	41	31

In the three Bantu tribes of Uganda, the only ones for which government records were adequate, the figures are much the same—some two-thirds of suicides are males. The Luo figures in Wilson's samples would seem to be reversed, but it must be remembered that his sample is smaller and was chosen for purposes of showing range of suicide situations rather than frequencies. The sex ratio for suicide in the United States was about 3 males to 1 female in 1920.[18]

[18] Father Adolph Dominic Frenay, *The Suicide Problem in the United States*, Boston, 1927, p. 31.

In all these tribes, females committed suicide predominantly in domestic situations. Suicide was, for the most part, the direct consequence of domestic strife in which a woman was unable, either through the fault of her husband, her father, of co-wives or of "fate," to play the role of wife and mother. Most of these cases had their origins directly in social relationships, but some of them were due to illness or to the death of some loved person. Barrenness is mentioned by several of our contributors as a situation in which women may be prone to suicide. There is, in short, no pattern save the domestic one for suicide among women in our samples.

For male suicide, the same pattern appears, but it is not the sole one. Impotence or fear of it is a constant theme in many African societies, which often leads to suicide. The pattern appears prominently among the Soga. In most of the tribes represented here, there are cases of men who committed suicide when their domestic situation was threatened, by faulty social relationships, by disease, or by some other misfortune. As is the case with homicide, men commit suicide for the same reasons as women do—and for some others as well.

These additional, non-domestic situations in which men commit suicide in Africa are for the most part seen by Africans in terms of over-all status or rank in the society. The high suicide rates for Gisu, for example, come at an age when a man's total status is in some doubt—in the years immediately following initiation, and in the years when a man should be settling down to assume the status of elder. The Luo, to take another example, phrase their loss or uncertainty of total social status in terms of shame. The loss of status or of "face" may occur in institutional contexts of the traditional tribal system or of the modern system of Kenya, but can nonetheless be recognized as status problems.

Thus, the suicide forms which we find primarily are the "jural," the domestic, and the status-linked situation. The "motives" in terms of which they are expressed, the cultural idiom in which they are found, varies.

These suicide patterns do not coincide with the Durkheim classification in terms of integration any more than they coincide with the folk classifications in terms of shame as among the Luo and Soga, or in terms of "anger" or *litima* among the Gisu. However, most of the suicide considered here is anomic in Durkheim's terms: it is committed by people who are not integrated satisfactorily into operating institutions. The patterns we have mentioned might, with some modifications, be made to appear as varieties of anomic suicide, depending on the institution which is inadequate—jural, domestic, or other.

It is also characteristically African that suicide is—except in cases of revenge suicide—not interpreted entirely as a volitional act, because (whatever else it may be considered) it is considered an irrational act: as Soga say, "an act of utter irresponsibility." Although suicide situations are recognized, only supernatural intervention can place a person into the situation. Among Gisu, the situation is created by ancestors—and specifically not by witches. Among Tiv and Luyia, suicide is a sure sign that the perpetrator was bewitched. Contagion of suicide is also recognized in most of these societies—the East African societies all destroy the tree on which or the hut in which the suicide occurred, burning it and the rope expressly so that an epidemic of suicides will not occur. Contagion is most easily expressed in supernatural terms, although Westerners now express it in psychological terms.

As in many other areas of the world, the overwhelming method of suicide in Africa is hanging. Hanging is surpassed in frequency in the United States only by firearms (37 to 19 per cent), and in England only by poison gas (34 to 16 per cent). In Germany, hanging is still the most prevalent method of suicide.[19] The Tiv are unusual in that all of the six cases

[19] A. J. Lotke, "Suicide," *Encyclopaedia Britannica*, 1953.

recorded were by stabbing—but the sample is insufficient to show whether or not this is a regular pattern.

Suicide rates in Africa would seem, on the basis of our data, to vary from moderate to low, but except for the Uganda tribes the rates are not computable in a way that makes them comparable with those of the record-keeping world.

Finally, a word should be said about the influence of rapid Westernization on both homicide and suicide in the societies considered here. We have two opposing viewpoints represented on the basis of different material—and, of course, there is every reason to believe that both are correct. The Fallers found that those areas of Busoga which had the lowest rates of homicide and suicide were those in which European influence was strongest. They postulated a causal relationship— that the impact situation had something to do with the low rates—but noted that this generalization was not intended to apply beyond Busoga. Southall found that for Alur crime rates in modern situations were higher than in traditional situations. The soundness of both these views is powerfully documented in a set of figures collected by Southall from records of the High Court of Uganda for the years 1945-1954. His findings, set forth in Table 52, indicate that the Soga are the only people in Uganda who have a smaller proportion of homicides (by killers) away from their home district than they have population away from home. In short, Soga are slightly more homicidal in Soga country than they are abroad—or at least in other parts of Uganda. All the other tribes save the Baganda (who show precisely the same proportion of homicide abroad as there are Baganda abroad) show a greater proportion of homicide away from home territory than the portion of population away: some of them as much as 28 times. Figures of this sort are very difficult to evaluate. Since presumably a greater portion of men are absent from home than women, the difference therefore is at least in part a reflection of the greater homicidal tendencies of the male. But, if that is the case, the

Soga figures are the more striking, and the fact that so many Soga murders are uxoricides is underlined. There may be many other explanations, but we do not have the data to venture them. It would seem, however, that this is a fertile field for investigation.

TABLE 52. PERCENTAGES OF HOMICIDE COMMITTED IN UGANDA OUTSIDE HOME DISTRICTS

Tribe	Percentage of Homicides Committed Outside Home District, 1945-54	Percentage of Population Outside Home District, 1948	Ratio
Alur	60.34	23.68	2.5
Nyoro	56.00	22.42	2.5
Konjo	44.44	1.59	28.0
Lugbara	44.05	12.19	3.6
Kiga	37.33	8.10	4.6
Kumam	29.17	12.09	2.4
Toro	28.57	9.94	2.9
Nyole	28.12	2.72	10.3
Ankole	27.88	14.37	1.9
Gwere	22.64	10.84	2.1
Gisu	19.00	9.63	2.0
Acoli	17.07	3.32	5.1
Teso	16.37	4.66	3.7
Lango	15.79	8.38	1.9
Madi	14.81	7.10	2.0
Ganda	5.85	5.79	1.0
Soga	4.86	5.04	.96
Karomojong	4.35	1.10	4.0

These figures do show that Western impact situations may have a very different effect on the homicide rates and practices of one tribe than on others. Western impact may even create stability in some traditional type villages at the same time that it creates *anomie* in migrant labor situations. In short, culture contact is too easy an answer. In any case, we do not need a catch-all, for we have found in Africa low homicide as well as low suicide rates, when compared with many countries of Europe.

In Durkheim's terms, there is little or no egoistic homicide or suicide in Africa. There is only a moderate amount of anomic homicide and suicide there.

In legal terms, we must note that the proportion of cases in which intent was proved was very small: premeditated intent was, among Gisu, found in only 4 of 99 cases; for the Luyia it was found in 14 of 114 cases. The Luo consider premeditated homicide a last resort, but one sometimes worth taking a chance on when all else fails. And yet, the rate was low. This factor must not be overemphasized, for "intent" is probably a very difficult notion to define cross-culturally in terms of any specific legal code. Nevertheless, the small proportion of "murders" compared with manslaughter (to put it into Anglo-Saxon terms) must be remarked upon.

It is our opinion, as a result of having done this study, that one of the best ways to approach problems of social norms is by studying examples of their breach.[20] It is also our opinion that tribal or recently tribal Africa, even though it has been shaken by Western impact and new social forms, beliefs, and institutions, even though it is in the process of political revolution, is still a solid, relatively stable community in which strife is controlled and the course of life usually predictable and often pleasant.

[20] See K. N. Llewellyn and E. Adamson Hoebel, *The Cheyenne Way*, Norman, Oklahoma, 1942, Chapter II.

INDEX

abuse, 223

accident, 32, 86, 131, 230, 254

actuaries, 14

adultery, 40, 42, 62, 69, 100-102, 138, 169-170, 172, 189, 234

age, as a factor in suicide, 14, 120ff.; as a factor in homicide, 82, 108-109

aged, 86, 121, 125, 127, 145, 176

age sets, 47

aggression, 18

agnates, murder among, 42-43, 44ff., 47

Akiga, 53, 63

alcohol (*see also* beer-drinks, drunkards), 161, 257

altruistic homicide, 13

altruistic suicide, 10, 11-12

Alur, 18, 214-229, 231, 233, 234, 240, 257

ancestors, 111-112, 195

anomic homicide, 12-13, 241, 266

anomic suicide, 9, 10, 11-12, 266

anomy, 8-9, 265

arson, 33, 70, 143, 166, 186

Ashanti, 232

authority, 105

Baganda, 155, 239

Bantu language, 66

barrenness, 114-115, 262

Bastide, R., 24

Basuto, 232

Beattie, J. H. M., 239

beer drinking, 32, 87, 95, 103, 139, 161, 162-163, 168, 171, 189, 200, 205, 210, 221, 224, 257

betrothal of children, 201

Bjerre, A., 16

blood-wealth, 97-99, 173, 174

Brearley, H. C., 5

bride-wealth, 67-68, 104, 113, 123-124, 149-150, 152, 189ff., 198, 201, 206, 208

Briffault, R., 22

British, 20

Bunzel, B. (*see also* L. I. Dublin), 15

business cycle, 118

"capture" at marriage, 191-192

cassava, 192

cause, 23, 25, 249ff.

Cavan, R. S., 5, 7, 9, 11, 23

Ceylon, 11

Chicago, 13, 54

children, killing of, 52ff., 60-61, 242

church, 165-166, 204

circumcision, 104, 108, 122ff., 128

comparative studies, 235

compensation (for murder), 59

courts, xiii, xvii, xviii, 94, 204

co-wives, 82, 88, 140, 170, 191, 192, 204, 206, 207, 209, 211, 212, 220, 261, 262

Crazzolara, J. P., 214

crime, of suicide, 19; of homicide, 6, 19, 217, 232

criminal–victim relationship (*see also* killer–victim relationship), 27-28, 235, 242

criminological theory, 6, 22, 247, 252

culture pattern, 27-29

Dagomba tribe, xv

Dahomeans, 24, 232

dangerous institutions, 230, 231-232, 252

death, indigenous ideas of, (Gisu) 96; (Luo) 181ff., 193; (Alur) 215-216

Denmark, 61, 242f.

divination, 41, 70, 133, 186-187, 195, 209

drunkards, 87, 94-95, 104, 136, 161, 221, 257

Dublin, L. I. and B. Bunzel, 14, 23

Durkheim, Émile, xviii, 5, 6-15, 17-18, 24-26, 116, 117, 118, 121, 177, 263, 266

267

Index

269

APPENDIX

ABBREVIATIONS IN THE CASE CHARTS

Acc	Accused
Access	Accessory
Acq	Acquitted
Ad	Adult
Aff	Affine
Ag	Agnate
Appr	Approved
B	Brother
BinL	Brother-in-law
Bond	Bonded over
"C"	"Cousin"
Ch	Child
Chg wtd	Charge withdrawn
cl	Classifactory
Comm	Commuted
D	Daughter
D	Death (when used in Judgment column)
d	Day
Dec	Deceased
F	Father
f	Female
FinL	Father-in-law
G	Guilty
GmuD	Guilty murder, death
Hgd	Hanged
HL	Hard labor
Hosp	Hospital

Imp	Imprisonment
Ins	Insane
Ki	Kinsman
m	Male
M	Mother
MinL	Mother-in-law
Mist	Mistress
mo	Month
msl	Manslaughter
mu	Murder
N	None
N.G.	Not guilty
No rec	No record
N.P.	Nolle Prosequi
Prob	Probation
Rel	Released
S	Son
U	Unknown
W	Wife
Wid	Widow
y	Year
yB	Younger brother
Yg	Young
Z	Sister

No.	Accused Sex	Accused Age	Victim Sex	Victim Age	Kin Rel	Weapon	Judgment Sentence	Remarks
1.	m	26	m	U	FclB	Axe	G ins Asylum	Epileptic. Afraid he was being bewitched by dec.
2.	m	35	f	U	M	Knife	G ins Asylum	Feared dec causing his illness by witchcraft.
3.	m	U	f	U	W	Knife	No rec	Dec wanted to marry someone else. Forced by guardian back to acc. She dared him to kill her. He did.
4.	m	U	m	U	N	Arrow	GmuComm 3yHL	Ran amuck. Fear of witchcraft for his children were dying.
			f	14	U			
5.	m	25	m	U	U	Beating	GmuComm 10yHL	Beat dec for not paying tax. Also rivalry over woman.
6.	m	U	f	U	W	Knife	G ins Asylum	Wife didn't please him. Fear of witchcraft.
7.	m	U	m	U	U	Stick	GmuComm lifeimp	Said dec committed adultery with his wife. Wife denied this.
8.	m	U	m	U	U	Arrow	No rec	Shot at tax collector. Hit dec by mistake.
9.	m	U	m	U	FB	Knife	Gmsl 15yHL	Acc had no explanation. An impulse. No previous desire to kill.
10.	m	35	f	U	U	Knife	Gmsl 2yHL	No apparent motive. Acc a deaf-mute.
11.	m	U	m	U	BS	Axe	G ins	Went beserk because B refused to pay a cow to akombo ceremony for acc's illness
12.	m	U	f	U	FW	Arrow	No rec	Sleeping sickness violence.
13.	m	U	m	U	FBDS	Knife	GmuComm 10yHl	Dec struck acc's wife in absence of acc.
14.	m	U	m	U	ZH	Arrow	1y	Watching for thieves in field. Insufficient evidence that wounds caused death
15.	m	U	m	U	U	Arrow	Gmu death	Acc claimed that dec gave him medicine to kill him.
16.	m	U	m	U	Ag	Arrow	NG	Long-standing argument over debt of horse.
17.	f	U	f	5	D	Knife	G ins	Frantic with fear because she had been accused of witchcraft.
			f	3	D			
18.	m	U	m	2	"C"	Arrow	Gmu death	Killed bystander while firing poisoned arrow at mother.
19.	m	U	m	20	U	Arrow	No rec	Dec challenged acc's right to take chicken to kill for father-in-law
20.	m	35	m	U	U	Horse kick	Gmsl 6moHL	Acc's horse kicked dec in head. Died 5 days later.
21.	m	U	m	U	U	Gun	Gmsl 1yHL	Hunting accident.
22.	m	30	f	U	W	Knife	Gmu death?	Killed wife and tried to kill himself.
23.	3m	U	f	U	U	Beating	2GmuD 1Acq	Obtaining head for ritual purposes.
24.	f	U	f	U	U	Arrow	No rec	Insanity from sleeping sickness.
25.	m	U	m	U	N	Knife	Rel	Drunken market quarrel over ownership of knife.
26.	m	U	m	U	1/2B	Gun	Gmsl 10yHL	Dec rich and would not pay for medicines for acc's full brother.
27.	m	U	m	U	U	Knife	Acq	Gambling fracas. Dice.
28.	m	U	m	U	U	Arrow	Gmsl 4moHL	Communal hunt accident.
29.	m	U	m	U	1/2 B	Arrow	Gmsl 6moHL	Communal hunt accident.
30.	m	U	m	U	FB	Arrow	Gmsl 6moHL	Communal hunt accident.
31.	m	U	f	U	W	Spear	Gmu death	Adultery of wife and young brother several days before killing.
			m	U	yB	Axe		
32.	m	U	m	U	FB	Arrow	No rec	Acc said dec had killed all his brothers.
33.	m	U	f	U	KiW	Fire	Gmsl 18moHL	Set fire to hut in anger. Dec dashed in to rescue belongings.
34.	m	U	m	U	U	Knife	Gmu death	Killed acc for sleeping with his wife.
35.	m	U	m	U	U	Gun	Case dis	Bystander killed by flying shrapnel.
36.	m	U	m	U	U	U	Case dis	Dec and acc's wife had intercourse on acc's farm. Insufficient evidence.
37.	m	U	m	U	U	Arrow	Case dis	Dec bumped into poisoned arrow held by acc. Insufficient evidence.
38.	m	U	m	U	U	Spear	Gmsl 1yHL	Hunting. Spear ricocheted from tree.
39.	m	U	m	U	F	Knife	Gmsl 5yHL	Dec struck acc in dark. Had knife in hand. No intent.
40.	m	U	m	U	U	Arrow	Gmu death	Quarrel over money led to fight.
41.	m	U	m	U	U	Arrow	Acq	Communal hunting accident.

No.	Accused Sex	Accused Age	Victim Sex	Victim Age	Kin Rel	Weapon	Judgment Sentence	Remarks
42.	m	U	m	U	Ag	Arrow	Gmsl 3yHL	Acc claimed dec was formerly head of thieves' ring who now refused to protect him when he stole.
43.	m	U	f	U	N	Knife	Gmu hgd	Dec daughter of a man believed to have taken payment to kill acc.
44.	m	U	m	U	U	Beating	Gmsl 7moHL	Dec defecated near house of acc. They fought. Blow in stomach.
45.	m	U	m	U	Ag	Knife	GmuComm 15y	Acc heard dec's wife had lover. Stabbed man in bed with her. It was her husband.
46.	m	U	m	U	U	U	Gmsl 14yHL	Killed wife's lover.
47.	m	U	m	U	U	Knife	Gmsl 7yHL	Acc took wife to her brother for sterility ceremonies. Dec her subsequent lover.
48.	m	U	f	U	W	Knife	Gmsl 4yHL	Killed wife for adultery.
49.	m	U	m	U	1/2B	Arrow	No rec	Communal hunt of 5 1/2 brothers.
50.	m	U	m	U	U	Arrow	No rec	Communal hunting accident.
51.	m	U	m	U	U	Beating	Rel	Fracas at "Christmas party".
52.	m	U	m	3d	U	Exposure	Gmsl 3yHL	Exposed infant of woman who died in childbirth.
53.	m	U	m	U	F1/2BS	Knife	Gmsl 2yHL	Hit acc on old scar in scuffle over division of meat.
54.	m	U	m	U	WAg	Knife	No rec	Dec jeered at Acc for living matrilocally. Acc attacked.
55.	7m	U	f	Old	U	Beating	Gmsl 1-5y	Caught dec stealing yams. Beat her. She died.
56.	m	U	m	U	U	Stick	No rec	Fight at beer party. Acc had been hit and could not see.
57.	m	26	m	U	U	Knife	No rec	Beer drink brawl. No former trouble.
58.	m	U	m	U	U	Arrow	No rec	Hunting accident.
59.	m	17	m	U	U	Stone	Gmsl 9moHL	Dispute about taking cloth in payment of debt.
60.	m	U	m	Old	Guar AccW	Knife	Gmsl 3yHL	Aiming at man who had been said to "spoil the marriage", he hit acc.
61.	m	U	m	U	U	Arrow	No rec	Communal hunt.
62.	m	U	m	U	U	Spear	No rec	Beer drink fracas.
63.	m	U	m	U	U	Spear	Gmsl 1yHL	Hunting accident.
64.	m	U	U	Yg	U	Fire	Gmsl no rec	Threw child in fire during epileptic seizure.
65.	m	U	m	U	B	Arrow	G ins hosp	"He deprived me of my things and laughed at me."
66.	m	U	m	U	U	Beating	G no rec	Acc suspected dec of sleeping with wife.
67.	m	U	m	U	U	Arrow	No rec	Hunting accident.
68.	m	U	m	U	U	Arrow	No rec	Hunting accident.
69.	m	36	m	U	FB	Knife Spear	Insane no rec	"He would not cure my illness."
70.	m	U	f	U	U	Arrow	Rel	Dec caught stealing. No evidence death caused by arrow.
71.	m	U	m	U	1/2B	Spear	Rel	Dec refused to answer acc when challenged at night.
72.	m	U	m	U	U	Knife	Ins Asylum	Acc stole knife of dec. Fight.
73.	m	U	m	U	U	Arrow	4yHL	Dec said Acc beat dec's wife who had tried to make him stop beating mother.
74.	m	U	m	U	U	Suffocation	18moHL	Attempted murder while trying to steal goods from Hausa trader.
	m	U						
75.	m	U	m	U	U	Arrow	No rec	Claimed self-defense. Dec stabbed first. Acc a slave and orphan.
	m	U						
76.	m	U	m	U	U	Arrow	No rec	Communal hunt.
77.	f	U	m	U	Ag	Knife	G ins hosp	Obsession about being bewitched.
78.	f	U	U	Yg	Ch	Knife	G ins hosp	Stabbed child. Attempted suicide. Epileptic.
79.	m	Old	m	U	Ag	Arrow	Died	Bridewealth dispute. Set fire to house then shot dec. Acc died during trial.
80.	U	U	m	U	U	Poison?	All rel	Classic witchcraft case for imborivungu rites.
81.	m	U	m	U	U	Burning	G ins hosp	After killing, fired 2 huts.
82.	m	U	f	U	Ward	Slap	No rec	Accident. Dec wanted to return to husband who paid no bridewealth.
83.	f	U	m	U	H	Blow	Rel	Misadventure. She felled him and walked off. He drowned.

No.	Accused Sex	Accused Age	Victim Sex	Victim Age	Kin Rel	Weapon	Judgment Sentence	Remarks
84.	m	U	m	U	U	Adze	Gms1	Argument over a woman. Provocation
85.	m	U	f	U	U	Knife	No rec	She took his money and then refused to sleep with him.
86.	m	20	f	20	FBSW	Arrow	Gmu death	Fear of witchcraft. Also wounded husband of dec.
87.	m	U	3f	U	Ds of Mist	Arrow	Life impris	No motive emerged. Ostracized and lonely life.
88.	m	U	m	7	1/2BS	Beating	No rec	To make medicine. (Acc's "confession" of doubtful value.)
89.	6m	U	m	U	U	Beating	Gms1	Punishment of thief.
90.	m	U	m	U	B	Arrow	Gms1	Quarrel over 9s.0d. No former quarrels known.
91.	m	U	m	U	BS	Arrow	No rec	Killed wrong person. Tried to kill 1/2 brother out of fear of witchcraft.
92.	m	U	m	U	N	Knife	No rec	Killed stranger at beer party.
93.	m	U	m	U	U	Medicine	No rec	Magical medicines proved fatal.
			m	U	U			
94.	m	U	m	U	U	Arrow	Gms1 10yHL	No record.
95.	5m	19-35	m	U	U	Beating	Gms1 4moHL	Beating thief.
96.	m	U	m	U	N	Knife	No rec	Fight between two lineages over theft of beans.
97.	m	U	m	U	N	Arrow	G ins hosp	No motives emerged.
98.	m	U	m	U	MB	Knife	G ins hosp	Peaceful division of meat at ceremony.
99.	m	20	m	U	U	Stone	Gms1 3 1/2 yHL	Bad blood. Argument over fish.
100.	m	U	m	U	MBki	Arrow	Gms1 3yHL	Acc's mother's people lax about medical treatment of acc's full brother.
101.	m	U	f	U	W	Beating	18moHL	Adultery suspected.
102.	m	U	m	U	U	Gun	No rec	Accident. Didn't know gun was loaded.
103.	m	U	m	U	U	Knife	Rel	Self-defense? Acc young and so put in charge of clan head.
104.	m	U	m	U	N	Arrow	No rec	Inadequate proof of cause of death.
105.	7m	U	m	U	N	Beating	1-4D 5-7Acq	Beating thief.
106.	m	30	f	U	M	Stick	G'ins	Sent to division jail.
107.	m	U	m	U	N	Beating	Rel	Not solved.
108.	m	U	m	U	U	Knife	18moHL rel	Acc I caught dec in *flagrante delicto* in adultery with his wife.
	m	U						
109.	m	U	m	U	U	Arrow	No rec	Communal hunt.
110.	m	U	f	U	U	Gun	6moHL	Accident.
111.	m	U	m	U	U	Arrow	6moHL	Hunting accident. Poisoned arrow hit dec in ankle.
112.	m	U	m	U	U	Arrow	No rec	Hunt. Arrow missed duiker, hit dec.
113.	m	U	m	U	U	U	2yHL	- - -
114.	m	U	m	U	U	Arrow	18moHL	Hunt. Arrow glanced off duiker, hit dec.
115.	m	U	m	U	U	Arrow	6moHL	Aiming at anteater.
116.	m	U	m	U	U	Knife	G ins hosp	Decs were husband and wife. Acc died in mental hospital.
			f	U	U			
117.	m	U	f	U	W	Matchet	Dis	Dec I forced into marriage. Dec II struck by accident as acc beat dec I. Insufficient evidence.
			f	Yg	Wch			
118.	m	U	m	U	U	Arrow	2yHL	Thief
119.	m	U	m	U	U	Arrow	No rec	- -- - - -
120.	m	U	m	U	N	Knife	6yHL	Fight over a woman.
121.	m	12	m	U	U	Arrow	Rel	Communal hunt. Acc released and given 12 strokes by father.
122.	m	U	m	U	U	Arrow	GmuComm 14yHL	Fear of witchcraft.

No.	Accused Sex	Accused Age	Victim Sex	Victim Age	Kin Rel	Weapon	Judgment Sentence	Remarks
1.	m	21†	f	21†	W	Pestle	Gms1 2y	Dispute between spouses.
2.	m	21†	m	21†	U	Stick	Gms1 9mo	Dec caught in act of theft.

No.	Accused Sex	Accused Age	Victim Sex	Victim Age	·Kin Rel	Weapon	Judgment Sentence	Remarks
3.	m	36+	m	U	N	Stick	Gmsl 2mo	Dec caught in act of theft.
4.	m	21+	m	36+	U	Hoe	Gmsl 2y	Dec a thief.
5.	m	21+	m	36+	-	Stick	Gmsl 12mo	Marital dispute. Dec step-parent of acc.
6.	f	36+	m	36+	U	Stick	Gmsl 12mo	Dec and acc were lovers.
7.	m	21+	m	36+	N	Stick	Gmsl 1d	Dec caught in act of theft.
8.	m	21+	m	21+	N	Knife	Gmu death	Acc killed people trying to arrest him when he was escaping from jail.
9.	m	36+	f	36+	W	Knife	Gmu death	Marital dispute.
10.	m	21+	m	36+	N	Blow	Gmsl 9mo	Beer party dispute.
11.	m	21+	m	21+	Ag	Hoe	Gmsl 4y	Dispute over land.
12.	m	36+	f	21+	W	Cord	Gmu death	Marital dispute.
13.	m	21+	m	-21	U	U	Gmsl 15mo	Beer party fight.
14.	m	21+	m	21+	N	U	Gmsl 1d	Dec caught in act of theft.
15.	m	21+	m	21+	Ki	Stick	Gmsl 3y	Self-defense.
16.	m	21+	m	36+	Ki	Knife	Gmsl 6y	Beer party brawl.
17.	m	21+	m	21+	U	Knife	Gmsl 2y	Dec bumped acc with bicycle.
18.	m	Ad	m	36+	U	U	Gmu death	Acc killed victim in order to rob him.
19.	m	21+	m	21+	U	Stick	Gmsl 1mo	Dec a thief whom acc caught with the goods.
20.	m	21+	m	21+	U	Whip	Gmsl 8mo	Dec caught in act of theft.
21.	m	36+	f	21+	W	Blow	Gmsl 6mo	Acc angry because child fell into fire.
22.	m	36+	m	51+	U	Stick	Gmsl 3y	Beer party brawl.
23.	m	21+	f	21+	W	Hoe	Gmu comm20y	Wife adulterous.
24.	m	21+	f	21+	W	Hoe	Gmu comm20y	Wife bit acc's finger during quarrel.
25.	m	36+	m	Ad	U	U	Gmsl 3mo	Beer party brawl.
26.	m	21+	m	51+	U	U	Gmsl 2 1/2y	Acc caught dec stealing.
27.	m	36+	m	21+	Aff	Spear	-	Dec hadn't given affinal gift of chickens. Acc committed suicide before trial.
28.	m	21+	f	36+	MinL	Panga	Gmu death	Dec advised her daughter, acc's wife, to desert.
29.	m	-21	m	21+	U	Stick	Gmsl 4y	Beer party brawl.
30.	m	36+	m	-21	Wch	Beating	Gmsl 3y	- - - - - - - - -
31.	m	36+	f	36+	W	Stick	Gmsl 7y	Wife committed adultery. Acc at large for one year before he was caught.
32.	m	21+	f	36+	W	Knife	Gmu comm20y	Dec ran away.
33.	m	21+	m	36+	U	Cord	Gmu comm20y	Killed dec while robbing him.
34.	m	21+	f	-21	U	Beating	Gmsl 4mo	Dec pupil of acc. Failed to learn lesson.
35.	m	21+	m	21+	U	U	Gmsl 8mo	Dec caught in act of theft.
36.	m	21+	m	21+	Aff	Stick	Gmsl 6mo	Acc protecting dec's wife from beating by dec.
37.	m	21+	m	21+	U	U	Gmsl 1y	Beer party brawl.
38.	m	21+	f	21+	W	Knife	Gmsl 14mo	Caught wife in adultery.
39.	m	21+	m	21+	U	Knife	Gmsl 10y	Rivalry over woman.
40.	{ m	21+	m	21+	U	U	Gmsl 12y	Dec a thief.
41.	{ m	21+			U	U	Gmsl 19m	Dec a thief.

No.	Accused Sex	Accused Age	Victim Sex	Victim Age	Kin Rel	Weapon	Judgment Sentence	Remarks
42.	m	21†	m	21†	U	Car	Gmsl 4y	Accident. Careless driving.
43.	m	~21	m	21†	Aff	Panga	Gmsl 5y	Wife ran away from acc to home of dec.
44.	m	~21	m	21†	U	Canoe paddle	Gmsl 3yprob	Quarrel over money.
45.	m	36†	f	36†	W	Stone	Gmsl 5y	Said wife refused to cook for him.
46.	m	36†	m	21†	U	Car	Gmsl 3y	Drunken driving.
47.	m	21†	f	~21	W	Knife	Gmu death	Wife ran away to parents.
48.	m	21†	m	~21	U	Panga	Gmsl 2y	Dec caught in theft.
49.	m	21†	f	21†	W	Axe	Gmu death	Wife undutiful. Tried to bewitch him.
50.	m	Ad	m	~21	U	Car	Gmsl 18mo	Accident.
51.	m	36†	f	~21	W	Knife	Gmsl 10y	Found wife in adultery.
52.	m	Ad	m	~21	N	Car	Gmsl 6mo	Speeding.
53.	m	Ad	f	21†	W	Kick	Gmsl 15mo	Marital quarrel.
54.	m	Ad	m	Ad	N	Car	Gmsl 1y	Drunken driving.
55.	m	21†	m	Ad	Ag	Stick	Gmsl 5y	Dec tried to stop acc fighting with wife.
56.	m	21†	f	21†	W	Knife	Gmsl 7y	Found wife with lover.
57.	m	Ad	f	21†	W	Spear	Gmsl 3y	Found wife in adultery with leper.
58.	m	36†	m	21†	U	Stick	Gmsl 3y	Found wife in adultery with dec.
59.	m	21†	f	36†	Ki	Stick	Gmsl 2y	Beer party brawl. Hit dec by mistake.
60.	m	21†	f	21†	U	Knife	Gmu death	Dec was the acc's concubine. She ran away from him.
61.	m	21†	m	21†	U	Cord	Gmsl 4y	Dec in adultery with wife.
62.	m	21†	m	Ad	N	Car	Gmsl 12mo	Accident.
63.	m	Ad	f	Ad	W	Fist	Gmsl 18mo	Argument about child.
64.	m	Ad	m	Ad	U	Stick	Gmsl 3y	Beer party brawl.
65.	m	Ad			U	Stick	Gmsl 3y	Beer party brawl.
66.	m	Ad	m	Ad	B	Axe	Gmsl 6y	Acc said dec tried to burn his house.
67.	m	Ad	m	Ad	U	Canoe paddle	Gmu death	Dec a public official. Disagreement over weight of fish.
68.	m	65†	m	21†	BS	Axe	Gmu comm10y	Acc thought dec had poisoned him.
69.	m	36†	f	21†	W	Stick	Gmsl 7y	Dec caught in act of adultery.
70.	m	Ad	m	Ad	U	Panga	Gmsl 6y	Dec caught in act of theft.
71.	m	36†	m	Ad	WS	Knife	Gmsl 6y	Acc fighting with wife. Dec intervened.
72.	m	~20	m	51†	F	Stick	Gmsl 2y	Father and son began fighting at funeral feast. Drinking. Later father came to son's house who hit him not knowing who it was.
73.	m	21†	f	21†	W	Knife	Gmu comm20y	Thought wife was making him impotent by sorcery.
74.	m	36†	f	21†	W	U	Gmsl 2y	Acc tried to stop fight between 2 wives. Beat them. Dec died from mild beating.
75.	m	51†	f	36†	W	Axe	Gmsl 10y	Both drinking. Wife refused to have intercourse and insulted him.
76.	m	21†	m	21†	U	Stick	Gmsl 9mo	Dec caught in act of theft.
77.	m	21†	f	21†	W	Adze	Gmu comm20y	Wife ran away from him after giving him VD
78.	m	21†	m	21†	StepB	Firewood	Gmsl 21mo	Quarrel over a fowl

No.	Accused Sex	Accused Age	Victim Sex	Victim Age	Kin Rel	Weapon	Judgment Sentence	Remarks
79.	m	Ad	f	21+	W	Knife	Gmu comm20y	Wife wanted separation. Chief disallowed. She left him regardless. Husband killed her.
80.	m	Ad	f	21+	W	Knife	Gmsl 10y	Wife ran away to parents. Resisted husband's attempt to take her back.
81.	m	Ad	m	21+	U	Hoe	Gmu comm20y	Dec having affair with acc's wife.
82.	m	Ad	f	Ad	W	Hoe	Gmu comm10y	Wife unfaithful. Refused to work. Insulted husband.
83.	m	Ad	m	Ad	N	Spear	Gmsl 2y	Beer party.
84.	m	Ad	m	Ad	U	Car	Gmsl 9mo	Accident.
85.	f	Ad	f	21+	U	Pestle	Gmsl 3y	Found husband and dec in adultery.
86.	m	Ad	m	21+	ZHFZH	Knife	Gmsl 14y	Beer party quarrel.
87.	m	Ad	f	21+	U	Knife	Gmu death	Dec was mistress of acc and was unfaithful.
88.	m	21+	f	Ad	W	Medicine	Gmsl 12mo	Accident while trying to cure wife of disease. Injection.
89.	m	36+	f	Ad	W	U	U	Worried about impotence.
90.	m	36+	f	Ad	W	U	U	Wife threatened to leave him.
91.	m	36+	f	Ad	W	U	U	- - - - - - - -
92.	m	21+	f	Ad	WM	Panga	U	Dec harboring wife of acc.
93.	m	21+	f	Ad	W	U	U	Wife wanted to leave him.
94.	m	36+	f	Ad	W	Panga	U	- - - - - - - -
95.	m	21+	f	Ad	Wki	U	U	Dec became involved in quarrel between husband and wife.
96.	m	21+	f	Ad	W	U	U	- - - - - - - -
97.	m	36+	f	Ad	W	U	U	Quarrel with wife's father who lived nearby.
98.	m	36+	f	21+	W	U	U	Quarrel over washing clothes.
99.	m	36+	f	Ad	W	U	U	Wife in mourning for death of father's sister. Not allowed intercourse. Husband tried to force her.
100.	m	21+	f	Ad	W	U	U	Wife gave goat to sister without acc's permission.

No.	Accused Sex	Accused Age	Victim Sex	Victim Age	Kin Rel	Weapon	Judgment Sentence	Remarks
1.	m	U	m	U	F"B"	Knife	Gmsl 3yHL	Dec tried to stop acc from beating his wife.
2.	m	U	m	U	Ag	Knife	Dis	Dec drunk. Not acc's fault in local opinion. Land
3.	m	25	m	43	Ag	Stick	Gmsl 1moHL	Dec came to acc's hut at night and attacked him.
4.	m	U	m	U	U	Kick	Dis	Dec drunk and insulted acc. No evidence.
5.	m	U	F	13	Ag	Arrow	Gmu death	Long feud with dec's father. Premeditated.
6.	m	25	m	Old	F	U	Dis	Local opinion that the 2 had quarrelled over dec's 3rd wife.
7.	4m	U	m	U	U	Stick	GmuComm 15yHL	Drunken brawl at beer shop. All set on non-Gisu.
8.	m	U	m	70	MAg	Stick	GmuComm 20yHL	Both drunk. Insulted each other. Acc said to have killed another man.
9.	m	U	m	U	Ag	Spear	Gmu death	Feud. Acc a dangerous character. Had killed another man.
10.	m	30	m	35	U	Pestle	Gmu death	Local opinion said it was political rivalry. Suspected wife's lover.
11.	m	50	m	U	FinL	Spear	GmuComm 20yHL	Dec refused to send acc's wife back.
12.	m	16	m	18	U	Knife	Gmsl	Quarrel over sale of shirt and money owed acc. Acc under-age. Bound over to village head.
13.	7m	U	m	U	U	Beating	Gmsl 3yHL	Beer party. One of acc made advances at dec's woman.
14.	f	20	m	U	N	Knife	Dis	Attempted rape after beer party.

No.	Accused Sex	Accused Age	Victim Sex	Victim Age	Kin Rel	Weapon	Judgment Sentence	Remarks
15.	m	35	m	U	N	Spear	Gms1 3moHL	3 men caught stealing cattle.
16.	m	U	m	U	BinLS	Spear	Gms1 6moHL	Dec found in theft.
17.	m	19	m	U	U	Stick	Gms1 3moHL	Acc found thieves in his hut.
18.	m	35	f	U	N	Panga	GmuComm 20y	Witchcraft.
19.	m	35	f	U	W	Knife	GmuComm 20y	Wife left him. 4th unsuccessful marriage.
20.	f	U	m	U	HB	Hammer	Gms1 4yHL	Acc barren. Dec tried to force her to let husband take 2nd wife.
21.	m	U	m	U	U	Firewood	Acq	Beer party brawl.
22.	2m	27	m	U	U	Firewood	Gms1 3yHL	Beer party brawl between 2 lineage groups.
23.	m	28	m	30	Wki	Panga	Gms1 6yHL	Blood feud. Habitually on bad terms. Row at beer party.
24.	m	26	m	U	FB	Knife	Gms1 12yHL	Dec tried to expel acc from land. Self-defense.
25.	m	U	f	U	W	Beating	Acq	Dec after beer party attacked acc and children.
26.	m	Yg	m	U	U	Stick	Gms1	Caught dec stealing goat meat. Acc under-age. Not imprisoned.
27.	m	28	m	U	U	Stone	Gms1 2yHL	Acc was refused beer at beer party for work.
28.	3m	U	m	U	U	Panga	2Acq 1 2yHL	Fighting over dec's claim that accs took cows.
29.	m	U	f	U	W	Panga	Gmu	Suspected wife of adultery. Tried to commit suicide.
30.	m	45	m	U	B	Hoe	Gmu death	Quarrel over disposal of their sister's bridewealth.
31.	m	32	m	U	F	Stick	Gms1 3yHL	Fight at beer drink. Father rebuked him for putting reed in beer pot.
32.	m	U	m	U	clF	Club	Gms1 3yHL	Acc said dec bewitched wife.
33.	f	U	m	U	H	Firewood	Acq.	Self-defense. Acc 7 months pregnant.
34.	m	U	f	U	M	Blow	Dis	Dec insane and attacked acc who later tried to hang himself.
35.	m	24	m	U	B	Knife	Gms1 2yHL	Quarrel over distribution of cows of sister's bridewealth.
36.	m	38	m	U	U	Firewood	Gms1 2yHL	Gambling quarrel.
37.	m	U	f	U	MinL	Panga	Gmu death	4th cow on bridewealth of dec's daughter not returned.
38.	m	U	m	U	N	Stick	N.P.	- - - - - - - -
39.	m	14	m	U	F	Wood	Rel	Father drunk. Attacked acc's mother.
40.	m	24	m	50	F	Stick	Gms1 2yHL	Family quarrel with insults.
41.	m	U	m	U	ZHF	Spear	Gms1 2yHL	Beer party brawl. Acc's sister supported him and was beaten too.
42.	f	U	f	U	M	Hoe	Gms1 6moHL	Dec scolded and insulted acc - an un-married adult living at home.
43.	f	U	f	U	U	Bite	U	Dec stole from acc's garden. Acc bit her. Dec got gangrene and died.
44.	m	U	f	U	M	Stick	Gms1 2yHL	Acc found dec and husband having inter-course. Husband beat him. Fight er ued.
45.	m	U	m	U	Ag	Stick	Gms1 18moHL	Dec forced way into acc's hut.
46.	m	U	m	U	U	None	Dis	Thief caught in flagrante.
47.	6 m	U	m	U	N	Beating	Gms1 6wkHL	Dec an escaped prisoner.
48.	m	U	f	45	clM	Panga	Gms1 7yHL	Dec involved in struggle in fight between her husband and acc.
49.	m	U	m	U	U	Knife	Gms1 7yHL	Exchange of insults when drunk. Then fight.
50.	m	U	m	U	Ag	Stick	Gms1 1dHL	Dispute between lineages over authority of chief.
51.	m	U	m	U	U	Spear	Gms1 3moHL	Attempt to escape from unjustified arrest. Beaten by dec.
52.	m	20	m	U	clF	Stick Panga	Gms1 5yHL	Acc got very drunk and attacked dec.
53.	4m	U	m	U	U	Stick	N.P.	Dec a thief. Attacked acc. Dec had been in jail twice.
54.	f	U	m	U	H	Spear	Gms1 2yHL	Dec drunk and attacked acc.

No.	Accused Sex	Age	Victim Sex	Age	Kin Rel	Weapon	Judgment Sentence	Remarks
55.	m	U	m	U	U	Stick panga	Gmsl 7yHL	Acc taunted publicly by dec for being afraid of circumcision.
56.	f	U	m	U	H	Hoe	Acq	Self-defense. Acc pregnant. Both hospitalized after fight.
57.	m	27	m	U	B	Fist	Gmsl 6moHL	Both drunk. Acc refused dec beer and they fought.
58.	2m	30	m	U	U	Beating	1Bond 2ReI	Dec had served previous sentence for theft.
59.	m	U	f	60	U	Beating	Gmsl 6yHL	Quarrel over marital trouble of acc's sister.
60.	m	U	m	60	U	Stick	Gmsl	Quarrel at beer party over giving child beer. Bonded over for 3 years for sh.100.
61.	m	26	m	U	F	Stick	Gmsl 2yHL	Quarrel over beer. Dec insulted acc by going naked in front of him.
62.	m	60	m	U	exWH	Spear	GmuComm 20yHL	Bridewealth had been returned and marriage dissolved by a council.
63.	m	30	f	W	W	Spear	Gmu death	Habitually of jealous and violent nature. "I thought she was going to poison me."
64.	m	U	m	Old	U	Beating Nail	Gmu	Dec hated and feared by all. Local opinion that acc had done a good job.
65.	m	35	m	U	U	Fist	Acq	Dec lay in wait for him following beer party brawl.
66.	m	50	m	U	U	Spear	Gmsl 9moHL	Thief.
67.	m	50	m	U	U	Stick	Gmsl 1yHL	Dec forced his way into acc's house, demanding payment of a debt.
68.	m	35	m	8	U	Knife	Gmsl 2yHL	No apparent motive. Acc drunk. Dec son of acc's neighbour.
69.	m	Yg	m	U	1/2B	Knife	Gmu	Angry at dec for trying to stop him from beating his wife.
70.	5m	U	m	U	U	Strangling	1GmuD 2-520yHL	Wife of acc I in adultery with dec.(?)
71.	8m	U	m	60	U	Stick	Gmsl 3yHL	Fight between lineages over fishing rights in river which formed boundary.
			m	U				
72.	U	U	m	U	U	Stab	U	U
73.	2m	U	m	U	U	U	U	U
74.	m	U	m	U	F	U	U	U
75.	m	U	m	U	U	Spear	U	Dec a thief. Acc heard movements at night. Threw spear thinking it was an animal. Justifiable homicide.
76.	m	U	m	U	U	U	U	Dec caught stealing cattle.
77.	f	U	m	U	H	U	--	Acc brought back forcibly from lover. Acc and dec found dead. She killed him and hanged herself.
78.	m	U	m	U	U	Arrow	U	U
79.	m	U	m	U	U	Knife	U	Acc sold dec a cow for 4 goats. One died. Dec tried to take replacement awarded in court case.
80.	m	U	m	U	U	Stick	Gmsl 2yHL	Dec a thief.
81.	m	U	m	U	U	Stick	--	Dec found having intercourse with acc's wife. Acc and wife escaped to Kenya and were not found.
82.	f	U	f	Yg	U	U	U	U
83.	U	U	f	U	U	U	U	U
84.	m	U	f	U	W	U	U	U
85.	m	U	m	U	B	Kicks	Acq	Acc going to steal a cow from sister's bridewealth. Dec attacked him.
86.	m	U	f	U	U	U	U	U
87.	U	U	m	U	U	U	U	U
88.	m	U	m	U	clB	Knife	U	Beer party quarrel.
89.	m	U	m	U	U	U	Rel	Dec was lover of acc's wife. Insufficient evidence.
90.	m	U	f	U	W	Kicks	N.P.	Dec refused to give acc the keys to their hut.
91.	m	U	m	Old	U	Hoe	U	U
92.	2m	U	m	U	F	U	U	Acc refused more beer by dec at mourning rites for his classifactory brother.
93.	m	U	m	50	U	U	U	Found dead in river. Evidence of violence.
94.	m	35	f	U	U	Spear	--	Acc committed suicide. Witnesses said he quarrelled with wife and killed her.
95.	2m	U	m	U	B	Panga	--	Dec found 2 acc ploughing his land. Fight ensued.
96.	m	U	m	U	U	Stick	Gmsl 2yHL	Dec a thief. Acc said he stole his maize.

No.	Accused Sex	Accused Age	Victim Sex	Victim Age	Kin Rel	Weapon	Judgment Sentence	Remarks
97.	m	U	m	U	U	Axe	Acq	Acc and wife prevented from fighting by dec. Death due to infection of wounds.
98.	2m	U	m	50	clB	U	- -	No evidence for trial. Indication that quarrel was over land.
99.	U	U	m	U	U	U	- -	Found dead with marks of violence.

BANYORO HOMICIDE

No.	Accused Sex	Accused Age	Victim Sex	Victim Age	Kin Rel	Weapon	Judgment Sentence	Remarks
1.	m	65	f	30	U	Arson	Death	Meant to kill man who had accused him of killing father by sorcery.
			f	5				
2.	m	50	m	60	WF	Stick Knife	Death comm20y	Believed that dec had caused his daughter to have many miscarriages.
3.	m	25	f	Old	U	Strangled	Death comm10y	Believed dec had killed acc I's elder brother by sorcery.
	m	23						
4.	m	Old	m	50	U	Spear	Death	Dec had defiled acc's house.
5.	m	42	m	35	U	Stick	Acq	Found dec cohabiting with mistress.
6.	m	50	m	38	U	Strangled	G D / Acq	Acc I believed dec danced promiscuously with his wife.
	m	35						
7.	m	30	f	Old	McoW	Knife	9y	Acc believed dec had killed his mother by sorcery.
8.	m	18	f	45	M	Spear	G ins	Resented mother's forbidding his return to beer party.
9.	m	50	f	45	W	Stick	G ins	Believed dec practising sorcery against him.
10.	f	37	f	40	coW	Knife	Death comm10y	Believed dec practising sorcery against her.
11	m	38	f	35	BW	Arson	Acq	Believed dec killed his brother by sorcery.
12.	m	36	f	18	U	Strangled	Death comm15y	Wanted to silence victim of rape.
13.	m	26	m	28	U	Stick	Gms1?	Accused jealous of sexual prowess of rival.
	m	24						
14.	m	45	m	40	U	Spear	Death	Dec refused to pay debt.
15.	m	25	f	50	WM	Spear	Gms1 8y	Dec would not allow her daughter to return to acc.
16.	m	40	f	30	W	Knife	Death comm3y	Wife had left him for another.
17.	m	35	m	30	U	Spear	Death	Thought victim was a thief.
18.	m	30	f	28	Mist	Spear	Death comm15y	Dec left him for another.
19.	m	55	f	20	SW	Spear	Death	Dec resisted his sexual advances.
20.	m	36	f	67	U	Knife	Death comm15y	Thought son of dec killed his relatives by sorcery.
21.	m	35	f	25	W	U	Suicide	Wife refused to return to him.
22.	m	50	f	U	U	U	Suicide	- - - - - - -
23.	f	30	f	50	HBW	Stick	N. P.	Resented accusations of sorcery.
	f	22			FBW			
24.	m	35	m	30	U	Spear	Gms1 7y	Found dec cohabiting with acc's wife.
25.	m	28	f	30	W	Axe	Death comm20y	Wife wanted to leave and go to her lover.
26.	f	Ad	-	Yg	Ch	Axe	Suicide	Acc jealous of husband's other wife.
			-	Yg	Ch			
27.	m	39	f	34	W	Knife	Death	Wife refused to return to him or to refund bridewealth.
28.	m	25	f	Old	M	Arson	N.G. / Acq	Believed dec to have killed wife of acc I by sorcery.
	m	19			MZ			
29.	m	20	m	55	F	Spear	Death comm20y	Resented rebuke by father who sent him home from beer party.
30.	m	37	f	60	WM	Spear	Death	Dec had persuaded her daughter to leave acc.
31.	m	48	m	40	U	Gun	Death	Resisting arrest.
32.	m	35	f	30	W	Knife	Suicide	Wife wished to leave him.
33.	m	17	m	25	B	Spear	Gms1 6y	Feared sorcery by brother, whose property he had stolen.
34.	m	40	m	45	U	Knife	Acq	Resented demand for payment of debt by dec whom he believed a sorcerer.

BALUYIA HOMICIDE

No.	Accused Sex	Accused Age	Victim Sex	Victim Age	Kin Rel	Weapon	Judgment Sentence	Remarks
1.	f	24	f	2	HkiD	Axe	Gms1 6moHL	Fight between acc and mother of dec over needle. Meant to strike dec's mother.
2.	4m	Ad	m	Ad	U	Knife fimbo	½Gms1-1d / 2-4 rel	Argument over walking stick.
3.	f	U	f	U	CoW	Panga	Gms1 2yHL	Argument over inheritance.
4.	m	U	f	U	W	Axe	Gmu hgd	Divorced. Crime followed sex before parting.
5.	m	U	m	2	BS	Panga	Gmu hgd	Land bickering for many years. Beserk.
			f	Ad	BW			
			f	6y	BD			
			m	Ad	AgKi			
6.	f	Ad	f	58	N	Fist	Gms1 1d	Dec causing trouble among co-wives. One hit her.
7.	m	Old	m	65	N	Panga	Gmu hgd	Dispute between neighbors over thatching grass.
8.	m	20	m	25	N	Stick	Gms1 3yHL	Argument over girls and money.
9.	m	29	m	30	"C"	Panga	Gms1 3yHL .	Dec abusing acc's wife about court case.
10.	2m	26	m	Ad	U	Stick	½Gms1-4y / 2-Acq	Dec broke lamp of acc at beer party which led to fight.
11.	2m	20 22	m	27	U	Stick	Acq	Beer drink. Fracas when one man refused to stop dancing and be quiet.
12.	2m	U	m	U	B	Stick	½Gms1-5y / 2 Acq	Acc I said dec stole sheep. Dec attacked.
13.	5m	U	f	17	U	Suffocation	N.P.	Acc acquitted murder and rape.
14.	2m	U	m	Old	U	Stick	Gms1 3yHL	Acc II stole dec's daughter. Dec killed acc II and was killed by Acc II's brother, acc I.
15.	m	U	f	Old	U	Stick	Gms1 5yHL	Dec stole 2 of acc's chickens. Both drunk at time of fight.
16.	5m	U	m	35	U	Beating	½Gms1-5y / 2-5-4yHL	"Bad blood" between acc I and dec. Honey beer.
17.	m	Yg	f	13	U	Stick	Gms1 6moHL	Accident.
18.	m	U	m	U	FinL	Panga	Gmu death	Beat wife for inadequate care of children. 3 had died. The 4th ill. Her father interrupted, was killed. Acc escaped to Uganda. Detained 2 years later.
19.	4m	U	m	U	U	Knife fimbo	Dis	Thief killed at night.
20.	3m	U	m	Old	ZH	Firewood	½Gmu / 2-3Acces	Dec wife said her brothers killed dec because he sent her away.
21.	m	U	f	55	DHB	Axe	Acq	Dec's daughter said dec trying to steal chickens.
22.	6m	U	m	U	U	U	Dis	Foul play suspected from husbands of 3 women dec had seduced.
23.	m	U	m	32	N	Axe	Gms1 5yHL	Acc tried to make dec stop beating decs wife. Dec attacked acc.
24.	m	U	f	U	W	Strangled	Suicide	Dec's father said that acc killed dec and feigned her suicide.
25.	m	U	m	U	N	Stick	Gms1 2yHL	Acc said dec burnt his father's house.
26.	m	50	m	U	U	Spear	Gms1 6yHL	Land case existed between father of acc and dec.
27.	m	25	m	U	B	Hammer	Gms1 1yHL	Dec used acc's house as chicken coop.
28.	m	U	m	U	DHZ	Panga	Gms1 6moHL	Dec attacked acc over bridewealth.
29.	m	30	m	U	N	Beating	Gsm1-1yHL / Gsm1-6mHL	Dec a thief with one previous conviction.
	m	40						
30.	m	U	m	U	N	Beating	Gms1 18moHL	Dec attempting to steal cattle. Acc had one former conviction.
31.	m	Ad	m	U	1/2B	Club	Gms1 8yHL	Dec wife said dec blamed dec for killing children by witchcraft.
32.	m	U	f	U	N	Illegal inject	Gms1	Acc practicing without license. 3 previous convictions for other things.
			m	U				
33.	m	U	m	Old	Ag	Poison	Dis	Dec a well-known witch-doctor thought to have killed acc's 2 children.
34.	m	U	m	U	N	Stick	Dis	Justifiable homicide. Dec stealing cattle. Attacked acc with knife.
35.	f	U	f	U	Hch	Arson	Dis	Dec said acc bewitched her co-wife's children. Acc insane. Taken to hospital.
			m	Yg				
			m	Yg				

No.	Accused Sex	Accused Age	Victim Sex	Victim Age	Kin Rel	Weapon	Judgment Sentence	Remarks
36.	m	U	f	U	BW	Stick	Gms1 4yHL	Dec provoked acc by interfering in quarrel between him and his wife.
37.	m	U	f	U	W	Beating	Gms1 3moHL	Dec refused to sleep with acc. She attacked him. He beat her.
38.	m	32	f	U	W	Stick	Gms1 18moHL	Adultery of wife. Husband beat lover. Killed wife for subsequent offense.
39.	f	U	f	U	U	--	Ms1 rel	Illegal clitorectomy. Dec pregnant. Pneumonia set in.
40.	m	21	m / f	U / 12	U	Spear	Gms1 5yHL	Land dispute between acc and dec. Dec II daughter of dec I. Beer.
41.	m	40	m	U	U	Spear	Gms1 9moHL	Old enemies. Dec liked acc's wife. Fought at all beer parties.
42.	m	30	m	U	U	Stick	Gmu death	Dec's child died. Acc asked for food during mourning. Dec refused. Acc hit him.
43.	m	21	m	U	F1/2B	Arrow	Gms1	No quarrel. Fear when dec came at night. Acc had arrow in hand. Dec subnormal.
44.	m	21	m	U	1/2B	Knife	Gms1 2yHL	Father drinking. Beat acc's mother. Acc stabbed father (non-lethal) and 1/2 brother.
45	m	Ad	f	12	D	Stick	1d prison	Father told daughter to mind child. She refused. He threw stick. Accident.
46.	2m	35	m	U	Ki	Stick	1-8moHL 2 rel	Dec started fight over girls. Provocation. Accident.
47.	m	27	m	U	U	Knife	Gms1 18moHL	Dispute over right of passage of bicycle led to quarrel
48.	m	30	m	U	1/2B	Spear	3mo prison	Acc found dec and his wife copulating. Dec tried to kill him with panga.
49.	m	35	m	U	U	Stick	Gms1 10moHL	Dec caught copulating with wife of acc.
50.	m	35	m	U	1/2B	Knife	No rec	Dec said acc bewitched his children.
51.	m	45	m	U	U	Stick	Gms1 2yHL	Accident. Dec tried to stop acc wife-beating. Acc habitual banghi smoker.
52.	m	55	m	Old	U	Operation	1dHL	Dec ill for years. Demanded operation.
53.	m	22	m	U	F	Stick	Gms1 7yHL	Dec drunk. Father and son on bad terms. Son did not help him.
54.	m	19	m	U	U	Knife	Gms1 5yHL	Fight at dance. No enmity.
55.	f	14	m	17	Ki	Hoe	N.P.	Acc corrected dec's young brother. Dec angry. Struck her. She struck back. "Children's quarrel".
56.	m	35	m	50	BwidH	Stick	Gms1 7yHL	Dec was husband of acc's brother's widow whom acc should have inherited.
57.	m	39	f / m	U / Yg	W / U	Knife / Strang	N. P.	Acc in mania from ablosufan, leprosy drug.
58.	m	U	f	U	U	Poison?	Dis	Poison tests found negative.
59.	f	U	m	U	U	Panga	Gmu hgd	Dec and husband of acc quarreled about land. Dec claimed acc had poisoned her husband.
60.	2m	U	m	U	U	Poison?	Dis	Dec drank medicine as protection against his enemy's medicine.
61.	m	36	m	U	FBS	Knife	Gms1 7yHL	Anger over land case. Beer.
62.	m / m / m / f	30 / 25 / 28 / 40	m	U	U	Beating	N. P.	All drunk. Dispute over payment of pot of beer.
63.	m	45	m	U	S	Spear	Dis	Accident. Recent thieves. Boy came in drunk. Did not answer challenge.
64.	m	22	f	U	M	Kick	Gms1 18moHL	Dec told that she and acc were bewitched. Dec refused to keep still about it as requested by acc. He kicked her.
65.	m	30	m	U	FB	Stick	Gmu death	Dec inherited mother of acc. Dec "spoiled" the name of acc. Premeditated.
66.	m / f	30 / U	m	U	U	Kick	18moHL Rel	Acc I and acc II man and wife. Dec made pass at acc II.
67.	m	20	f	U	c1M	Kick	18moHL	Dec struck acc's children. Acc struck back.
68.	m	22	f	U	FW	Jembe	Gms1 6moHL	Acc threw hoe at cow to head it off. Accident.
69.	m	32	f	U	U	Kick	Gms1 3yHL	Both drunk. Dec called acc a thief.
70.	m	42	m	U	U	Panga	Gms1 8yHL	Argument and fight at beer party. No previous ill feeling.

No.	Accused Sex	Accused Age	Victim Sex	Victim Age	Kin Rel	Weapon	Judgment Sentence	Remarks
71.	m	U	m	U	U	Panga	Gms1 8yHL	Dec demanded toll at bridge. Acc refused to pay. Fight.
72.	m	U	m	U	U	Knife	Acq	Dec's wife insulted acc at wedding party. Fight. Beer.
73.	m	U	m	U	FB	Arrow	Gms1 8yHL	Drinking.
74.	m	32	m	U	U	Panga	Gms1 8yHL	Acc claimed dec bewitched his 4 children
			f	U		Spear		
75.	m	U	m	U	U	Poison	Dis	Report of government chemist does not support charge of manslaughter.
76.	m	U	m	U	N	Beating	Gms1 1dHL	Beating as result of bicycle accident. Blow would not normally kill.
77.	m	U		Yg	N	Kick?	U	Thought dec was a thief.
78.	2m	U	m	Old	U B	Kick	Acq	Argument at beer party. Denied any motive.
79.	m	Old	m	U	U	Spear	Gms1 1yHL	Thief.
80.	m	45	m	45	U	Stick	Gms1 4yHL	Dec's wife said they were not on good terms. Land case.
81.	m	U	m	U	U	Spear	Gms1 12yHL	Fight at beer drink. Acc said dec stabbed himself by accident.
82.	m	U	m	U	WF	Knife	Gms1 5yHL	Acc beating wife. Dec tried to stop him. Wife had deserted acc.
83.	m	27	m	U	U	Knife	Gms1 3yHL	No apparent motive. Acc said "You are my enemy".
84.	m	U	f	U	N	Panga	Gms1 4yHL	Dec interfered in fight between acc and another. Got hit. Drinking.
85.	m	32	m	20	U	Knife	Gms1 3yHL	Fight over who would buy next bottle of Nubian gin.
86.	m	32	m	25	U	Medicine	N. P.	Acc a witch doctor. No intent. Acc had used this medicine before with good effects.
87.	m	16?	m	3	U	Arson	N. G.	Father of dec accidently burned hut of father of acc who swore revenge. Assessors all said guilty. Released on technicality.
			m	8mo				
88.	m	14	m	Yg	U	Knife	Acq	Witness said dispute was over 40¢
89.	m	30	m	40	U	Knife	Gms1 3yHL	Dispute over price of table. Beer and Nubian gin.
90.	m	40	m	60	U	Stick	Gmu	Land dispute. Dec threatened to curse acc.
91.	m	U	m	30	U	Iron	Gms1 2yHL	Thief.
92.	m	16	m	U	U	Stick	Gms1 rel	Argument in dice game.
93.	m	28	m	20	U	Knife	Rel	Self-defense. Acc attacked on road by 3 men said Mau-Mau.
94.	m	U	m	U	F	Panga	Gms1 8yHL	Father attacked him and tried to kill his bridewealth cattle.
95	m	U	f	U	U	Knife	Gmu	"My head was bad". He dreamed he would kill a woman. Appeal dismissed.
96.	m	49	m	U	U	Stick	Rel	Self-defense. Dec and his brother were drunk.
97.	m	U	m	22	U	Knife	U	Beer party fight.
98.	m	U	m	U	S	Knife	Gmu death	Dispute over land. Son took out knife and attacked.
99.	m	15	m	U	N	Hoe?	Appr school	Acc defending 10 year old sister's honor. Said he was being taunted for being Luo.
100.	m	19	m	U	U	Spear	Gms1 5yHL	Acc had girl in house. Dec knocked several times. Acc said thought it was a thief.
101,	m	20	m	32	F1/2BS	Stick	Gms1 3yHL	Acc claimed dec was taking his blanket. Both drunk.
102.	m	U	f	Old	U	Beating	Gms1 10yHL	Acc denied crime. Judge said it was not sexual assault.
103.	m	50	m	60	N	Stick	Rel	Dec refused right of way over fenced farm. Acc said fight not cause of death.
	m	48						
104.	m	U	m	U	F	Stick	Gms1 2yHL	Father attacked son who took stick and beat him after father had told him to go to boma of his genitor.
105.	m	50	m	U	B	Jembe	Rel	Self-defense. Dec attacked.
	m	46						
106.	m	35	f	U	W	Knife	Gms1 5yHL	Both drunk. Acc thought someone was having sex intercourse with her.
107.	m	U	m	Yg	1/2B	Stone	Rel	Accident. Fighting over a cow that died.

BALUYIA HOMICIDE

No.	Accused Sex	Accused Age	Victim Sex	Victim Age	Kin Rel	Weapon	Judgment Sentence	Remarks
08.	m	U	m	25	U	Stick	Gmu death	Dec spent night at "hotel" with wife of acc.
09.	m	U	m	28	U	Knife	Gmu death	Argument at beer drink.
10.	m	U	m	U	MB?	Spear	No rec	Drunk on Nubian gin. Celebrating dec's wedding to Luo girl.
11.	m	U	m	U	B	Spear	N. P.	Beer. Drunk.
12.	m	U	f	U	W	Scythe	G ins prison	Insanity. Said her father was killing him.
13.	m	45	f	U	W	Beating	Msl rel	Dec attacked acc and beat their daughter for staying out all night.
14.	m	U	m	Old	U	Slasher	Gmsl 6yHL	Dec sneaking into acc's boma.

LUO HOMICIDE

No.	Accused Sex	Accused Age	Victim Sex	Victim Age	Kin Rel	Weapon	Judgment Sentence	Remarks
1.	m	U	m	U	U	Club	Dis	Quarrel over woman at dance and beer drink. Lack of evidence.
2.	m	U	f	U	W	Beating	Dis	Quarrel during preparation of beer.
3.	f	U	f	U	CoW	Panga	Gmsl 4yHL	Jealousy (NYIEKO) between wives over custody of orphaned child.
4.	m	U	f	U	CoWD	Poison Z	Dis	Inadequate cooking of raw cassava.
5.	2m	U	f	U	Z	Stick	6moHL	Bridewealth dispute. Dec tried to leave husband for lover. Her brothers killed her.
6.	m	U	m	U	Ag	Panga	3yHL	Quarrel when drinking.
7.	m	U	m	U	U	Spear	Gmsl	Dec took acc's wife.
8.	m	U	f	U	W	U	Dis	Medical report could not determine cause of death.
9.	2m	U	m	U	Ki	Stick	Dis	Both drunk. Quarrel at dance and beer drink over girl.
10.	m	U	m	U	Ki	Fight	Not proven	Dec had reported a theft committed by acc.
11.	m	Yg	m	U	Ki	Stick	3yHL	Drink and "Bhang".
12.	2m	U	m	U	Ag	Fight	Rel	Dec refused to return plow chains. Fight ensued.
13.	m	U	f	U	W	Club	3yHL	Discipline. Woman was lazy.
14.	m	U	m	U	U	Stick	Dis	Cattle were allowed to stray. Death after beating.
15.	m	U	f	U	W	Spear	Gmsl	Quarrel over wife. Acc bound over for sh. 100.
			m	U	Ki			
16.	m	U	f	U	W	Kick	Dis	Acc claimed he kicked at dog and hit wife by accident.
17.	m	15	m	U	F	Knife	Prob 3y	Killed father after having been out all night.
18.	m	U	m	U	U	Knife	Dis	Argument over property. No evidence.
19.	m	Yg	m	U	U	Spear	Dis	Acc a juvenile, confused. Killed playmate.
20.	3m	U	m	U	U	Knife	Acq	All drunk. Dec stabbed a man. Others beat him.
21.	f	U	f	U	U	Axe	Ins	Quarrelled about food.
22.	9m	U	m	U	U	Spear	1Gd 2-9dis	Avenging father's death. Father wrongfully imprisoned by dec and died as result. Acc I released on appeal.
23.	m	U	m	U	U	Knife	6yHL	Quarrel at beer party.
24.	m	U	m	U	U	Knife	6yHL	Quarrel at beer party.
25.	m	U	m	U	U	Spear	Rel bond	Dec stealing cattle.
26.	m	U	m	U	U	Knife	8yHL	Quarrel over debt at drinking party.
27.	m	U	m	U	Ki	Knife	1yHL	Beer. Quarrel among kinsmen.
28.	m	U	m	U	U	Knife	Gmu	With 4 friends tried to "pull" girl. Dec killed in trying to stop them.
29.	m	U	f	U	W	Stick	Chg wtd	Discipline.
30.	f	U	m	U	U	Stone	3mo prison	Quarrel about making a fire.
31.	m	U	m	U	B	Knife	Dis	Quarrel in bed between brothers. Drunk.
32.	m	U	m	U	U	Club	Chg wtd	Drunk.

No.	Accused Sex	Accused Age	Victim Sex	Victim Age	Kin Rel	Weapon	Judgment Sentence	Remarks
33.	m	U	m	U	U	Knife	8yHL	Quarrel at beer party.
34.	m	U	m	U	U	Kick	Prob3y	Quarrel about a bicycle pump at beer party.
35.	m	U	m	U	U	U	Dis	Quarrel over land. No evidence.
36.	m	U	m	U	U	Knife	U	Quarrel over women. Drunk.
37.	m	U	m	U	U	Club	3yHL	Acc set dog on dec. Fight set in.
38.	m	U	m	U	U	Stick	Dis	Fight over girl. Guilt not proven.
39.	m	U	m	U	U	Stab	Dis	Longstanding quarrel involving women and pride. Self-defense.
40.	m	U	f	U	U	Knife	Dis	Quarrel about sheep theft. Lack of evidence. Collected blood and tongue to use in cleansing ceremony.
41.	m	U	f	U	1/2BW	Stick	4yHL	Dec interfered in quarrel between acc and dec's wife.
42.	m	32	f	U	U	Kick	3yHL	Beer.
43.	m	U	m	U	U	Knife	Acq	Fight at wedding. Beer.
44.	m	15	m	U	U	Hoe?	Gmsl	Killed in blind anger over insults. Sent to approved school until 18.

No.	Accused Sex	Accused Age	Victim Sex	Victim Age	Kin Rel	Weapon	Judgment Sentence	Remarks
1	m	30	m	35	N	Stick	GMs1 5yHL	Beer party. Victim Muganda. Occurred Buganda.
2	m	Ad	m	Ad	None	Hoe	GmuD	Occurred West Nile.
3	m	44	m	30	None	Stick	Ms1 7yHL	Victim Muganda. Occurred Buganda
4	m	Ad	m	30	None	Stick	Ms1 10yHL	Victim Muganda. Occurred Buganda.
	m	Ad					Same	
5	m	Ad	m	Ad	None	Car	Ms1 1yHL	West Nile.
6	m	35	m	35	None	Car	1yHL	Drunk while driving. In Teso country.
7	m	Ad	m	Ad	None	Stick	NolPros	Dec Muganda thief. Happened in Buganda.
8	m	14	m	22	Neighbor	Pestle	Ms1 3yHL	Provocation. Victim Acholi, occurred in Buganda.
9	m	Ad	f	Ad	Wife	Bottle & hoe	3yHL	3 yrs. for unlawful wounding; no intent.
10	m	40	m	U	U	Knife	Ms1 3yHL	Acc 1 & 2 man 7 wife. Victim was Lango employed by Acc 1 as carrier.
	f	40						
11	m	Ad	f	Ch	D	Stick	Ms1 3yHL	Claimed provocation and no intent.
12	m	36	m	30	N	Fall?	NolPros	Acc prisoners; victim a guard. Wrestling and no intent proven. Victim Lugbara. Occurred Buganda.
	m	28						
13	m	Ad	m	25	Thief	Sticks	NolPros	Occurred Buganda
	m	Ad						
	m	Ad						
14	m	Ad	m	20	None	Knife	GmuD	Occurred in Buganda; victim Muganda
15	m	Ad	m	Ad	None	Stick	2yHL	Acc 1 Alur, guilty of bodily assult.
	m	Ad					4yHL	Acc 2 Rwanda, guilty Ms1.
	m	Ad					9moHL	Acc 3 Rwanda, guilty only of beating. Occurred in Buganda.
16	m	Ad	m	Ad	Neighbor	Knife	G	Provocation. Acc committed suicide.
17	m	Ad	m	30-	Neighbors	Club	NG	Discharged.
				40				Acc 2 is Dama; Acc 3 Teso.
	m	Ad						
	m	Ad						
18	m	30	m	Ad	Neighbor	Sticks	Acq	Dance; beer. Occurred in Buganda; all principals Alur.
	m	Ad						
19	m	Ad	m	30-	n	Spear	Ms1 18moHL	Members of rival clans.
				40				
20	m	Ad	m	30	None		NolPros	Beer party; victim Ankole; occurred Buganda.
21	m	36	?	30	Wife child	Knife	GmuD com20	Alur, occurred Buganda.
22	m	Ad	m	Ad	None	Panga		Incapable of defense, of unsound mind. Victim European trader.
23	m	30	f	30	Wife	Knife	GumD comm 20yHL	Jok session.

No.	Accused Sex	Accused Age	Victim Sex	Victim Age	Kin Rel	Weapon	Judgment Sentence	Remarks
24	m	40	m	25	Step S	Spear	2yHL	Provocation; attempted murder.
25	m	45	m	12-13	U	Knife?	Acq.	Only bones found. Acc 1 - 3 Acq; Remaining Acc, Nol Pros.
	m	35						
	m	50						
	m	Ad						
	m	Ad						
26	m	Ad	m	Ad	None	Knife	GmuD	Fellow employee. Occurred in Buganda.
27	m	39	m	Ad	F	Spear	G Att Mu	Impotence
28	m	20	m	Ad	½B	Knife	GMs1 4yHL	
29	m	Ad	f	60	Neighbor	Kick stick	GMs1 4yHL	Acc known as witch.
30	m	Ad	m	Ad	None	Stick	GMs1 3yHL	Dec. Congolese. Market fight, occurred in Buganda.
31	m	25	m	30	Neighbor	Pocket knife	GMs1 7yHL	Beer party.
32	m	35	m	Ad	½B	Spear	G Att Mu 10yHL	
33	m	Ad	m	36	None	Sticks	Acq	
	m	Ad					Acq	
34	m	19	f	14	None	Hands	Acq	Dance between rival villages.
35	m	Ad	m	30	None	Pestle	GmuD comm 20yHL	Dec non-Alur occurred Buganda. At auction sale.
36	m	30-35	f	11	Visitor	Hands	Acq	
37	m	50	m	40	Fellow employee	Pestle	GMs1 18moHL	Occurred Bunyoro.
38	m	35	m	Ad		Sticks	Acq	Fight at dance.
	m	35						
39	f	25	f	25	co-wife	Knife	GmuD comm	
40	m	24	m	Ad	Neighbor	Knife	10yHL	Occurred Kampala.
41	m	Ad	m	32	None	Stick	GMs1 Acq	Beer party; rival bands. Arrested by detectives in Congo after flight. Acc Ankole; occurred Bugunda.
42	m	Ad	u	u	None	Sticks	GMs1 6yHL 4yHL 1½yHL 1yHL	
	m	Ad						
	m	Ad						
	m	Ad						
43	m	Ad	m	35	None	Spear	Acq	Beer party between rival villages.
44	m	24	m	30	Neighbor	Stick	Nol Pros	Beer party.
45	m	Ad	?	?	None	Syringe?		Suspected antiminy poisoning. Remitted to district court.
46	m	30	m	Ad	Neighbor	Hands & sticks	GMs1 10yHL	Beer party, with gambling, among neighbors.
	m	20					6yHL	
	m	22					6yHL	
	m	20					6yHL	
	m	21					6yHL	
	m	25					6yHL	
	m	30					6yHL	
47	m	Ad	m	40		Sticks	Nol Pros	Dec Muganda; occurred Buganda. Beer party.
	m	Ad						
	m	21						
	m	21						

No.	Sex	Age	Means	Circumstances
1.	m	Ad	Hanging in house	Suffering from hernia.
2.	m	36+	Hanging in house	Impotence - killed wife first.
3.	f	Ad	Hanging on tree	Grief over death of husband.
4.	f	-21	Hanging on tree	Quarrel with husband over another woman. Husband had beaten her.
5.	m	21+	Hanging on tree	Impotence.
6	m	21+	Hanging on tree	Grief over death of sister.
7.	m	36+	Hanging on tree	Wife threatened to leave him. Killed wife first.
8.	m	51+	Hanging on tree	Shame because son convicted of stealing chicken.
9.	f	36+	Hanging on tree	U
10.	m	21+	Hanging on tree	U
11.	m	36+	Hanging in house	Quarrel with wife - killed wife first.
12.	m	21+	Hangig on tree	Disease.
13.	m	21+	Hanging on tree	Wife left him. Killed wife's mother before committing suicide.
14	m	21+	Stabbed himself	Unknown - but stabbed wife first.
15.	m	21+	Hanging in house	Wife wanted to leave him. Killed wife first.
16.	m	-21	Hanging on tree	Unknown.
17.	m	Ad	Hanging in house	Depressed by having leprosy.
18.	m	Ad	Hanging in house	Shame - was caught stealing maize.
19.	m	Ad	Hanging in house	U
20.	m	-21	Hanging on tree	Impotence and V.D.
21.	m	36+	Hanging on tree	V.D.
22.	m	21+	Hanging in house	V.D.
23.	m	36+	Hanging on tree	Grief over suicide of his brother.
24.	m	36+	Hanging on tree	Insanity.
25.	m	21+	Hanging on tree	Depressed over hernia.
26.	f	51+	Hanging in house	Felt unwanted by children. No husband.
27.	f	36+	Hanging in house	Grief over illness of daughter.
28.	m	21+	Stabbed himself	First stabbed wife and young son. Motive unknown but suspected madness.
29.	f	21+	Hanging on tree	U
30.	f	36+	Hanging on tree	Depression over sickness.
31.	m	21+	Hanging on tree	Insanity.
32.	m	51+	Hanging in house	Had TB. Wife deserted him.
33.	m	Ad	Hanging in house	Ill and partly out of his head.
34.	m	Ad	Hanging in house	Impotence.
35.	m	65+	Hanging in house	Blindness.
36.	f	21+	Hanging on tree	Depressed by disease and childbirth the day before.
37.	m	Ad	Hanging in house	Shame - appears he may have helped kill another man.
38.	f	21+	Hanging in house	Disease.
39.	m	36+	Hanging in house	First killed wife. Cut off her head with panga. Motive unknown.
40.	m	21+	Hanging on tree	Epilepsy - first set fire to hut.
41.	f	36+	Hanging on tree	Leprosy and V.D.

No.	Sex	Age	Means	Circumstances
42.	f	21+	Hanging on tree	Quarrel with husband who suspected her of unfaithfulness.
43.	m	21+	Hanging in house	Had quarrel with wife and had killed wife's "female relative". Reason unknown.
44.	f	65+	Hanging in house	Blindness.
45.	f	51+	Hanging in house	Felt unwanted by her son who refused to take her in.
46.	f	21+	Hanging in house	Quarreled with husband who wouldn't let her go home to her parents.
47.	m	21+	Hanging in house	Impotence. 2 wives had left him.
48.	m	65+	Hanging on tree	Illness.
49.	m	36+	Hanging in house	U
50.	f	21+	Hanging on tree	Husband had taken second wife. Felt neglected.
51.	f	36+	Hanging on tree	Forced to live with husband she didn't like.
52.	m	21+	Hanging in house	Had been drinking at beer party. Motive unknown.
53.	m	21+	Hanging in house	Followed violent quarrel with brother.
54.	m	51+	Hanging on tree	Shame because he couldn t raise money to pay back bridewealth of daughter who left her husband.
55.	m	36+	Hanging on tree	Impotence.
56.	m	36+	Hanging in house	Illness from being bitten by a pig.
57.	m	36+	Hanging on tree	Grief over death of son. Also had eye disease
58.	f	21+	Hanging on tree	Had quarrelled with her husband about not giving her enough clothes.
59.	m	21+	Hanging on tree	Killed wife first - reason unknown.
60.	m	36+	Hanging in house	Quarrelled with wife's father and killed wife Also had leprosy.
61.	f	Ad	Hanging in house	Had had quarrel about sharing work with co wife.
62.	f	21+	Hanging	U
63.	m	51+	Hanging on tree	Hernia for 3 years.
64.	m	Ad	Hanging on tree	Syphilis - thought it was caused by sorcery.
65.	m	36+	Hanging in house	Leper - wife left him.
66.	f	21+	Hanging on tree	Lunacy and "swelling" believed caused by sorcery.
67.	m	21+	Hanging on tree	Insane.
68.	f	36+	Hanging on tree	Grief over death of son.
69.	m	36+	Hanging in prison	Remanded on trial for murder - also ill.
70.	m	21+	Hanging on tree	Blindness.
71.	m	36+	Hanging on tree	Had run away from own village where he thought he had killed his wife during quarrel.
72.	m	36+	Hanging	Had killed wife in quarrel over washing clothes
73.	f	51+	Hanging in house	Blindness
74.	m	21+	Hanging in house	Hernia
75.	m	36+	Hanging on tree	Wife left him - refused to return.
76.	m	21+	Hanging on tree	Impotence.
77.	m	36+	Hanging in house	Illness.
78.	m	36+	Hanging on tree	Leprosy. Wife refused to sleep with him.
79.	f	51+	Hanging on tree	Leprosy, bad teeth, hernia.
80.	f	65+	Hanging in house	Blindness.
81.	m	-21	Hanging on tree	Was in habit of running away from home - particularly after arguments with father. Most recently was his going to school which he refused to do.
82.	f	51+	Burnt herself in hut.	Leprosy.
83.	m	65+	Hanging	Man was 80 years old. Wife refused to have intercourse.
84.	m	36+	Hanging	Had killed wife who refused to sleep with him because she was in mourning.
85.	f	21+	Hanging	U
86.	m	36+	Hanging in house	Leprosy.
87.	m	36+	Hanging on tree	U.(Had been drinking at beer party).
88.	m	36+	Hanging in house	Had fought with wife and injured her badly.
89.	m	65+	Hanging	Had been ill for 3 years. Wife also ill.
90.	f	21+	Hanging on tree	Insanity.
91.	f	21+	Hanging on tree	Illness. Sounds like leprosy.

No.	Sex	Age	Means	Circumstances
92.	m	36†	Hanging in house	Impotence.
93.	m	21†	Hanging	Had killed wife for giving goat to her sister without his permission.
94.	f	~21	Hanging	Husband paid more attention to co-wife who was her sister.
95.	m	36†	Hit by train	Run over – had been drinking heavily. Reason not known. People tried to pull him off track but he wouldn't move.
96.	m	51†	Hanging in house	Deserted by wife and children. Felt unwanted.
97.	f	~21	Hanging	Had quarrelled with husband. Her mother said she was not a good wife.
98.	m	51†	Hanging	Quarrelled with wife who said he didn't support her properly.
99.	f	51†	Hanging	Very ill. Said she was tired of life.
100.	m	21†	Hanging	Insanity.

GISU SUICIDE

No.	Sex	Age	Means	Circumstances
1.	f	U	Set fire to house	Was a leper.
2.	f	25	Hanging	Had V.D. Feared prosecution and adultery case of husband.
3.	m	30	Stabbed self	Stabbed uncle in rage then in remorse himself
4.	f	U	Hanging	Quarrel with husband who beat her.
5.	m	U	Hanging	Brother died. Committed suicide on day of brother's funeral.
6.	f	U	Hanging	Had been ill for some time.
7	f	35	Hanging	Alleged to be a lunatic.
8.	m	19	Hanging	Beat his mother in fury and then father who tried to intervene.
9.	m	50	Hanging	Had had V.D. for 21 years. Lately much pain.
10.	m	60	Hanging	Had V.D. for long time.
11.	m	32	Hanging	– – – – – – –
12	m	48	Hanging	Leper. Lost finger and couldn't work.
13.	m	Old	Hanging	Ill for 3 years Had threatened suicide. Wife dead, living alone.
14.	m	29	Hanging	Ill for some time. Often in hospital.
15.	m	70	Hanging	Complained of pains in chest.
16.	f	29	Hanging	Epileptic and chronic wound on leg Had threatened suicide before as tired of suffering.
17.	f	37	Hanging	– – – – – –
18.	m	35	Hanging	Had been suffering from V.D. for some time.
19.	m	29	Hanging	Ill for 4 years.
20	f	U	Threw self off cliff	Row with husband. Real trouble her barrenness.
21.	m	70	Hanging	– – – – – –
22	f	55	Hanging	Second daughter had gone to live with man not husband.
23.	f	U	Hanging	
24.	m	U	Hanging	Beat wife badly. Heard she'd died in hospital (false). Feared murder charge.
25.	f	U	Hanging	Unsound mind.
26.	m	U	Hanging	Had chronic gonorrhea.
27.	m	U	Hanging	On remand for murder charge. Committed suicide in jail.
28.	f	U	Hanging	Killed husband then committed suicide. (This guesswork – no witnesses)
29.	m	U	Hanging	None but letters found saying case against him for laziness and asking for transfer – ill.
30	m	13	Hanging	Playing with another child who was injured Feared parents.
31.	m	U	Hanging	– – – – – – – –
32.	m	U	Hanging	– – – – – – – – –
33.	f	U	Hanging	Mentally deranged. Epileptic
34.	m	U	Hanging	Left letter but no mention of contents.

No.	Sex	Age	Means	Circumstances
35.	m	U	Hanging	- - - - - - - - - -
36.	m	U	Hanging	Letter of instructions left.
37.	m	U	Hanging	Member of DYM and knew chiefs were going to arrest him.(DINI YA MSAMBWA)
38.	f	U	Hanging	Was ill.
39.	f	U	Hanging	- - - - - - - - - -
40.	f	U	Hanging	- - - - - - - - - -
41.	m	U	Hanging	Ill for 4 years.
42.	f	U	Hanging	- - - - - - - - - -
43.	f	37	Hanging	Accused by husband of adultery Had been on remand for this.
44.	m	35	Hanging	Beat up wife and killed her.
45.	f	U	Hanging	- - - - - - - - - -
46.	m	18	Hanging	Had recently had disease which affected his mind. Stepfather chaffed him for this.
47.	f	40	Hanging	Mad. Used to live in bush and throw stones at people.
48.	m	40	Hanging	A leper for 6 years. Chief came that day and told him to go to hospital. Refused.
49.	f	39	Hanging	Mother and her children kept on dying.
50.	m	24	Hanging	Ill for 3 months.
51.	f	60	Hanging	Stomach trouble and coughing a lot.
52.	m	80	Hanging Stabbing	When in temper used to try to commit suicide. This 3rd try. Stabbed himself in stomach when hanging rope broke.
53.	m	68	Hanging	Not sound in mind. Had threatened suicide before.
54.	m	65	Hanging	Suffering from V.D. Couldn t walk.
55.	f	45	Hanging	Bad illness. Hemorrhage very bad that night.
56.	m	35	Hanging	Married the week before. Proved impotent.
57.	m	32	Drowned in river	Used to beat his wife. Then she went to hospital. Chiefs came to arrest him. He ran away and committed suicide.
58.	m	20	Hanging	Had had intercourse with brother's daughter. Suicide next morning.
59.	f	22	Hanging	Row with parents who were trying to make her go back to her husband.
60.	m	65	Hanging	Abdominal pains. Couldn't urinate for 2 weeks.
61.	f	35	Hanging	No apparent motive.
62.	m	28	Hanging	Discharged from hospital with incurable sore.
63..	f	30	Hanging	Epileptic This her 3rd attempt.
64.	f	45	Hanging	Just told she was a leper. Daughter a lunatic.
65.	m	14	Hanging	Stole some money. Found out and scolded - not beaten.
66.	f	55	Hanging	Leper and had been taunted with it.
67.	m	28	Hanging	Had complained he wasn't feeling well that day. No apparent motive.
68	m	12	Hanging	No apparent reason.

BANYORO SUICIDE

No.	Sex	Age	Means	Circumstances
1.	m	Yg	Hanging on tree	U
2.	f	45	Hanging on tree	Long and painful illness.
3.	m	15	Hanging on tree	U
4.	m	29	Hanging in house	U
5.	m	20	Hanging on tree	Poverty - no money to pay tax and "afraid of being imprisoned".
6.	m	70	Hanging in house	Long and painful illness (gonorrhea) for 13 years.
7.	m	35	Hanging on tree	After killing wife who had left him and would not return.
8.	f	50	Hanging on tree	Grief at death of son killed by car.
9.	f	30	Hanging on tree	Grief at death of child who died 2 days previously.
10.	m	50	Hanging in house	After killing wife.
11.	m	50	Hanging on tree	Ill with TB for many years.
12.	f	60	Hanging on tree	U
13.	m	50	Knife	Mental illness.
14.	m	Ad	Hanging in house	Long and painful illness (VD)

No.	Sex	Age	Means	Circumstances
15.	m	50	Hanging on tree	U
16.	m	29	Hanging in house	Painful illness for 2 years. Left explanatory note.
17.	f	Ad	Hanging on tree	Jealous of husband's other wife. First killer her 2 children with axe.
18.	m	Old	U	Old man. Relatives all dead.
19.	f	70	Hanging in house	Long illness.
20.	m	U	Knife	(attempt only) - leprosy and poverty.
21	m	25	Hanging in boys' quarters.	Unknown, but had been ill.
22.	f	U	Hanging in house	Unknown, but 3 of her relatives had hung themselves.
23.	m	28	Hanging on tree	Had been sick for a few days.
24.	m	50	Hanging in house	Ill for about 10 years.
25.	m	36	Hanging on tree	U
26.	f	40	Hanging in house	Jealous of other wives of husband.
27	m	Old	Hanging in house	Ill and without relatives
28.	f	16	Hanging on tree	Under pressure to return to husband she disliked.
29.	m	U	Spear	Attempt only. Unknown.
30.	f	Ad	Hanging on tree	Attempt only. After quarrel with husband who suspected her of having lover.
31.	m	Ad	Hanging in house	Wife refused to return to him.
32.	m	15	Hanging on tree	Resentment at being forbidden to smoke.
33.	m	70	Hanging in deserted house	Leper for 24 years.
34.	m	70	Hanging on tree	U
35.	m	35	Hanging in house	U
36.	f	Ad	Hanging	After quarrel with husband.
37.	m	65	Hanging in house	Ill with paralysis - could only crawl.
38.	f	28	Hanging on tree	After mental illness.
39.	m	65	Hanging in house	After quarrel with wife.
40.	m	29	Hanging on tree	Leper.
41.	m	Ad	Hanging in prison	Had been taken into custody as a lunatic.
42.	f	25	Hanging in house	After quarrel with husband whom she suspected of adultery.
43.	f	30	Hanging on tree	After quarrel with husband and arrest for theft of his property.
44.	f	60	Burnt herself in house	Epileptic for 5 years. Had often threatened suicide.
45.	f	19	Hanging on tree	Under pressure to go home to husband she disliked.
46.	f	22	Hanging on tree	Unwilling to be married to ex-lover by brother whom she disliked.
47.	m	30	Spear	Epileptic - believed himself and his mother to be victims of sorcery.
48.	f	60	Hanging in house	Suffered from painful affliction of eyes.
49.	f	30	Hanging on tree	Bereaved, and accused of sorcery by husband.
50.	m	22	Hanging on tree	Ashamed after assaulting mother and being arrested by chief
51.	m	35	Hanging in house	After killing wife who had wanted to leave him.
52.	m	50	Hanging in house	Illness (gonorrhea)
53.	f	28	Hanging on tree	Grief at death of husband who died after being stabbed at beer-drink..
54	m	45	Hanging in kitchen	Long and painful illness.
55.	f	18	Hanging on tree	Unwilling to be married to elderly man.
56.	m	38	Hanging in tree	Believed himself neglected by wife.
57.	m	45	Hanging in house	Ill for many years.
58.	f	Old	Hanging in house	Ill for many years.
59.	m	42	Hanging on tree	Gonorrhea
60	f	75	Hanging on tree	Long and painful illness.
61	f	19	Hanging on tree	U